Research Methods, Statistics, and

M000204289

A Guide for Students in Family and Consumer Sciences

By Jerry L. Cook, Ph.D., C.F.L.E.

Research Methods, Statistics, and Professionalism:

A Guide for Students in Family and Consumer Sciences

By Jerry L. Cook, Ph.D., C.F.L.E.

Publisher: CreateSpace.com
ISBN-13: 978-0983688013

ISBN-10: 098368801X

Printed in the United States of America

Note: This book is in "draft" form, and will likely have spelling, grammatical, formatting, and content errors.

Contents

Chapter 1: An Introduction

Skeptics make the best researchers.

Chances are good that you are at least a little skeptical about this book and the course that requires this book. You may have heard how important research is, but you remain unconvinced. Or perhaps you see research as an important skill, in a general sense, but you do not see its relevance to your future career.

In each situation, you remain open minded to the possibility of learning about research, but you may also feel you need more information about what research is and what it can do for you before you embrace it with open arms. And for that, I say, "Welcome!"

One of the greatest ironies about being skeptical toward research is that ~~you need to be skeptical to be a good researcher. Research is a very long process of gaining evidence~~ (which we more commonly refer to as "**support**") about things we do not fully understand; it is being wary toward things that have not been proven to us. In summary, true researchers are often cautious, and perhaps even skeptical, about what they have heard or learned from others, and are passionate about wanting to try things out on their own before determining what to accept as "truth."

The very doubts or reservations you may have about research actually can make you a great researcher. I'm not claiming you will throw on the white lab coat at the end of this semester to become a full-fledged researcher, but I am suggesting that you will soon find that you have more in common with researchers than you may now think you do. Research is not only about learning new information, it is also about improving the skills you already have; your ability to investigate, analyze, and create resources for your organization or employer are in great demand!

Important Information About This Textbook

The majority of textbooks fall flat. They are essentially designed to lull you into the Dark Side of Academia, to convince you to adopt the ways of the farce.

You will quickly see that I am a big critic of the psychobabble used in academia, and it is frustrating to see that research and academia often use big words and vague concepts that—outside of the class—find little connection to reality. This isn't to say that we won't learn the jargon, but we'll do so in a way that will actually make sense. Students often enter "research methods" courses with a bit of apprehension and confusion about the course, and most textbooks make things worse –not better. My hope is that this book will be very user-friendly and that you will find that many of the concepts in it are relatable to your needs and future goals. I hope you will feel as if I am talking directly to you.

Many of the "research/statistics" courses I teach are filled with students who have already taken a "research methods" or a statistics course (or both). Admittedly, it is very difficult to take a course if you feel you have already learned the concepts and vocabulary, and you may wish you could be doing something else. I've been there.

If you are in this situation, I would like to let you know that chances are very good that I will present the concepts in a very different way than what you learned them. Initially, it may sound like the same song-and-dance you have heard in other classes, but as we move throughout the semester, it is likely that you will see some major differences from what you had learned and experienced in other courses. Please do not close the door on learning (or re-learning) these concepts, as we will start from the beginning to ensure that your learning can be applied to your future career.

If you haven't ever had a research methods course, or a statistics course, or perhaps you haven't ever written a research paper, please understand that there will be a lot of concepts that may seem foreign to you. In a way, it is like learning a new language, but if you stay confident and dedicated to studying, chances are very good you will surprise yourself with what you are able to learn. I have seen this time and time again; it may take time, but it is well worth it.

 As mentioned, many of the research methods textbooks students have used about research and statistics fall flat. It isn't because they aren't useful, but rather because they focus on memorization of concepts rather than genuinely understanding those same concepts. Some research methods textbooks try to indoctrinate you with terms many professors struggle to fully understand. Some textbooks try to water down (or dumb down) the principles so they are easier for students to understand, and others are focused on entertaining you that they miss the opportunity to teach serious concepts.

Perhaps the greatest challenge, however, is that many research methods and statistics textbooks aren't presented in the fields of study the students are currently in. With the course I am currently teaching, our students are in a "Family and Consumer Sciences" major, and yet the majority of "methods" textbooks are devoted to Psychology or Sociology majors. Family and Consumer Sciences, or FACS, is a collection or fields of study that include Family Studies, Consumer Studies, Nutrition, and Fashion Merchandising. Two additional foci within FACS may sometimes also include Child Development and Home Economics, which tends to be a generalist/teacher credential program with expertise across all the fields of study within FACS.

At first glance, it may not always be easy to see the similarity or overlap between the concentrations or fields of study within FACS. It isn't uncommon for students from all of these different perspectives to join into one "core" course, and wonder why they *should* all be together in one class. However, the number of topics crossing two or more foci or concentrations is nearly limitless, and there are opportunities for learning from another person's perspective. A small sample of topics that overlap the fields of study is given below.

Body Image	Eating disorders	The elderly
Identity	Mood/Emotion	Maternal well-being
Obesity	Infant development	Marketing of products
Gang colors	Program evaluation	Depression/Anxiety
Welfare	Teen pregnancy	Drug use
Shopping trends	Parent-Adolescent conflict	

As you continue through these pages, many of these topics (which are not well-addressed in other research methods or statistics textbooks) will be discussed. However, this book is *not* designed to teach you about what research previous scholars have conducted; rather, it is to help you better understand the research *process* so that you can become a better consumer, educator, and expert in your given field. Being a better researcher will help you better understand, anticipate, and evaluate the trends in your field. There are a lot of "research" concepts most professionals take for granted and only pay lip service to, and being able to articulate and apply these concepts in your field will improve your chances for employment, and they will make you the leader others will look to.

You, the Researcher

You likely have participated in or conducted research, at least to some degree, before reading this book. Because academia is the most common employer of researchers, it isn't surprising that students are one of (if not) the most commonly researched populations in the world. For this reason, you likely have completed one or more surveys in college.

If you have ever left a review for a product or a service, perhaps on Yelp or Amazon.com, then you have also participated in research. Research is the process or mechanism for collecting data, and sites designed to get your data (i.e. feedback) are research-based. You probably have looked at previous customer reviews (i.e. data) to determine what level of trust you should have for a company, product, or service being promoted.

Most students have also conducted research by searching for what scholars have found on a particular topic. If you have had to write a paper about a country, a product, a service, or a trend, then you have likely researched what previous scholars have found or said about that topic.

If you have ever purchased a car, a home, or shopped around for a loan, chances are good you did your research to ensure that you got the best deal you could. If you were interested in learning about someone, chances are you went online to research them through social networking sites or Google. (Have you really done that?)

Technology has made research more accessible, but with a heavy price. At our fingertips and with the click of a button, we literally have hundreds of thousands of options to sift through on a given topic, and Internet search providers (and not us) have determined which results are more valid and have priority over others. Interestingly, these search results are manipulated and competed for by businesses, organizations, and individuals who spend enormous amounts of money to be listed in the Top 10 search results for the thing you are looking for online.

Getting information quickly doesn't always lead to getting the information you need or that is the best for you. Most of us have searched for something, and once clicking one of the results or links, realized that our computers were infected with a virus. If we are lucky, we identify it quickly and have it removed. Too often, however, we miss the malware or viruses that come with the click of a mouse, and it slows down everything else we want to do. Or worse, it crashes our computers and we have to spend our hard-earned money to buy a new one.

Similarly, we live in an age where we are overloaded with information; it is all around us. Identifying the information we can trust, and becoming more able to avoid information that is less trustworthy, are more important (and more difficult) than ever.

Much of what we learn in our fields of study can be comparable to looking at the results from an Internet search engine. Each and every textbook is essentially giving you the links and information it believes are most important and most valid. But that information is often very subjective, and as humans with their own biases, textbook authors (and instructors) may sometimes attempt to sway you to believe the way they do; they can sometimes present opinions as facts.

Here's an example: Recently I watched a presentation from a registered dietician about a nutrition workshop designed to improve the well-being of African American families. The dietician touted her workshop to be the best thing since sliced bread, and was passionate about making sure that other families were able to receive this same workshop (in order to improve their well-being as well). She kept pointing to her "highly statistically significant" results as proof that her workshop needed to be shared with every community in the nation. When she said there was a .08 correlation between how much time participants spent in her class and their well-being, that was the first red flag. Although we will learn more about statistical significance and correlations later in this book, a .08 correlation is similar to saying that I am somewhat related to Michael Jordan, the professional basketball player. Yes, my second-cousin's sister's boyfriend is a nephew of Michael Jordan's cousin's grandmother's friend's second-cousin's grandson's friend. (Okay, I did make that up, but I am trying to make a point here). The point is that dietician, like most scholars, focused on the statistics that support her bias and overlooked other aspects that completely discredits what she is trying to "prove" to us. It is a human tendency, and textbook authors (including myself) are prone to do it. The lesson to this is that we can't always believe what we read or hear, even if it comes from someone with an important title or who has authority over us.

I want to make it very clear that I am a huge believer and advocate for nutrition; my example is *not* given to make you doubt everything you have read or heard about nutrition (or any other field of study). It does, however, give us the motivation to find out, for ourselves, what is true and what isn't; it tells us to watch out for the times when even experts can exaggerate the truth. (The same would be true when experts tell us to change our parenting "style" or when clothing companies are told by business experts that they need to invest a lot of their money into a particular fashion trend. How do we know if they are presenting us with truth or half-truths?) There are two ways to find out what is true and what isn't: (1) test everything on our own, or (2) have a better understanding of how others conduct their research.

Of course, many times we rely on our instincts to determine what is true or not. We tend to judge people by how we feel about them (or around them), and we often make purchases based on how we think those things would make us feel. Comparably, we could try to determine what truth is based on how we comfortable we feel when companies, textbooks, and instructors are telling us something. Matter of fact, your gut is filled with bacteria so complex and that have such a powerful effect on our brains that researchers often call the human gut the "second brain."

So should we rely on ourselves or the data?

To answer that question, we should first understand the word **Postmodernism**. "Modernism" is an era, or more particularly, an ideology that believes that truth can be verified by results or data. In this view, truth can be proven scientifically.

Postmodernism, in contrast, recognizes that truth can be found or experienced in a variety of ways, and that one source of truth doesn't hold truth for all people or all situations. The value of Postmodernism is that it is much more tolerant of people and situations that do not fit the norm, and it also is better at recognizing that science is not the definitive authority on everything. When our personal beliefs conflict with science, Postmodernism suggests that there is truth in what we feel is true. The era of Postmodernism has also created a great deal of conflict, however, where more and more people tend to ignore science and go with what they believe or feel in their hearts, or perhaps because of what they heard from a friend or authority figure. (Perhaps you have learned about something in your field of study, but your personal experience does not agree with what science says is "fact"). The debate over vaccinations and global warming are just two examples where people debate over whether science or other sources of knowledge are more credible and trustworthy.

It is true that science, as well as "facts" that stem from science, have not always been as trustworthy as we would like them to be. Fields of study evolve, and our "truths" about parenting, marriage, eating fatty foods and salt, and the use of animals (e.g.

13

vegan vs. vegetarian diets, "tanning" and the wearing of apparel made with leather) are in constant change as well.

It is my opinion that research and our beliefs, wherever they come from, act as Checks and Balances for each other. Much like the Executive, Judicial, and Legislative branches were designed to act as checks and balances for each other, to ensure that neither would have too much power over the other, our beliefs serve to check (watch over) and balance (put into context) what we discover from research. In the same light, research may also serve to check and balance our personal beliefs, or to provide a mechanism for helping us ground ourselves in reality.

Years ago, a program called D.A.R.E. was created to keep children from using drugs. The program cost the government (and its taxpayers) millions if not billions of dollars, and it consisted primarily of law enforcement personnel educating the students about the dangers of drugs. Some of the assumptions were that students would learn to trust law enforcement, that they would have positive role models in the community, and that they would feel discouraged from taking drugs.

Despite the popularity of the program, the research consistently showed that the program did not work. Matter of fact, in some communities, it seemed to *increase* the likelihood that students would take drugs. If it wasn't for research putting personal and political beliefs in "check," our government would still be paying billions of dollars for something that did not work.

Myths about Research

As mentioned, our beliefs and research (or science) act as checks and balances for each other. Although I am a big believer in the

14

value of research, I also recognize why an increasing number of people doubt the value of research and findings from scientists.

At the same time, there are still those who believe in Modernism principles more than in Postmodernism principles; this is to say that some people will only believe what is proven by data. For the person who will only believe when there is scientific proof, and to the person who prefers to consider science and to remain true to their personal values and beliefs, understanding the myths of research will be helpful.

The first myth is that all research is scientific. There is an assumption that, just because research is conducted by scientists, you can trust what they have to say. As we will see in greater detail throughout this textbook, scientists are human and make mistakes, have biases, and although rare, intentionally mislead us. More often that human intent, however, is the fact that the tools for collecting the data may not be the best, leading to faulty conclusions.

The second myth is that numbers and statistics don't lie. The counterargument is that statistics don't lie, but sometimes people do. More often is the fact that certain numbers and statistics are given, but others are left out, to justify a bias (like the dietician-scholar's presentation I shared earlier in this chapter). There is also the possibility that the calculations or methods for developing those statistics may not have been correct. And finally, there is the possibility that the interpretation of those numbers and statistics may also be in error.

I often share a story about three college students who went to an academic conference. They are poor, and so they look for the cheapest hotel they can find. The rooms cost $30 per night, but they can get a $5 discount if they tell the hotel manager that they are staying there because they are attending a conference. What a great deal, right?

When the students get to the hotel, they paid the $30 (or $10 each) for one room and explained they were going to go to the conference the next morning. The manager completely forgot about the discount, but fortunately remembered a few minutes later, when the students were up in their room. The manager walked up to the room with five one-dollar bills in his hand, but then reasoned, "I can't split five one-dollar bills among three people," and so he pocketed (i.e. kept) two dollars and gave each of the students one dollar back.

Do you remember how much each student paid when they first got to the hotel? $10. Do you remember how much they each got back? $1. How much then, did they each pay? (Hint: $10-$1 = $9). If each student paid $9, and there were three students, how much did they pay altogether ($9 X 3 = $27). And how much did the manager keep? Two dollars. Twenty seven dollars that the college students paid plus the two dollars the manager kept equals $29. Where did the other dollar go?

Just like understanding the magician's (or in this case, a mathematician's) secrets will help you see there isn't any magic at all, demystifying the steps in research will help you recognize where the errors are, and it will help you better determine what (and who) you can trust. Understanding what the numbers are, how they're obtained, and how they are interpreted are important steps for understanding the research process.

The third myth is "they said it was significant." In a classic movie, The Princess Bride, there is a mastermind attempting to start a war, but a pirate continually foils his plans in ways the mastermind finds unbelievable. "Inconceivable!" the mastermind exclaims. Over and over again he says the word "inconceivable," and finally a swordsman (who has been following the mastermind) says, "You keep using that word. I do not think it means what you think it means."

In research and throughout academia, we often hear the word "significant" or the words "statistically significant" as if they determine whether the results or meaningful, powerful, or useful. Although the true meaning of these words will be given to you later (when we focus exclusively on statistics in the textbook), I wish I could tell other scholars, "You keep using those words. I do not think they mean what you think it means." In short, significant does not mean that the results are meaningful, powerful, or useful. And yet so many of us have been taught that is what they mean. In part, many believe the myth because they think that the words "statistically significant" means the same thing as the word "significant" that we use in our everyday language. Unfortunately, they do not mean the same thing. We have been taught a myth.

Summary

Research can be an incredible tool for helping us understand people and the world around us, but not all research is useful, meaningful, or trustworthy. In this book, we will uncover some of the strategies for recognizing good (and bad) research. We will also look at how research affects our fields of study, our politics, and how it can affect our employment.

Review Questions

1. Why do skeptics make some of the best researchers?

2. What attitudes or beliefs have you learned about research (or research methods) that may serve as barriers to learning?

3. What topics may be of interest for students across a variety of fields of study?

4. In what ways do our personal beliefs act as Checks and Balances for research? In what ways does research act as Checks and Balances for our personal beliefs?

5. What is Postmodernism, and in what ways is it connected to Checks and Balances?

6. What are three Myths about Research?

Personal Application

1. If you want to be a full-time researcher, or if you absolutely HAD to be a researcher (because it was the only job in the world), what would you choose to research?

_____

_____

_____

_____

2. Are there any myths about research you have been taught to believe in? Which ones?

_____

_____

3. When has your personal values or belief systems been at odds with (or had a different viewpoint than) research? How did you respond to that difference?

_____

_____

_____

4. How much of a commitment are you willing to make for learning the content and principles in this book? How are you going to structure your time so that you can successfully learn these principles?

_____

Chapter 2: Where to Begin as a Researcher

Now that we have some recognition about the importance of research, or at least for good research, we still need more specifics as to what the research process consists of. In the previous chapter, I tried to convince you that you have already used many of the principles that researchers use: you have a question and you look for information to answer that question.

In research, when we follow the **Scientific Method** we are more likely to get to the truth (eventually). The Scientific Method also gives researchers a moral obligation to share what they have learned. In short, the Scientific Method is about having questions and getting the answers to those questions, but the specifics in the steps provide (below) is what guides our research:

Step 1. Ask a question.

Step 2. Complete background research.

Step 3. Develop a **hypothesis**, which is a testable research question or assumption.

Step 4. Test the hypothesis. This is usually done by collecting **data** (i.e. information) from a survey, observation, or other measurement tools.

Step 5. Analyze the results and draw a conclusion as to whether the hypothesis was supported.

Step 6. **Disseminate** (i.e. share or publish) the results.

Step 7. If the hypothesis was not supported, or if you need more information about the topic or data, you may need to start at Step 1 again.

For example, let's say you are interested in how female teens can improve their self-esteem (Step 1). You go to the library, or onto a library website, and look for **peer-review journal articles** about "self-esteem" and "female teens" (Step 2). The reason peer-review journal articles is preferred over textbooks, self-improvement literature, and videos is that peer-reviewed journal articles are generally considered of higher quality (or more trustable) than other sources because of the steps involved in getting published. This process is also frequently referred to as a **review of the literature.**

After you reviewed the research about teen females and self-esteem, perhaps you see find a pattern: teen females who judge themselves by their talents---rather than by their physical appearance---tend to have higher levels of self-esteem (than those who judge themselves by their physical appearance). That may be good to know, but the question is: How can we motivate teen females to focus on their talents rather than obsessing with how they look? You may guess that the way to do this is having a motivational speaker visit with the junior high schools to talk with them (Step 3). But you haven't yet tested your hypothesis.

Before the motivational speaker visits a junior high school, you ask that all females in that school take a survey to determine how much they value their talents, how often they focus on their physical appearance, and how high (or low) their self-esteem is. After the motivational speaker visits with the school, you give them another survey and see if there are any increases in how they value their talents, and whether this change in perception is associated with an improvement in their self-esteem (Step 4).

At this point, all you have is the surveys and what the respondents said on those surveys. You have data. But if you asked 500 females a bunch of questions, it can be very difficult to summarize what you have found. That is why there are statistics. With statistics or statistical tests, you can test whether you hypothesis is supported (Step 5). If your results can show that the motivational speaker helps female teens focus more on their talents (and less on their physical appearance), and if this change is associated to an increase in their self-esteem, then you can say that your hypothesis was **supported**.

As mentioned in the previous chapter, the process of research is a long journey because it takes a great deal of evidence before one can say something is proven. In our example, can we prove that it was the motivational speaker that caused the changes, or is it possible that something else may have happened to cause the changes in female self-esteem and body image? Is it possible that the results were obtained by chance, or were a fluke? Is it possible that the female teens filled out the surveys, but filled them out randomly, without paying attention to what they were reading or marking? Perhaps completing surveys gave the students extra credit, and so they quickly marked answers (that may not be truthful) only to get the extra credit. And perhaps there were hundreds of female teens who did not complete the survey; would your results have been different if they had completed the survey?

There is a very high standard for "proving" something, and the word (i.e. "prove") in research is met with a great deal of skepticism. This is why we tend to say that the results "supported" our hypothesis, because the data or the results are in agreement (but do not prove) our testable hypothesis.

Now that you have some evidence (i.e. support) that motivational speakers can help increase female teen self-esteem, you can share this information with others. You may tell the schools, other researchers, share the information in a conference presentation, or publish your results in an academic journal. This process is referred to as "dissemination" (Step 6).

Although the Scientific Method encourages researchers to share their findings, whether they support their hypotheses or not, the reality is that studies failing to support their hypotheses are much less likely to be published or shared in academic conferences than are studies that are statistically significant. As noted earlier, with regard to the myths about research, there is a very strong bias in academia that says (falsely) that only statistically significant results are important.

Commonly, after a study is complete, the results will generate more questions than they will give answers. Perhaps in our example, we find that all but one group (e.g. ethnicity, socioeconomic status, age) of teen females tend to improve their perception of their talents and their body image; we may question why that one group did not improve, and work through the scientific process again.

The truth of the matter is the very few researchers say, "We are on step number 3 now." Again, the Scientific Method is really more about an ideology than a "How-To-Guide" for conducting research.

The Anatomy of an Article

When I was in high school, I quickly realized that the easiest way to write a book report was to read the front and back covers, and then to read the first and last 20 pages of the book. Many college students take this same approach when reading a journal article. There are many reasons for this, including they are trying to save time, the readings are boring, or more commonly, that they do not understand what is in the middle of the article.

Like me and my high school reports, chances are good that you may not feel that skipping the middle of the articles is much of a problem. When you write a research report, it is unlikely that your graders or instructors have asked you, "Which section of the article did you read that from?" In all frankness, for most students there is very little motivation to read all of the sections in an article because they may seem boring, complicated, and time-consuming.

I have to be honest here, and say I am not sure if I can convince you to read an entire peer review article from now on, but I can give you reasons or a sense of purpose for doing so. The short answer is that our primary goal as researcher is to find or uncover the truth, and you may be surprised to find that there is much in a research article, even a peer review journal article, that may not contain the highest level of truth or evidence.

For example, let's say you are interested in a new medication that treats diabetes. At the beginning of the article, it will likely summarize its findings in an easy-to-read format. Perhaps it may say something like this:

A study was completed that tested the effectiveness of a new diabetes medication. After using the medicine for a period of six weeks, the results indicated that the medicine (on average) improved sugar levels, with the results being statistically significant.

That sounds pretty good, doesn't it? And perhaps it is. But what might it leave out? The beginning of the article (i.e. the Abstract) likely does not explain that 20% of the individuals on the medication actually developed more problems with their diabetes (as a result of the medication) than it helped; because most of the participants improved, the 20% does not really reflect the "average" result. Similarly, does the beginning of the article talk about how many patients dropped out of the study into the third week? Perhaps the reason the "average" results seemed so good is because most of the patients who experienced problems from the medication did not want to continue with the study; their experiences would not have been reflected in the "average" results.

Whether you are interested in medicine, fashion, parenting, or nutrition, the reality is that the biggest part of the "story" in your article is going to be in the middle of the article (particularly the Methods and Results sections). That is where you will be able to determine what you can trust and what you cannot trust. How many times have you read from articles or from the textbooks about the "average" parenting style, nutritional status, or consumer fashion experience? Are we certain that their use of the word "average" actually means what we think it means?

Let's take a moment to look at the anatomy of an article, and determine where we can find these sections. As we review these sections, it is important to understand that different journals have different requirements for headings or levels, and so there is considerable variation as to what the anatomy could look like. We will go over the most basic anatomy found in most academic (i.e. peer reviewed) journal articles.

The most noticeable words in a peer review journal article is the **title of the article.** Some people also refer to this as the title of the study. The title of the article is usually very brief, meaning that is very few words, and is designed to reflect what the study is about. Its purpose is also generally to attract attention; journal editors want people to read their journals, and creative titles are one way to do that.

Speaking of journals, the **name of the journal** is also part of the anatomy of a journal. Many times the name of the journal has the word "journal" in it and the name of the journal is also usually italicized. For example, there is the *Journal of Adolescence*, the *Journal of Fashion Merchandising*, and the *Journal of Nutrition*. The name of the journal is commonly near the top or the bottom of the page where the title of the article is printed; it may also be on every page of the article. Occasionally, the names of journals can be quite long, and may be abbreviated; for example, the *Journal of Family Issues* might be abbreviated as *Jrnl Fam Iss.*

Typically near the title of the article you will also see the **authors of the article.** The author who is given the most credit for the article is listed first, or is commonly referred to as the "first author." This author typically has taken the lead or given the most effort toward the study, and is typically the person to contact if you have questions about the study.

The **Abstract** consists of a very brief summary (typically 150 words or less, although some journals allow for longer Abstracts) of what the study is about; it will almost always provide at least some information about the results, but it rarely will talk about the weaknesses of the study. The Abstract commonly cites how many people were in the study, and sometimes it will cite what kind of measurements (e.g. survey, observation, etc.) were used to collect data.

Consider the Abstract to be like a teaser or a trailer for a movie. Its primary goal is to encourage you to watch the rest of the movie (or in this case, read the rest of the article). Understandably, there are movies where teasers or trailers have shown all the best parts of the movie, and sometimes we are left with wondering why we spent time and money watching the full show. However, in a peer review journal article, even though it may give you nice bullet points for your next research paper, it seldom, if ever, provides the context needed for understanding its results; relying on the Abstract without reading the rest of the article leads to mistakes, generalizations, and exaggerations that would not happen if you read the rest of the article.

Another part of a peer review journal article is the **Introduction**. This is often referred to as a **Literature Review**, because this is where the authors write what they learned from a review of the literature (or past studies and articles on the subject their study is about). The objectives for an Introduction are to (1) cite and describe previous research, and (2) lay the foundation or purpose for their own study. If their hypotheses were not cited in the Abstract, you can generally find that information (sometimes direct, sometimes a little vague) in the Introduction section.

The **Methods** section, in contrast to the Introduction, transitions into what the authors of the study have done. It typically presents information about the participants or sample (including age, gender, and race), the type and name of the measurement used (e.g. survey or observation), and the procedures for enrolling the participants into the study, as well as the steps taken to collect data.

The **Results** section is where the authors cite statistics and statistical tests to indicate what level of support existed for their hypotheses. Here you may read information about means, correlation coefficients, ANOVAs, and more. (It can feel a bit intimidating and/or annoying if you do not understand these statistics, but I will give you the basics for learning about these in a future chapter).

To be completely honest, the Methods and Results sections are the only sections of the article that focus on the complete facts from their (the authors') study. Everything else is a collection of opinions, interpretations, summaries, and/or descriptions of other studies. If you truly want to know the truth about a study, and nothing but the truth, the Methods and Results sections are the only place you will find it. As we progress throughout this book, you will gain the knowledge and skills you need to read, understand, and even critique journal articles.

Because these sections of an article can be difficult for some to understand, there is another section called the **Conclusion**. Sometimes this is also called the **Discussion** section. In this section, the authors of the study usually summarize and interpret their results within the context of their previous research completed on that topic, but this time, the language is more user-friendly or easier to read.

When I say they interpret their results, you should know that this means that there is a great deal of guessing involved. For example, in our previous example, they may have found that having a motivational speaker was associated with an increase in self-esteem. They may even guess why there was an increase in self-esteem, but the reality is they did not know, or have proof, as to why that would be the case. Many students take these Discussion sections, interpretations, and guesses to mean that there is "proof" for something, when nothing could be further from the truth. Yes, these interpretations are often educated guesses, but they are guesses.

Because of there is so much uncertainty and a high probability for mistakes in research, the Conclusion or Discussion section will also often address some of the greatest mistakes or "threats" to their study. On one hand, researchers will let you know that you need to take their results with a "grain of salt," and in the next paragraph they will often say something like, "Our results are so important they will change the world!"

The final section (discussed here) of a peer reviewed journal article is the **Reference List**. In an article, it is usually just called **"References."** The reference list will include a list of all the studies referenced in that article. It is important to add here that a Bibliography and a Reference List are quite different from each other; a bibliography points readers to studies that may be of interest, while a reference list will only cited the studies if it was previously cited in the study. (We will learn more about APA citation methods a little bit later).

If you have written a research report or research paper before, chances are high that your report would consist of a literature review, a conclusion, a reference list, and perhaps an abstract and a title page (or title of your paper). Student research papers are unlikely, however, to include a methods or a results section.

Behavioral Sciences Goals and Types of Behavior Research

We learned earlier that there are many reasons to conduct research, and for many of you, there may be even more reasons to understand research. If you were to conduct your own research, you really need an end-goal, meaning what you hope you will get when you're done with a particular study.

These end-goals can simply referred to as Behavioral Sciences Goals (BSG) and Types of Behavior Research (TBR). The first, and simplest, BSG is "**Description**." If this was your goal, you would likely look at averages, trends, and existing attitudes among a certain group of people, your customers or clients, or any other given population. You may be interested in describing what percentage of population is married, how many people enjoy your product or are satisfied with your company's service, or how many juniors or seniors are in a given classroom. The Description goal is pretty much like taking a snapshot and describing what you see from your data.

The next BSG is **Prediction.** Prediction is a much more difficult goal to accomplish, because it essentially goes beyond the Description goal of "What is going on right now?" to estimating what will happen in the future as well. For example, research on obesity is filled with "predictive" studies, indicating that those with obesity are increasingly at risk for other health problems in the future.

Another example of a Predictive study could involve our hypothetical study where we have motivational speakers attending junior high schools, and *then* we see what happens to their self-esteem. The idea is "If-then."

Similarly, college entrance exams are excellent examples of Predictive research. Why are colleges so interested in your SAT or ACT score? It is because they can predict how well you will do in school (at least, to some degree) by how well you do on your college entrance exam.

The third Behavioral Science Goal (BSG) is **Explanation**, or to Explain, what is going on the research. If Behavioral studies describe the *what*, and the Predictive studies predict the *when*, the Explanation studies explain the *why*.

As mentioned, there are many Descriptive studies about obesity, indicating how many people in a given population are obese. We could also *predict* how likely a person will be obese based on their age, gender, where they live, their socioeconomic status, their diet, and their exercise levels. We could go even further to explain why their risk for obesity will go up or down based on those factors. It may seem obvious, but that isn't always the case.

A great deal of research has been interested in the social development of teens who spent enormous amount of time on video games, and many of these authors were concerned about the social and emotional consequences for spending all that time on video games. It is not surprising as to what they found: teens spend a lot of time using technology, and males, in particular, spent a great deal of time on video games. What was surprising about many of these studies is that a large percentage of teen males who spent a great deal of time playing video games actually have strong social skills and friend networks. As mentioned before, being able to explain why this was the case is very difficult, and in a later chapter about "experiments," we will learn why.

In addition to the three Behavioral Science Goals, the purpose for research can often be classified as one of the Types of Behavioral Research (TBR). The most simple or basic type of research is called, well, "**Basic**" research. The primary goal of Basic research is to understand something; you are not trying to change anyone or anything. You are just observing things or data.

For example, you may be interested in understanding why some customers frequently return to your store while others do not. As they leave the store, you might invite them to complete a survey describing their reasons for shopping at your store, and if they plan on returning.

In contrast, the second type of behavior research is **Applied** research. The goal of applied research is to change behavior. In our earlier example, if customers were willing to give you their phone number, and then you called them to get them to shop at your store more frequently, that is an example to see if you can "manipulate" their behavior. (Ironically, in the social sciences, the word "**manipulate**" simply means to change, and it does not necessarily involve anything unethical). When stores offer "Rewards" programs, or when they collect information about you and your shopping behaviors, as well as reward you for returning, that is also be an example of applied research.

Let's look at one more example. Perhaps you are interested in understanding how many new mothers nurse their infants. In that particular study, it would be "Basic" research because your goal is to understand how many new mothers are nursing, and perhaps you could have also asked them what barriers exist to nursing. In contrast, if your goal was to increase the number of new mothers who nursed their infants, then anything you did to increase those numbers, as well as collecting information through that research, would be classified as Applied research.

With shrinking budgets and increased scrutiny toward academic institutions, many are calling on researchers to focus their efforts on applied (rather than basic) research. If you could understand gun violence, or actually reduce gun violence, which would be more useful? If you could understand child malnutrition, or actually decrease the number of children who were malnourished, which would you choose? If you could understand fashion trends, or if you could start fashion trends, which one would be more useful?

Despite the usefulness and pressure to develop applied research (more than basic research), most scholars continue to engage in basic research for several reasons. Some of these reasons include (1) the turnaround time from start-to-finish for basic research is much quicker than applied research, (2) you could publish several basic research studies before you could complete one applied research study (i.e. tenure is often determined by how many publications a faculty member has), and (3) some researchers continue to passionately believe that basic research is very important.

Relationships

Most research involves looking at the relationship between two or more variables. Although we will look at "relationships" in greater detail later in this book, understanding what a "relationship" looks like will help you with the rest of this chapter, as well as future chapters.

A relationship is a pattern or link between two things, and it can usually be classified as one three types: positive, negative, curvilinear, and no (or zero) relationship. Let's take a brief look at each one.

In a positive relationship, you will see that one variable increases (in general) when the other variable increases. This probably sounds quite vague, so let's look at an example.

There is a positive relationship between eating out and calories consumed. This means that the more we eat out, the more calories we tend to consume.

For a negative relationship, you will see that as one variable increases the other variable will tend to decrease or decline. An example of this is the temperature outside and our heating bill for our houses; as the temperature rises, our *heating* bill tends to fall.

For a curvilinear relationship, it looks like a positive and negative relationship combined; at first, as one variable increases, the other one decreases, but then, at some point, as the first variable increases, the second variable decreases. Again, this may sound incredibly vague, so let's look at an example. Let's look at the relationship between our own cell phone use and how happy others feel about us.

We typically use our phones to communicate with others, and typically the greater the communication with others, the happier they will be with us. However, let's say we start bombarding them with text and phone calls when they are working or sleeping or at all times of the day; when our communication becomes intensified, others will become less happy with us.

The final relationship is a *no relationship*, often signified by a zero. This means that there is no predictable pattern or link between the two variables. You may be surprised to hear that very few combinations of variables can actually have a zero relationship, but we will re-examine this when we talk more in detail about statistics.

Hypotheses

Earlier in this chapter, we learned about the Scientific Method, with developing a hypothesis as one of its steps. A hypothesis will often hint at the Type of Behavioral Research or Behavioral Science Goal it is looking to meet.

For example, if I was interested in family dinner time, I could simply ask, "How many children under the age of 18 are having dinner at least five times per week with at least one of their parents?" (The ages of the children and the number of times they have dinner isn't required, but have some level of specificity does help narrow the research focus). In this particular example, the research question centers on "how many" or to get a general picture of what is currently happening. We can say that would meet the Descriptive Behavioral Science Goal or perhaps even the Basic Type of Behavioral Research.

How about if I asked, "How can we increase the number of meals that children under the age of 18 have with their parents per week?" At that point, we are either interested in *predicting* change or perhaps *explaining* how to increase meal times, or even causing change (i.e. applied research).

In my opinion, and I admit many researchers would adamantly disagree with me, I see very little use in separating the words "research question" and "hypotheses." Admittedly, a hypothesis is a testable research question, and a research question isn't *always* testable, but the two are so inseparably connected it's hard sometimes to tell the difference. What is more useful than arguing over semantics is being able to write different forms of research questions (ahem, I mean "hypotheses").

For example, I could ask, "Is there a link between vegetable intake and energy levels?" I could also ask, "Is there a relationship between vegetable intake and energy levels?" Similarly, "Do those who consume more vegetables experience greater levels of energy than those who consume less vegetables?" Learning how to ask questions in a variety of ways is beneficial for a variety of reasons; it helps us understand what researchers are talking about, and it will also help us understand what statistics are most useful under certain types of wording in the hypotheses (which will be addressed in a later chapter).

APA citation

Perhaps one of the first things that comes to mind when you are writing a research report is the format you are to use and how you should cite your references. **APA citation** is a very common form of citation, and the most popular form of citation in the social sciences.

In reality, writing a paper using "APA" includes more than the citations, but in this chapter, we will focus exclusively on referencing. Please keep in mind that APA referencing guidelines often change, but I will try to provide some of the most basic, as well as consistent, rules used in APA citation.

APA stands for **American Psychological Association**, and there is a great deal of pressure (for scholars and students) to follow their guidelines. Some criticize the APA for being so heavily invested in making money, as each new edition of APA leads to yet another very large book with its new set of standards we need to memorize, although with these resources being online now, that particular criticism may not hold as much merit.

One advantage for understanding and using APA format is appearance. For example, if you were to apply for a job, chances are that you would dress up to show the potential employer that you are serious about wanting to work there and that you respect yourself and their organization. After you get the job, there may also be some rules about uniforms or "dress guidelines," meaning what was appropriate or inappropriate to wear. Admittedly, organizations over time have become increasingly relaxed on these guidelines, but appearance and uniformity are still important to serious scholars. Whether you are able to follow the APA guidelines reflects whether you are serious enough or invested enough in a sense of professionalism.

APA referencing also gives readers an easy way to access the studies you use in your research report. For example, if you write about body image and cite several authors, I may be interested in learning more from those authors as well. Having a uniform approach for how to list and cite authors takes a great deal of guessing work out from those who want to learn more from those who influenced your writings.

I will list five common rules in APA citation, but as mentioned, there are many more, and if your instructor or organization expects you to follow APA to the "T," please understand there are other resources that are much more useful than this book. In addition to the APA Manual, there are several online sites available.

The first rule is that anything that is listed in the "body" of your paper must be cited in the reference list. The body of the paper is also often referred to as in-text referencing.

With in-text referencing, your goal is to be as brief as possible. For example, I would not want to say:

In a study by Dr. Jane L. Johnson, Ph.D. and Dr. Jason Fredrick Johnson, Ph.D., of the University of Alabama, in the Department of Family and Consumer Sciences, published on March 31, 2016, they found that exercise improves metabolism.

In contrast, a much better way is to say:

In one study, Johnson and Johnson (2016) found that exercise improves metabolism.

In in-text referencing, the only things you want are the authors' last names, the year it was published, and if it includes a quote, the page number the quote was taken from. I could also say this:

In one study (Johnson & Johnson, 2016), they found that exercise improves metabolism.

Notice how this differs from the previous example. The authors' last names are now within the parentheses, and the "and" is now an "&".

Another rule within APA citation deals with the format of the Reference List. As mentioned previously, it is labeled "References" when it is typed on the page. It will be listed, or more precisely centered at the top of the first page following the end of the Discussion or Conclusion.

In the reference list, this is where you provide more information for your readers. For example, for our earlier Johnson and Johnson reference, it may read:

Johnson, J. L., & Johnson, J. F. (2016). Metabolism and energy among teenage athletes with GPAs above 3.5 in a rural community. *Journal of Exercise, 54 (2)*, 22-34.

What did you notice about this reference?

1. The "&" is not within parentheses in this particular example.

2. For this particular APA edition, the first line is not indented, but subsequent lines are.

3. The name of the journal is always italicized, along with the volume number (i.e. 54) and its accompanying issue number (i.e. 2) in parentheses, are also italicized. The page numbers follow and it ends with a period. (The page numbers are not italicized).

Summary

The Scientific Method consists of several steps to help researchers discover, analyze, and share their results. The Scientific Method is also a standard or ideal that researchers may seek to meet; not all research is shared.

Research can often be classified by its "goal" or "type." These are more specifically referred to as Behavioral Sciences Goals and Types of Behavior Research. Hypotheses will often imply which goal or type the research study would be.

APA citation is an important characteristic or attribute of social science research. Not only does it provide a standard method for checking references, but it also symbolized a high standard of research and professionalism.

Review Questions

1. What is the purpose of the Scientific Method?

2. What are the specific steps of the Scientific Method?

3. Identify the anatomy of a peer reviewed journal article.

4. Identify the value and purpose of the Methods and Results sections.

5. Name the three Behavioral Science Goals.

6. Name the two Types of Behavioral Research.

7. What are some reasons why APA citation methods are heavily required in some classes?

8. What are some basic rules or guidelines for APA referencing?

9. What is a hypothesis?

Personal Application

1. Goal-setting has a lot in common with the Scientific Method. Identify a goal you would like to work on and could potentially complete within the next week. Write it here:

_____

2. Research (however you define it at this point) what benefits your successful completion of the goal are likely to bring. List them here:_____

3. Write your research hypothesis. For example, it may be something like this: Will my _____ (insert your goal here) improve _____ (include what the research suggests it would help you improve on)?

4. Track your progress and how it affects you for one week, and then draw a conclusion about whether your hypothesis was supported. Write your conclusion here:

_____

Chapter 3: Ethics

Professionals, including scholars, across a wide variety of fields are expected to follow a set of ethics (or ethical guidelines). **Ethical guidelines** are provided to protect others, as well as yourself. At the very minimum, they are provided to keep you from getting into trouble, and they are designed to help professionals keep their priorities straight.

Although we will be covering some very specific terms and ethical guidelines, the reality is that not every professional or scholar is given a list of specific guidelines. Sometimes they are implied rather than written down. And sometimes the ethical guidelines aren't always as clearly presented as we'd like them to be.

Maximizing benefits and decreasing risks

Take, for instance, a general guideline for research, which is to **maximize benefits and minimize risks.** It sounds simple, but sometimes it can get very tricky. Recently I conducted research about the steps trauma victims go through in order to experience healing, and my research involved interviewing individuals to learn about their stories of trauma and healing. Although I am pleased that my research has helped others, one of the academic criticisms of my research is that it is very subjective, meaning that how my interpretations were drawn was based on what I thought as much as what the data showed.

As mentioned earlier, there is a lot of pressure (especially among scientists) to have the data speak for itself, essentially, rather than having my conclusions being so subjective. On a practical note, to have my subjective research backed up by more empirical data would also mean that my research could be used by more professionals.

There was a long list of rewards or benefits possible, for me, for other professionals, and for a much larger number of trauma victims and survivors. So I crafted my research questions, developed my survey, and identified a group of cohabiting and married women who were at high-risk for domestic violence I could give my survey to.

One of the ethical guidelines, however, is to get permission or approval before you hand out your survey. I tried to get approval from the university, but I did not get it because the group I wanted to collect information from was already considered "high risk" and the questions from my survey were considered too sensitive.

It was clear to me that there would be potential benefits from my project, but I was informed that the risks were too high to offset the benefits. What if the questions would re-traumatize those who were asked to complete the surveys? What if their partners found out I was asking about violence, safety, and trust? Would that put the group I was interested in helping in greater jeopardy than they already were?

Scholars and other professionals are frequently confronted with these types of dilemmas. They are passionate about a topic and about helping others, and it is difficult to know when the benefits offset the risks, or even with the risks offset the benefits. Even outside observers do not always agree on where the line is between what is acceptable and what is not. Fortunately, there are some general guidelines that most professionals do agree with. Sometimes, however, it is easier to recognize when ethical guidelines have been violated rather than when they have been kept.

Perhaps the most frequently cited example of ethical violations, at least in the social sciences, is commonly referred to as the **Milgram Experiment.** (Stanley Milgram actually conducted more than one experiment, but because of the attention this one received, it is referred to as "the" experiment). In the early 1960s, Milgram was very interested in the Holocaust, and more particularly, why citizens (who knew better and had a conscience) did not stop it earlier. That was essentially his research question: Why do people do bad things when they know it is wrong to do so?

Milgram hypothesized that it may be that there are other values or social pressures that cause people to "look away," or to avoid doing things they know are just and right. One of these values, especially in the 1950s and in earlier decades, was "obedience." There was a sense of thinking that authority figures knew best, and that following their instructions was the right thing to do for family and country. "Rocking the boat" disrupted family life and threatened the unity of family and country; you could not be a good citizen (which was an important value) by going against your authority figures.

Using "obedience" and "authority" as the centerpieces of his study, Milgram devised an experiment to test his hypotheses. When participants agreed to the study, and understood that they would receive a small level of compensation for their study, they were introduced to two people: a scientist dressed in a lab coat a supposed second participant (hereafter often referred to as the "learner").

The participants were informed that this study was about learning, and that the first participant (hereafter often referred to as the "teacher) would read pairings of words and then later test the learner to see what he had remembered. To ensure that the learner did not see the pairings of words, and to ensure that the teacher could not see the learner, each of the participants were in separate rooms communicating to each other through a speaker.

When the learner failed to repeat a word pairing, the teacher was instructed to administer a "mild" shock to the learner by pushing down a lever that sent electricity from a device and through the probes (i.e. wires) attached to the learner. Each additional time the learner made a mistake, the teacher was instructed to increase the amount of shock given to the learner.

As you might imagine, the learner made plenty of mistakes. What was shocking was that the majority of teachers ended up administering the highest level of electricity to the learners, even when the learners indicated that they had a heart condition, would plead for mercy, or at the end, would no longer say anything, suggesting that the learner had died from the experiment.

Where the "teachers" evil or did they lack a conscience? On the contrary, most if not all of the participants assigned as teachers would pause and ask to stop the experiment to check on the other participant. The scientists, however, would remind them that they agreed to participate, and "for purposes of the experiment," they must continue. Some participants asked if the scientist would accept responsibility for what would happen, or what might have already happened, if they continued the experiment; the scientist agreed to take full responsibility, and then most participants went on to seemingly administer lethal doses of electricity to the participant in the next room.

The good news to this story is also the bad news: The "learner" participants were actually scientists themselves, and the "shock" given did not happen at all. It was all an act. Although we can take some comfort that no one was physically hurt, the psychological risks (of thinking a person had killed another human being) were very high.

Most of us would agree that there was considerable value to this experiment. We did learn a great deal from this experiment about morality, obedience, and choices that hurt other people. And we did learn why people would continue to be obedient, even when it was uncomfortable to do so. Participants in the study were also provided with some monetary compensation, or **incentive**, to reward them for their help.

Although there were benefits to this experiment, there were many more issues or problems. Whereas there is a societal belief in **beneficence**, meaning doing good and by providing help or charity, this experiment was closer to that of **malfeasance**, or the willful act (usually of someone who is in authority) of hurting someone, which is unethical. Milgram betrayed the values of humanity by using his authority to put the people who trusted him in harm's way.

Even though Milgram informed the participants of the true purpose and nature of the study after the experiment had been completed, the use of **deception** and the risk of psychological harm violated (at least, today's) ethical standards for research. Typically the **debriefing** or explaining the nature of the study or experiment should be done before the study or experiment

47

begins, not after, to ensure that participants can make an informed and educated, willful decision about whether they should continue to participate. Their participation should be **voluntary**, not mandatory or coerced.

Having participants who are considered "high risk" for harm, especially the elderly, children, individuals who cannot read or speak your language, and those with psychological or physical disabilities, makes the standard for ethical guidelines more rigid, and researchers must prove that there is little to no risk that their participation will lead to any type of emotional or physical harm. Participants from these populations set off "red flags," not because the people are dangerous, but rather because it indicates a greater level of caution and scrutiny before approving research projects that involve these populations.

Institutional Review Boards and Consent Forms

Fortunately, scholars are not left alone when trying to determine whether their research should move forward given certain levels of risk. In universities, there are Institutional Review Boards, more commonly abbreviated as IRBs, with colleagues who help determine what risks are involved, and who give the final determination as to whether the research project can move forward.

Many times, especially when IRB's consider your project to be more than minimal risk, you will be required to provide a **Consent Form,** also referred to as an **Informed Consent,** to debrief potential participants about the nature and purpose of the study. In the Consent Form, you would also outline the benefits and possible risks associated with the study, as well as give the participants information on how they could ask questions if they had any.

Of course, if the participants could not read, or if there was the likelihood that they could not read, you would need to read the Consent Form to them. When I assisted with the Early Head Start Research project, which consisted of low-income families, I would read through the Consent Form and ensure that they understood what the study was about and to give them opportunity to ask any questions.

There are many different types of Consent Forms, and each has its advantages and disadvantages. The key is to ensure that, whatever you use, it is used to help the participant best understand the nature of the study and whether they should (based on their own interpretation) participate or not.

Sometimes research proposals are classified as "exempt," which basically means there is no risk in that study. Students who develop or administer a survey may want to check with a faculty advisor, who can help them navigate to the right committee or resource to ensure that they have approval before handing out their surveys or conducting certain types of research.

The Importance of Anonymous and Confidential Responses

Before moving onto the next section, let's look at two different tools designed to protect participants and clients. The first is when a person's identity is **anonymous**, meaning that you do not know who participate in the survey. Anonymous surveys are useful when trying to collect sensitive information, including sexuality, drug use, violent or illegal behaviors, or perhaps even income or politics, including attitudes toward same-sex marriage, abortion, and legalizing marijuana. Providing anonymous surveys often helps participants feel more comfortable with answering the questions truthfully.

If the participants' identities cannot be anonymous, they certainly can still remain **confidential**. This means that you know who participated, and you can connect their identities to what they said, but that you will not reveal their identities or personal information (in a way that will reveal their identities) to other people. For example, you would *not* want to say, "A 43 year old construction worker who lives at 2345 Tallyho Drive in Sacramento, California, let us know that he is not happy with his marriage."

In my earlier example with the Early Head Start Research project, I got to know the participants very well because I interviewed and videotaped them several times over a period of three years. Matter of fact, I would frequently see these participants in the grocery store or when going to see a movie, and maintaining their confidentiality was not easy. Was it rude of me to say "hello" to them (because then they may feel I was letting everyone know they were low-income) or was it rude of me to *not* say "hello" to them (because I knew them and perhaps they thought I was dismissive of them)? More often than not, these participants would approach me in public to say "hello," and I would have to tell those I was with (i.e. my family or friends) that I could not tell them how I knew those who came up to me to say "hello." How awkward is that?

Confidentiality is all about showing respect for others, and showing your participants and clients that they can trust you with their need for privacy. Breaking confidentiality or sharing information you should not is breaking others' trust in you, and can lead to serious legal or other workplace penalties.

Two recent debates about the collection of data can also be given here, and each could be a case study on the intersection between technology, ethics, and the law. First, Facebook has often been in the news because of concerns that our personal (i.e. private) information is collected, and potentially seen or used by others who have less than kind intents toward us. Another debate involves the collection of data or information from our cell phones, including whether we should have the right to determine how identities and conversations (i.e. data) are being collected. In each situation, the violation of trust may be just as harmful as the violation itself.

Plagiarism

Although fraud and plagiarism can certainly be part of the research process, as well as issues confronting professionals from a variety of fields, the seriousness of these issues merits their own sections. You are more likely to be more aware of plagiarism (than fraud) because college campuses bring the topic up more than fraud, and because plagiarism *is* more common than fraud. However, there are essentially two sides of the same coin of dishonesty.

Plagiarism refers to using someone else's work without giving them credit. It is also refers to receiving credit for something that you should not get credit for. In academia, plagiarism is considered a serious offense, and penalties can range anywhere from failing an assignment to losing your right to attend that college and having a record of dishonesty on your school records, which potential employers typically look at before they consider hiring you.

In this digital age, it is admittedly very easy and convenient to copy things, including movies, music, and books. Simply selecting "copy/paste" from the document you are reading to transfer information onto your research paper will also save you an incredible amount of time.

Some even argue that information (and other resources) should be free, and/or feel that just because they have one copy (of music, a movie, or a book), that they should have the right to make copies for personal use or to loan out to friends. And like speeding on a highway, most people do it because they won't get caught. This debate about what our rights are for accessing, maintaining, and sharing resources with digital content will likely continue for decades, and will fill the courts with endless cases.

For now, the important thing to recognize is—not exactly what plagiarism is—but why it is important to understand how serious plagiarism is. Let me provide a personal example. Although I have written several books, the amount of money I have made off those books is nominal. It is even a bit embarrassing that, given the amount of time researching, analyzing, writing, editing, and promoting a book, as well as paying others for their assistance, I make less than minimal wage for each of my books. Matter of fact, for most of my books, I have *lost* more money than I have earned. Most of my books require an intensive working period of more than two years from start to finish, so when I see unauthorized electronic copies of my book on the Internet or with students, it is a bit frustrating. Matter of fact, it is theft, and it shows that they do not value my work.

The point I am trying to make is not about me. It is about you. When you plagiarize, you are using someone else's work for your own gain, and not valuing their efforts enough to give them the credit they deserve. That is why plagiarism is so serious in nature; it cuts to the core of your integrity as a student, and it is predictive of type of employee you will be.

Of course, students are not the only ones who might plagiarize. Other professionals, including researchers, have plagiarized (for the same reasons some students plagiarize), and it has often ended their careers.

Now that we have established the seriousness of plagiarism, let's look at what plagiarism can consist of. Most of us recognize the general definition of plagiarism, of using someone else's work without giving them credit, and assume this must mean that we need to cite everything we use. That is part of it, but it goes well beyond that.

When we hand in a paper that is largely a "copy and paste" product filled with quotations or minor adjustments (i.e. substituting the word "use" with the word "utilizes"), we may not meet the strict definition of plagiarism but we certainly meet the spirit of it. It isn't uncommon for me to ask students, "What part of the paper is yours?" As their instructor, I can do my own research on a given topic, or perhaps I already am familiar with the research on a given topic, but I am looking for originality, creativity, and work they can call their own.

Similarly, it isn't uncommon for students to use portions or sections of their own previous research papers and copy/paste them onto assignments or papers for other classes. I understand the reasoning and the temptation to do so, and I also understand

the sense that "I should be able to do what I want if I wrote it."
Again, instructors are looking for originality, creativity, and
work separate from other activities; similarly, employees are
seldom paid for work they did from projects in previous months
or years. Employers pay for and expect something that is more
current and displays a commitment to that certain project or
organization, not just the past.

Whether or not you agree with my interpretation of plagiarism,
you should check with your department, instructor, or agency as
to what their definition or standard of plagiarism is. Ignorance is
unlikely to save you if you have committed plagiarism (by their
standard).

Fraud

Fraud, similar to plagiarism, is a form of deceit with the intent
to gain something when it isn't deserved or merited. More often
than not, it consists of the fabrication of data or identities.

Fraud can occur by misrepresenting what you have accomplished
on a resume, or it can be fraud if you make up (rather than
collect) data. Sometimes researchers have committed fraud; a
few examples will be provided here.

I knew of a faculty member who was responsible for a financial
counseling center. He presented himself in a way where others
believed he was a certified financial counselor, but he was
nothing of the sort. He ended up embezzling money from the
clients, lost his job, and faced legal penalties.

In another situation, a scholar who researched the effects of
divorce presented her findings to politicians, who ended up

making policy based on results. The only problem was that the researcher didn't have any findings; she made them up.

In a third situation, a recent news article discovered that some faculty members rigged the peer review system to increase the number of publications they could get, and thereby increase their status and income. They did this by sending their qualifications along with fake identities (i.e. names) to journal editors, and after they submitted an article they hoped would be published, they also offered (under a fake identity) to review that article. Not only did they do this for themselves, but there was a "ring" of scholars, who agreed to expedite the publication of articles for each other.

In each of these situations, I am confident the accused started with the best of intentions. "I want to help families with their finances." "The lives of divorced families and children need to be improved." "I need to get publications to receive tenure and keep my job." But the line was crossed where they pretended to be someone they were not in order to get what they wanted, and in the process, no amount of their good deeds can cover up the lack of trust others now have in them.

Ethical Dilemmas in Your Profession

In addition to building and maintain trust, ethics is a collection of values designed to guide and protect individuals. Unfortunately, as alluded to earlier, there will be times when one of your values will compete with another value.

Some of these dilemmas may involve being expected or required to do something unethical at your job. Perhaps it may mean "tweaking" the results of a report to make your organization look better than it is. Perhaps you will be faced with the knowledge that someone in your company is taking things (i.e. office supplies, money) when you know the company does not pay them what they need or deserve. And perhaps, like me, it will be struggling with keeping your clients' identities and stories confidential when they make it difficult to do so. Although there are some advantages for taking a wait-and-see approach, or keeping an open mind during this time, making up your mind right now as to what ethics are important (to you) can relieve some anxiety and provide the framework for the kind of employee or professional you want to be (and be seen as by your colleagues).

Summary

It will be interesting to see how our understanding of ethics or ethical guidelines, in research and in practice, change over the next decade with advances in technology. Questions will be raised and further debates will be waged of what is appropriate, ideal, and legal.

One of the legal and ethical battles of the future will involve the rights of teens who have differing values than their parents. For example, is it ethical to ask teens about their sexual behaviors or drug use, and is it ethical to ask teens about how they differ with their parents' religious views? This issue, over what is an adult, and whether one enters gradually into it, has had huge ethical implications, and will certainly remain that way for many years to come.

There are many ethical guidelines or vocabulary lists to memorize, but the true test of one's ethical principles is whether that person abides by the ethics they say they believe in. Following ethical guidelines may be the difference between keeping a job and getting fired, as well as the difference between maintaining or losing the trust of a client. It seems that, while many ethical standards may evolve with advancing technology, many of the core ethical principles will likely remain in place for the next several generations.

Review Questions

1. What are ethics? How would you define the word "ethics"?

2. Why are ethical guidelines provided or important to scholars and other professionals?

3. What does maximizing benefits and minimizing risks refer to?

4. What is the Milgram Experiment?

5. How would you define the following words: "incentive," "beneficence," and "malfeasance"?

6. How would you define "voluntary," "debriefing," and "deception"?

7. What is a Consent Form, and what is its purpose?

8. Compare plagiarism and fraud. How are they similar? How are they different?

9. Define "anonymous" and "confidential." How are they similar? How are they different?

Personal Application

1. Google "Milgram's Obedience Experiment" to learn more about this famous study. You may also be interested in learning more about the Belmont Report and the experimental study with Lil' Albert.

2. Imagine yourself in your future occupation. Who will trust you? Why will they trust you? How will you avoid a loss of trust?

_____

_____

_____

3. After reading through the text, has it changed your attitudes or beliefs about plagiarism and fraud? If so, in what ways?

_____

_____

_____

Chapter 4: Developing a Survey

One of the biggest myths about research is that it is easy to create a good survey. If we left one word out, or "good," then I would agree; it is easy to create a survey. But it is not easy to create a good survey. Good (or valid) surveys take time, patience, and work.

In most of the "research methods" courses I teach, I ask students to form groups and to create four good survey questions. I offer some guidance, but for the most part, there is a lot of flexibility in the kinds of questions they can create.

Once the survey questions are complete, I ask for their feedback on the process. Most are very confident, perhaps even extremely confident, that their surveys have really good questions.

We then talk about validity, reliability, and operationalization, and discover that every survey created in class needs serious revision. The goal, after all, is to create a good survey, or to measure what we hope it measures; if it doesn't do that, then what is the point of the survey?

The process of creating four questions, evaluating or critiquing them, then writing four new questions that we feel good about often takes two full class periods. This timeline is often needed because measurement concepts are some of the most difficult to understand, and even more difficult to apply.

And I'm not just referring to students. I have tried to write dozens of surveys, and I can tell you that, initially, the survey looks awesome, but when I test it I feel like I had wasted my time with writing a survey. Similarly, one semester my colleagues and I were assigned to write a survey to evaluate our students' knowledge of ethical guidelines, and despite several weeks of work and dedication, when everything was said and done, let's just say that the survey was not what we hoped it would have been.

You might be asking, "If my professors can't develop a good survey, then what are my chances?" Actually, your chances are quite good. Creating a good survey may involve a little luck, but it has more to do with five principles than it does with luck, and we (as professors) should have used them more faithfully. When we follow these principles, we (eventually) come up with a good survey. When we fail to follow the principles, our surveys usually flop.

The Five Principles for Creating a Good Survey

Principle #1. Know what your variables are.

If you want to have a good survey, it's important to know (and then remember) what you are measuring. A **variable** is anything that varies, and in the social sciences, it often refers to individual attitudes, beliefs, or behaviors.

For example, you might be interested in how many times teen males look in the mirror. One teen male may look in the mirror once per day, and another teen male may look in the mirror 100 times per day. Because the answer can vary, we call our topic a *variable*.

A variable usually has an abbreviated title or name of the question you ask. For example, if you asked teen males, "How often do you look in the mirror?" the name of your variable may be "Looking in mirror frequency." More commonly, the variable is even shorter than four words in length. Things like "self-esteem", "fashion preference", and "current dieting practices" may serve as variables, whereas the questions that ask about those things will likely have more words, and will likely have response options (i.e. answers) as well. You may also consider variables as topics, whereas your survey will ask questions about your topic. A sentence or survey question is not your variable; it is a measurement of that variable. Many times, when people start writing questions, they focus too much on writing a lot of questions and are side-tracked from what they initially set out to learn about. It is a little like getting into your car and forgetting where you are driving to.

What else can vary (between one person and the next)? Ice cream flavor consumption, parenting status, marital status, income level, race/ethnicity, sexual preference, amount of money spent on clothing per month---just to name a few!

Principle #2. Know what options you can use to ask your questions with.

It is important to know there are many options for how to measure most variables. Some of these options involve **Comparative Scales of Measurement**. The most popular comparative scale of measurement, at least in the social sciences, is the **Likert Scale**, which measures the relative intensity of a response. For example, you may be interested in how likely a customer would return to your store, which we'll pretend is called "Fashion-Wise." Your survey questions may be:

	Strongly Agree 5	Agree 4	Neutral 3	Disagree 2	Strongly Disagree 1
I enjoy shopping at Fashion-Wise.	5	4	3	2	1
I look forward to returning to Fashion-Wise.	5	4	3	2	1
I prefer Fashion-Wise to other retail stores.	5	4	3	2	1

When you look at the response options, or the answers participants can give, you can see that participants can have a "strongly disagree" response or a "strongly agree" response, with other options in between. The key here is that each number represents something.

Although strongly agree, agree, neutral, disagree, and strongly disagree are very common response options, there is the possibility for other options, including differences in wording and numbering, as well. Some scholars prefer to remove the "neutral" option because it can sometimes be difficult to interpret (ranging from 1-4), and sometimes surveys will even range from 1-7.

The key here is to make sure the survey fits your needs. If, for example, you wanted to know how much your consumers like your new ice cream product, some response options may include: 7-loved it; 6-liked it, 5-it was okay, 4-neutral, 3-not bad, but wouldn't want again, 2-definitely disliked it, and 1-hated it. However, it is generally a good idea to ensure similar wording with polar opposites.

Using **semantic differential** response options (another comparative scale of measurement) may be particularly useful when you are interested in opposing adjectives for one concept. One of my colleagues was interested in how junior high students rated their friends, and especially their best friends, by using a survey with semantic differential response options.

My best friend is: Loyal   _: _: _: _: _: _: _ : Disloyal

Fun   _: _: _: _: _: _: _ : Boring

A variation of the semantic differential method can also be seen at pediatrician's offices; children are asked to point at the face (much like the space above) that best represents how much pain they are feeling. It would also be interesting if teaching evaluations (for your professors) would use a semantic differential format:

My teacher is: Kind_: _: _: _: _: _: _: Mean

Open_: _: _: _: _: _: _: Intolerant

The third comparative scale of measurement is the **Guttman Scale**. Scholars who use the Guttman Scale are primarily interested in a single score that represents an inclusion or exclusion of other responses. For example, if I was interested in running, my survey could look like this:

1.   I have gone running in the last month. Yes/No

2.   I have gone running in the last week. Yes/No

3.   I ran at least a mile within the last week. Yes/No

4.   I ran more than three miles within the last week. Yes/No

5.   I ran a marathon within the last week. Yes/No

You will notice (above) that someone who marked "yes" on item 3 should have also marked "yes" on items 1-2. Similarly, if another person marked "no" on item 1, then they would have marked "no" on the rest of the items as well.

Principle #3. Know what <u>level</u> of measurement your survey can use.

Another option to consider when creating your own survey is what **level of measurement** your survey will be in. The level of measurement usually refers to the type of answers participants can respond with (to your survey questions). There are some similarities to comparative scales of measurement, in that they are each resources when writing survey questions, but they also have their differences. For now, you should know that the level of measurement will determine what kind of statistics you can use; comparative scales of measurement are not always as straightforward as to what statistics could be used when testing your research question. Additionally, the level of measurement helps you determine how precise your response options (or the answers respondents will give) will be. For example, which of the following questions below would give us greater precision or specificity?

1.   What is your height? (Please mark one). Short   Tall

2.   What is your height? Please list feet and inches. ___ ft ___ in.

From the examples above, you can see that the first question's responses options are not very specific. What determines short and what determines tall? Does it vary by gender or age? Similarly, you could ask a person if they ever shop at your store or you could ask how many times they have shopped at your store in the last month. It would also likely be more beneficial to find out how many servings of fruits and vegetables a client consumes rather than asking them if they eat fruit and vegetables.

In general, the more specific the answer the more information and options you have to work with. In order of specificity, from least to greatest, the levels of measurement include nominal, ordinal, interval, and ratio. Let's take a look at each level of measurement.

The first, **nominal**, is best used when considering categories or groups. It is also used when you can't really rank something to be more or less than something. For example, if I asked which flavor of ice cream you liked most, I could not say that chocolate is more of an ice cream then vanilla. More importantly, scholars use the nominal level for concepts like race/ethnicity, job titles, and gender. You could also use it in market research by asking which store a person likes to shop at the most; one is not "more store" than another, and would thereby considered under the nominal level category.

The second category is the ordinal level of measurement. **Ordinal** literally means "order," where you can rank one from least to greatest. For example, you can order class rank from least to greatest: freshmen, sophomore, junior, and senior. You could also rank your teachers by your least favorite to favorite with everyone in between.

The **interval** level of measurement is the third category. You can rank or order data, but with much greater precision. The one thing that interval data can do that ordinal data cannot is that it has equal distance between units. For example, consider if two people step on a scale, and one person weighs 150 pounds and the other person weighs 151 pounds; there is one unit or one pound that separates the two people. If two more people got on the scale, and one person weighs 200 pounds and another person weighs 201 pounds, that is also a difference of one unit or one pound. The one pound that separates the first two people is the same amount of weight (i.e. one pound) that separates the last two people; one pound means one pound, and it means something very clear to us. Many times, researchers will treat their data gained from the questions using the Likert-scale (comparative scale of measurement) as interval data, although I acknowledge that some researchers passionately believe it should be treated as ordinal data.

The final level of measurement is the **ratio** level. The difference between ratio level data (or responses) and interval level data is that the ratio level data has a zero point. Recall the earlier example of height; is there any possibility that anyone in your class is zero feet and zero inches tall? That's why height would likely be measured at the interval (and not the ratio) level.

In contrast, look at the following survey question (below). There is the possibility that some respondents will answer "zero," some may say "one," and others may say more than that. For the person who said "one" and the person who said "zero," there is a difference of one ticket; in this sense, it is very similar to the Interval level but because "zero" is an option, and there is an equal distance between units, this survey question is considered ratio-level.

How many speeding tickets have you ever received?_____

Remember that ratio is more precise than the others, but sometimes variables can only be measured a certain way. For example, there is no "zero" point for race/ethnicity.

Principle #4. Make certain your survey is valid.

One key for developing a good survey is making sure that your survey is valid. This sentence is a bit repetitive because valid does, in fact, mean "good." More than that, a **valid** survey will measure what it intends to measure; validity is the most important characteristic you want your survey to have. Without *accuracy*, the survey will not measure what its intended to measure.

When creating a survey, one of the most common mistakes is trying to ask a lot of questions about a wide variety of things. Sometimes it works well, but many times it doesn't. Why?

Let's say you are interested in creating a survey about body image. Perhaps you create three questions (below), where the response options range from strongly agree (5) to strongly disagree (1).

1.   I feel good about myself.   5 4 3 2 1

2.   I feel good about my body.   5 4 3 2 1

3.   People tell me I am good-looking.   5 4 3 2 1

If we look more closely, each question does appear to ask about how a person may feel about themselves, or it may ask about things that may help them feel better, but do they all ask specifically about body image or could the questions be addressing something else? Question 1 asks how a person feels about themselves, not their body; question 3 asks how others perceive them, not how they (themselves) view their bodies. Although I would argue that Question 2 may be a good question, some may misinterpret it; could the reader wonder if it refers to how well their body works or how healthy they are?

This is why "validity" goes hand-in-hand with "measurement precision," because the more precise we are in measurement, the more likely we will have a valid survey (and vice versa). If you had a bath scale, you would know if it was valid because it would provide you with a precise and accurate weight; if you stepped on it and it said "You look good today," that may be interesting information but it does not measure what you intend it to measure. It would not be a valid measure of what you set out to measure.

(Note: I often use the words "**measure**" and "**survey**" interchangeably. Although all surveys consist of one or more measures, not all measures are surveys. Some measures include instruments or other options. However, surveys are the most common form of measures in the social sciences, and that is why we are focusing on them in this chapter).

It is important to keep in mind that validity is seldom a "have it or don't" kind of thing. Validity falls on spectrum, where we can have a great deal of confidence the survey measures what it's intended to measure, no confidence that it measures what it's intended to measure, and anywhere in between.

Just as there are different methods for asking a question, there are different avenues for assessing the validity of a survey. These types of validity include face validity, construct validity, criterion validity, and content validity.

Face validity is the weakest of all assessments of validity. Face validity means that a measure appears to measure what it is intended to measure. It is basically an opinion and lacks concrete evidence of whether the measure actually measures what it's intended to measure. One person could have the opinion that their survey is valid, and another person could have the opinion that the first person's survey is not valid; either way, there is no real proof.

Construct validity is more useful and powerful than face validity because it demonstrates how well one survey compares to or is linked with another survey or topic that it should be linked to. For example, imagine that you created a survey to measure how satisfied individuals are with their marriage. Because you do not know how valid it is, you may want to compare it with another survey that has demonstrated strong validity. To do this, you could ask married couples to complete two measures: the questions you created about marital satisfaction, and additional questions from a measure (about marital satisfaction) that previous research has found strong validity for. If your measure of marital satisfaction correlates or closely mirrors the results from the other measure (which already has demonstrated validity), then that would show that your survey is valid as well.

You may be asking, "Why would you give to measures that ask the same thing?" One reason may be that your measure only has three questions, and the other measure with established validity has 54 questions; if you could show that your measure is just as effective at assessing something as the 54-item measure, and which could save clinicians a lot of time using it, that would be something both research and clinicians would be very interested in. In this instance, you are likely trying to establish **convergent validity**, which means how much your measure and another measure's results mirror each other.

It may also be possible that the reason you have developed your measure is that you want it to measure something slightly different than the measures already out there. Take the marital satisfaction measure, for example, that you created; perhaps your measure of marital satisfaction focuses exclusively on how meal planning as a couple affects the marriage. Because it measures marital satisfaction, you would expect it to assess some of the same things that would be measured by the more, well-established measure (and valid measure) of marital satisfaction. You also would hope that it shows how much it differs because you believe that "meal planning as a couple" is a unique attribute of a satisfied marriage. When your focus is on how much the two measures differ, you are then looking at **divergent validity.** Convergent and divergent validity are each components of construct validity. Researchers who develop surveys often are interested in both convergent and divergent validity to determine how useful and unique their surveys are.

Criterion validity is used for establishing the effectiveness that surveys results can predict future events, attitudes, or behaviors. If you were interested in how successfully college entrance exams (e.g. SAT, ACT) predicted college GPA, then you would be interested in those exams' criterion validity. (For this reason, criterion validity is also often referred to as "*predictive validity*"). You could ask couples to take your "marital satisfaction" survey, and follow up with them after another two years to see if they are still married; if couples who are very satisfied (according to your divorce) are getting divorced, and if couples who were very dissatisfied are still married after two years, then that survey would not have criterion validity.

Content validity is another approach for establishing validity. To establish content validity, you need to have (their) agreement that your survey is an accurate representation of what is needed. For example, with the marital satisfaction survey, perhaps you ask about their conflict, communication, dating/recreation, and sex life; if experts in the field of marital satisfaction agreed that your questions accurately reflected what goes into marital satisfaction, and that your questions asked about those things in a valid or precise manner, your survey would have content validity.

Principle #5. A good survey is reliable.

Another key principle for developing a good survey is to ensure that your survey is reliable. You might be thinking, "I thought you already said it should be a good survey. Isn't a reliable survey the same thing?"

Think of it this way: Validity and reliability are two sides of the same coin. They are both needed for measurement precision.

Reliability refers to the degree your measure is consistent. Let's go back to the bath scale example. What if I stepped on the scale and it said I weighed 50 pounds, and then I stepped off, then back on again and it said I weighed 595 pounds? Could my weight have realistically changed that quickly?

Having a bath scale that changes its report of my weight (when I know my weight doesn't change that quickly) is evidence that my measurement, the bath scale, is not consistent. In other words, it is not reliable.

Similarly, if I stepped on the scale, then off the scale, then quickly back onto the scale and each time I weighed myself I saw dramatically different results, then I would know that my measurement (i.e. my scale) is neither consistent nor accurate. Surveys are essentially like my bath scale, as they are looking to measure something. Having both reliability (consistency) and validity (accuracy) are essential for developing a good survey.

Just as there are different types of (or different ways for establishing) validity, there are also different types of reliability. Let's look at them one at a time.

Test-Retest reliability is a popular form of reliability, and it is found by comparing the consistency of response (or answers) between two or more points in time. For example, examine the questions from a survey we looked at in an earlier section, where the scale ranges from "strongly agree" (5) to "strongly disagree" (1).

1. I feel good about myself.   5 4 3 2 1

2. I feel good about my body.   5 4 3 2 1

3. People tell me I am good-looking. 5 4 3 2 1

Let's say John (a hypothetical name, of course) took this survey and marked "4" on the first question, a "3" on the second question, and a "2" on the third question. If John took the survey again, we would look to see how closely his second survey responses matched the first survey responses. If he marked "4" (again) on the first question, a "3" (again) on the second question, and a "2" on the third question, that would be as consistent as could be; that would be perfect test-retest reliability. The more John's second survey responses varied from the first survey responses, the less test-retest reliability that survey would have.

What would happen if you could not see John again, and you could only give him a survey once? Another method for establishing reliability refers to *internal* consistency, a category of reliability that involves at least three types of reliability methods.

Recall that reliability refers to consistency. Instead of looking for consistency *across* time, we might be interested in looking at consistency *within* the measure. The most popular method for establishing internal consistency involves a statistic called the **Cronbach's Alpha**.

For this example, let's assume John marked a "5" for each of his responses, meaning "strongly agree." Marking the same number for a survey that has three questions, all designed to ask about the same thing (i.e. body image satisfaction), indicates consistency within the survey. If John marked a "4" for each and every question, that would also be perfectly consistent. When there is perfect consistency in these instances, Cronbach's alpha would equal 1.0; anytime questions 1-3 yielded different responses or numbers, the alpha or statistic would go down, potentially to 0. (Cronbach's alpha ranges from 0-1.0).

1.   I feel good about myself.   5 4 3 2 1

2.   I feel good about my body.   5 4 3 2 1

3.   People tell me I am good-looking.   5 4 3 2 1

Another option, somewhat similar to using Cronbach's alpha, is **"Split-half reliability**." For split-half reliability, after John finishes his survey, researchers will add up half of the survey responses, then compare the sum of the other half. For this example, let's add one more question to our survey (below, #4) and change the participant's name (from John to Susie).

1.   I feel good about myself.   5 4 3 2 1 Susie=5

2.   I feel good about my body.   5 4 3 2 1 Susie=3

3.   People tell me I am good-looking.   5 4 3 2 1 Susie=1

4.   I always feel good about how I look. 5 4 3 2 1 Susie=3

Imagine Susie takes this survey and marks a "5" and a "1" for questions 1 and 3 (or the odd numbered questions). On the even questions, or questions 2 and 4, she marks a "3" for each. If you

75

add up Susie's responses for the odd questions (5+1=6), you will see that they equal her responses for the even questions (3+3=6). Even though she did not mark the same answer or number for each question, the total for the odd questions equals the total for the even questions; this shows that there is consistency within the measure. (You could also take the sum from questions 1-2 and compare them with the sum for questions 3-4). The more the sums for each half differ, the less split-half consistency it would have.

A third type of method for establishing internal consistency involves observation (rather than paper-pencil surveys). This type of consistency is called **interrater reliability**.

Some scholars who study marital satisfaction invite couples into their lab and videotape their interactions. At the end of the session, "coders" will examine the facial features and body language of the spouses to determine how each spouse is interacting with the other. One coder will see the husband frown, and but another coder may think that spouse is grimacing, and not frowning. The less consistency between coders with interpreting facial responses, the less interrater reliability there would be.

One last paragraph before we move on to the next set of ideas: Do you recall when I said that reliability and validity are two sides of the same coin? Both are needed for measurement precision, or for having a good survey. Imagine if I stepped on a bath scale and it said I weighed 12 pounds. If I stepped on it again (just seconds after the first measurement) and it again said I was 12 pounds, my bath scale would demonstrate "test-retest reliability," but it certainly would not be valid. That is why we need both for a good survey; it needs to be consistent and accurate (or consistently accurate).

Operationalization

Most measures or surveys contain more than one question about a variable. We may know what the variable is, but we may not know what to do with all the data once we have it. Imagine we had 50 people fill out our survey on body image satisfaction; what would we do to summarize or understand all the data?

Operationalization is the process of defining the variable, as well as explaining how to interpret the survey results. It consists of everything that shows how the survey operates. In our sample survey, we would first need to define "body image satisfaction." It may seem obvious, but it is still necessary, especially with abstract or vague variable or variable names. Perhaps we could define "body image satisfaction" as the level of content one feels toward how they view their body. Next, we look at how to interpret the results. In our earlier example with Susie (given below for convenience), Susie marks a "5" on question #1, a "3" on question #2, a "1" on question 3, and a "3" on question #4. To simplify the results, we could add up Susie's responses: 5+3+1+3= 12. Because the highest possible score on the survey was 20, we now need to interpret what a 12 out of 20 means. Would a 12 out of 20 mean that Susie has a high level, a moderate level, or a low amount of body image satisfaction? Knowing what each number means is part of the operationalization process.

1. I feel good about myself.   5 4 3 2 1 Susie=5

2. I feel good about my body.   5 4 3 2 1 Susie=3

3. People tell me I am good-looking.   5 4 3 2 1 Susie=1

4. I always feel good about how I look. 5 4 3 2 1 Susie=3

Additional Measurement Concerns

In addition to developing a valid survey, social scientists are especially concerned with **social desirability bias**. This happens when participants' responses may change because of sensitive cultural norms. For example, if we gave a survey to junior high students about drug use, there may be a tendency for many of them to under-report their drug use because of the disapproval their teachers or parents have towards drug use.

Any sensitive topic may lead participants to alter their responses from what they believe or know to a response that is culturally more acceptable. This is more common when there is the possibility that the researchers knows the participants or where participants worry that others will find out what they marked on their survey.

Do you remember my earlier example of developing a survey for women who were at high-risk for domestic violence? Although the survey was not approved, and the study did not end up taking place, if it had taken place there would been a good chance for social desirability bias; women may have been worried that their partners or spouses would ask what they reported, and so they might have under-reported abuse.

Social desirability bias is particularly more common when the survey is in the form of an interview. Have you ever had someone knock on your door and ask for your opinion about a political candidate, same-sex marriage, or abortion? You do not know that person asking the questions, and you do not trust what they will do with your answers, and so you may revise or change your answer in a way that they will be more accepting of it.

Similar to social desirability bias is reactivity. **Reactivity** refers to anytime a participant may alter their behavior because of the conditions around them. (Social desirability bias refers to the reasons why participants give an answer they don't believe but would conform to what is expected or preferred, and reactivity refers to changing their behavior). Because of the overlap or similarity between the two terms it isn't always easy differentiating them.

When I was young, my parents would discipline me by making me put my hands high on the wall; the punishment usually came because I was fighting with one of my brothers. After a few minutes, my arms would start to lower, and my parents (especially my dad) would tell me to get my arms up higher than they were. In response, I usually made my arms shake (to simulate being in pain); when my parents saw my struggles, they would have compassion on me and tell me that I could then put my hands down. They would then immediately ask if I learned my lesson. "I did," I said. But the truth is I had no idea what lesson I was supposed to learn by putting my hands on the wall.

Did they seriously believe I would not (ever) fight with my brothers again? And what would happen if I said I had not learned my lesson? The choice was easy: Tell them you learned your lesson and the punishment stops. I knew they wanted me to have learned my lesson, and so I told them I learned it. In that silly example, having my arms shake was an example of reactivity (i.e. altering my behavior because I was aware of my surroundings), and telling my parents that I learned my lesson (even when I didn't) was an example of social desirability bias.

Note: Although we have looked at examples of social desirability bias and reactivity, researchers refer to *social desirability bias* more often when they are talking about surveys, and reactivity typically when they are talking about *experiments*. Each can affect the validity of the survey).

Summary

Developing a good survey is one of the most difficult, and most important, things a researcher can do. Scholars, clinicians, and businesspersons make decisions based off the results from surveys, and if the survey is not a good survey then the results may not be accurate. Treating a person with a chronic disease, moving a business location, or working to change a family's perception of things can have serious repercussions, and it is important that our information comes from a source that is valid to help us make the best decisions.

Review Questions

1. What is a variable?

2. What are Comparative Scales of Measurement?

3. What are Levels of Measurement?

4. What is validity? Why is it important?

5. What is reliability? Why is it important?

6. What does "operationalization" refer to?

7. What is social desirability bias?

8. What is reactivity?

Personal Application

We have definitely learned a lot of new information, but sometimes having additional examples can be quite useful. For many of my classes, I ask students to complete a "silly survey," or a survey that has a bunch of ridiculous questions.

Look at the "silly survey" in Appendix B (toward the end of this book) and take a few minutes to look over those questions; you may even consider answering the questions. Look for any questions that may not be good questions, and, using your own words, explain *why* they aren't good questions. When you understand why survey questions may not be good questions, that is when you will truly understand the purpose for "validity" (or having a valid survey). For example, consider the question that asks how many people they have kissed; would this include all forms of kissing or just romantic kissing?

It will also be helpful to look for nominal, ordinal, interval, and ratio-level questions. Can you find an example for each? Next, look for Likert-scale questions.

To learn more about reliability, please turn to Appendix A, which is an actual survey developed by some of my students. In the two-thirds of Appendix A (where it is numbered 1-33), you will see Likert-scale questions. For each of the questions (again, in the last two-thirds of the survey), look at the combination of questions and do the following:

1.   Guess what they are trying to measure.

2.   Guess whether they are consistently measuring exactly the same thing.

The pairings that were written to measure the same variable include:

1-3   4-6   7-9   10-12 13-15 16-18 19-21

22-24 25-27 28-30 31-33

In all fairness, these questions were written before they really understood the concept of "validity" and "reliability." But reviewing these questions again and again helped them, so hopefully they will help you as well for learning about validity and reliability.

Chapter 5: Samples and Survey Techniques

Now that you have created your survey, you will need people to "take" or complete it. This is true whether your goal is to collect information about a group of people or if it is simply to establish validity and reliability for your new survey. (Of course, as mentioned in a previous chapter, you will want to ensure you have approval from the Institutional Review Board, or an appropriate organization, before proceeding).

Recall the purpose of research: You want to find something out, and in the social sciences and in marketing, you want to find something out about people. Let's continue with our previously cited survey about body image satisfaction; who would you want to fill out the survey?

If your answer is "everyone," that is a very popular answer. Another answer might be "anyone who is willing to complete the survey." Unfortunately, most researchers quickly find out that getting people to complete their survey is difficult work; how many people do you think are *happy* when a telemarketer calls them and asks them to take a "few minutes" for a survey?

One of the things that researchers tend to do to limit the scope of their study, and to increase the likelihood of representation of their target population, is to narrow down who the population is. For example, if I was interested in body image satisfaction, I could focus exclusively on females between the ages of 12-14 living in Sacramento. My research question could then be: Among females between the ages of 12-14 living in Sacramento, how satisfied are they with their body image? Compared to getting everyone in the universe to complete my survey, finding a sample large and representative enough of Sacramento females between the ages of 12-14 is much more doable.

Notice I have frequently used the word *"representative."* That is the primary purpose of a sample, to represent the larger population.

Let's consider an example outside of the social sciences. When you go to a grocery store, sometimes they offer "samples" of a particular product. Sometimes the deli or bakery will provide a piece or portion of something they hope you will buy. (I remember the last time I had a sample of ice cream, and although I had no intention of buying ice cream when I went into the store, I left the store with a large carton of ice cream).

What *is* a sample? By definition, it is a smaller piece or part of the whole. The sample chocolate chip cookie you eat at the grocery store is supposed to represent what a bag of chocolate chip cookies will taste like when you buy them.

You may be thinking: Well, duh! Why wouldn't it?

But let's look at it this way: Perhaps you went back several times (in the same day) to get several samples of that same chocolate chip cookie. What if each of the chocolate chip cookie samples did not taste the same? Perhaps it would be because the dough had not been mixed well, or perhaps the cookies came from different batches. Even though a sample cookie should represent the other cookies that look like it (or are the same kind of cookie), people are not cookies. There is so much diversity in

84

people that it is impossible to find one person who represents every other person as well.

We differ on gender, race, religion, politics, geographic residence, family background, socioeconomic status, and the list goes on and on. While getting everyone to participate in your study is ideal, it is far from likely (or even possible). Your next best bet is to get a sample that accurately represents a larger group, also known as a population.

Before looking at the different categories and types of sampling techniques, let's provide additional clarification about the differences between a sample and a population. Let's assume you would have a survey about university student eating experiences.

Getting your survey to everyone may be somewhat complicated, even at your own university. Even if you had the permission and technology to email your survey to every student at your university, the *response rate* (i.e. those who complete your survey) for emailed surveys is usually very low. Of course, you could call every student, but you would need to have their phone numbers, and that is unlikely and would require an enormous amount of time. You could post a banner or sign asking for volunteers to take your survey, but that usually leads to few volunteers and low response rate.

If there is a central location where students on your campus tend to eat, that may be the best place to look for students who would be willing to complete your survey. They have an investment or interest in the food. Once you've made your decision, you go to the eating area, which holds 12 restaurants, and you ask how many diners eat at their restaurants each day. The number or total is around 800.

You may want to consider optimizing your time, and you realize the two hour block for the most patrons will be between 11 am and 1 pm. Two hours sounds reasonable and you go to each restaurant, asking individuals to participate in your survey; up to 100 students agree to complete your survey. The population for one day is around 800, but how many students had ever ate there? This is why sampling can get very complicated; sometimes it is difficult knowing how large the population really is.

Probability Sampling

When you do know the size of your population, you might consider probability sampling techniques. **Probability sampling** is where everyone in the population has an equal chance for participating. Polls for politicians are often reasonably good (but far from perfect) at predicting a winner because they use probability sampling; everyone within a certain population (i.e. state, nation) starts with the same chance for being enrolled in the study, but then the pollsters only call on a small percentage of people. **Randomness** is a key characteristic of probability sampling; when there is true randomness, the chances for obtaining a representative sample is quite good.

Imagine you are in charge of a retail store that provides a "rewards" program for loyal shoppers; most of these programs require you to give them at least some of your contact information in exchange for the rewards (i.e. discounts, coupons, etc.). Occasionally, you may want to send an email to your most loyal shoppers and asking them to participate in a survey about their experiences with your store. You could, of course, send the email to every one of your loyal shoppers, but because you want to send out a different survey every quarter, you do not want to annoy your customers with excessive emails. Instead, you could randomly select a portion (e.g. 25%) of your loyal customers to email to every three months; every three months a different set of customers receives an email invitation to participate in a survey.

To make sure the 25% that you send an email to each month reflects the other 75% of your loyal customers, it is important that you use a truly "random" technique. For example, if you take the first 25% of the customers on your list, is it possible that they may differ in tastes and spending habits than the rest of your loyal customers? Perhaps the 25% who signed up first for your program signed up first because they were more frequent shoppers than the other 75%, and so you could not make assumptions about all of your loyal customers based on the 25%.

As an alternative, there are plenty of software programs and websites designed to give you a list or **table of random numbers**. The purpose of the random numbers is to remove bias as well as to increase the likelihood that the sample (and survey data) represents what you want it to represent. From the table of random numbers, you could then select which customers to send a survey invitation to. The 25 customers, when chosen randomly, should do a good job of representing the rest of your customers' attitudes and shopping habits; the greater the number you select randomly, the better it will represent your population of loyal shoppers.

Nonprobability Sampling

There are times when it is difficult (or impossible) to know how many are in a given population, let alone making sure that you know everyone's chance for being selected for your sample. Do you remember our earlier example, where you surveyed those who at on-campus? Sometimes you simply have to start somewhere, and get who you can get to take your survey. This is particularly true when you work for an organization (or are on your own) with limited money and other resources. During these times, convenience is both an asset and a challenge.

A "**convenience sample**" is a sample that you gain by convenience; it does not rely on probabilities. For example, if you developed a survey, who would you ask to complete the survey? Who would be most likely to complete the survey? Perhaps your friends, classmates, and family members?

The strengths of convenience sampling is that it is relatively quick, at least compared to probability sampling, and it is at least a start for answering your research question. But there are serious concerns with **generalizability**, or **external validity**, which is the ability of your results applying to a group outside of the sample you surveyed.

Let's look at an example. Let's say that, you create a survey about text messaging; you are interesting in how often others send and receive text messages and whether it interferes with their social and family lives. Out of convenience, or to save time, you ask your friends if they will fill out the survey; after expressing their joy in being asked, they complete your survey.

You now look at your completed surveys, and you are able to answer at least two important questions. You were able to find out, on average, how many text messages have been sent and how many are received. (Let's guess than is 112 per day, total). You were also able to determine, from the survey results, that text messaging helped more than it hurt their social lives.

Given the hoopla about how much technology interferes with "real life," you decide that you need to publish what you found, and you start telling everyone that they will need to increase their text messaging. What is wrong with this scenario?

Being able to answer that question depends on us being able to answer the following questions:

1.   What population does your convenience sample represent?

2.   How well does your convenience sample represent the larger population?

3.   Who is part of the larger population?

With convenience sampling, we don't even really know who we are trying to represent. Can we say that your convenience sample accurately represents all college students? Would your results accurately represent non-college students? And would your results accurately represent those whose lives are different than those you studied?

Because convenience samples often do not represent the larger population, many scholars use "replication." **Replication** is a process for which studies are repeated, often under different circumstances or which different groups of people than previous studies have been completed with. For example, research has found that parents who demonstrate high levels of warmth and moderate levels of strictness tend to be the best type of parents for their children. This may make sense to many of us, but could other types of parenting be more beneficial for children in circumstances that we did not grow up with?

Indeed, as this study was replicated, or tried again with different cultures, they occasionally found that very strict parents (who we might consider less kind) were sometimes the best type of parents, especially when children were at-risk for some of life's greatest challenges. Research often uses replication, not only to be more certain of the original results, but to see how the results might change under different circumstances. Consider, for example, whether blood pressure holds the same level of risk for people regardless of their race or ethnicity. Or whether the shopping attitudes of those who live in Seattle would apply to (or be the same as) those living in Green Bay, Wisconsin.

Another type of nonprobability sampling is "Purposive Sampling." **Purposive sampling** is best used when you are looking for a very specific population to study from. For example, you may be interested in color-blind females, and instead of surveying a large group, you may go directly to the leader of a support group for color blind females, and ask for their participation.

For my dissertation, I was interested in couples who were becoming parents for the first time. More specifically, I was interested in the transition to parenthood, which most researchers consider to be the time between of pregnancy and the first child's second birthday.

My purposive sample consisted of couples who were participating in child birth classes; most couples who attend child birth classes are preparing for the birth of their first child. Going directly to a place that focused or helped the population I wanted to study made the process much easier than it would have been if I had simply tried to interview everyone I knew—or if I had tried to interview people at random.

Longitudinal and Cross-Sectional Approaches

In addition to considering the sampling technique you should (or could) use, you will also want to consider whether a longitudinal or a cross-sectional study would best fit your needs. **Longitudinal studies** are often referred to as ideal (at least compared to cross-sectional studies) because longitudinal studies are able to look at *individual change across time.*

Many "aging" studies, or those that study changes in individuals as we get older, use a longitudinal method. For example, if we want to look at how wisdom, motor coordination, diet and lifestyle change over time, then we need to have a study that measures these variables over that same time period.

In my dissertation work, where I studied the transition to parenthood, I surveyed couples who were expecting to have their first child with the next few months. I again surveyed those same couples once their first child was about six months old. Some of my results included:

-the more satisfied couples were with their marriage or relationship, the more active fathers were with raising their children

-couples who were the most satisfied before having a child were the most satisfied after having a child, but couples who were the least satisfied (with their relationship) before having a child experienced a steep decline in their relationship after their child was born

-having similar world views, as well as similar (albeit not identical) problem solving strategies within marriage was associated with a slight increase in marital satisfaction; however, in heterosexual relationships, men's and women's problem solving strategies tend to be quite different from each other, especially after having a child for the first time.

Although longitudinal studies are often considered the gold standard of research, relatively few studies use a longitudinal approach because it is time consuming. Instead, most studies use a cross-sectional method for studying variables.

Cross-sectional studies are essentially one-time snapshots, comparing one or more groups. For example, in my dissertation work, if I had used a cross-sectional method rather than a longitudinal method, I could have surveyed a group of expectant parents and then I could have surveyed a *different* group who had been parents for at least a few months. These two groups could have been compared with regard to their relationship quality, and I could have made assumptions about what impacts relationship quality during the transition to parenthood. However, these assumptions could not always be made with as much confidence as I would like to have in my results.

Let's imagine we want to look at "financial cautiousness," or how protective individuals are of their finances, over their lifetime; our sample consists of young adults and senior citizens.

When we look at our results, we can see that senior citizens are more conservative or cautious with their finances than are young adults; does that mean that getting older will make us more conservative or cautious with our finances?

The immediate answer is "perhaps," but the full answer lies in what is called "*cohort effects*." My grandma grew up during the Depression, and learned to conserve just about everything. "Make it last. Wear it out. Make it do, or do without." My grandma, even when she had a decent amount of money in her elderly years, still shopped for clothes at thrift stores and yard sales. Because she had lived such an important time in her life without money, she was as protective as she could be with it.

Although we may have lived through some economic uncertainty, the political culture and government resources for dealing with those stressors is very different than when my grandma was a child. Government welfare was basically non-existent during the times of her greatest poverty.

A **cohort effect** is something that is unique to a particular period of time, like the Depression. You may also be interested in looking at technological literacy, so you compare the elderly with teens and find that teens are more technologically literate; does it mean that teens are smarter or does it mean that the elderly did not have the kinds of (unique) experiences that teens have today with technology? A cohort effect may also help explain why senior citizens are less likely than young adults to wear their seatbelts; the enforcement of seatbelt use wasn't mandated until 1984 (or after, depending on the state one lived in).

Ironically, whereas longitudinal studies give us greater confidence in our assumptions about how things (and people) change over time, we can only make assumptions about the group of people being studied. Cross-sectional studies can show us differences between groups, but they cannot explain if those differences are caused by time (or age) or by cohort effects. Then which one is best, a longitudinal or cross-sectional design?

The truth is that each has its advantages and disadvantages. Although very rare, some studies combine the two designs and use a **cross-sequential** design. For a cross-sequential design, researchers will gather longitudinal data from two more groups of people. For example, if we are interested in diet patterns as we age, we could:

-collect survey data from today's teens, and then again when those teens are senior citizens

-after today's teens become middle aged adults, we could start collecting data from a new generation of teens

Summary

There are actually a large number of approaches researchers can use, some being quite complex. Remember that the goal is to answer the question, or the research question, and each can be used to answer that question in different ways.

Researchers are human, and there are reasons for going with the easiest and quickest approaches for answering their research question. But that convenience often comes with a price, of not being able to have as much confidence in the results as we would like to have.

Remember that a sample is a piece or portion of the whole (or a larger group). Its primary design is to represent that larger group; some sampling techniques do a good job but are difficult to employ, while others are relatively easy to use but do a poor job of representing their group.

While samples can usually be classified as probability or nonprobability, study designs are usually either longitudinal or cross-sectional. Which one you use depends on your resources and goals for the study.

Review Questions

1.   What are some important differences between a probability sample and a nonprobability sample?

2.   What are some advantages for using a convenience sample? What are some disadvantages?

3.   What are some differences between a longitudinal and a cross-sectional design?

4.   What is a sample? What is its purpose?

Personal Application

This section is broken down into "steps." Follow these steps to ensure that you understand the concepts in this chapter.

Step 1. Look at the following questions below and choose which one you are most interested in.

-Are parents with one child more permissive or strict than those with more than one child?

-When considering young adults and senior citizens, which group is most likely to want assistance with retail/clothing purchases?

-Are teens or middle-aged adults more likely to experience a Vitamin D deficiency?

Step 2. What would a probability sample (for the population in the above research question) look like? What would a nonprobability sample look like? What are the advantages and disadvantages for each?

Step 3. Which would be better to answer your question: a longitudinal or a cross-sectional design? Why?

Step 4. Imagine your ideal job. The CEO of that organization calls you and said that you might just be the perfect person they want to hire, but that they want to see "samples" of your work. What will you send them? What kind of a "sample" will it be (i.e. probability, nonprobability)? What are the advantages and disadvantages for each (in this situation)?

Chapter 6: Observation

Thus far, we have primarily focused on one type of measure: surveys. However, it is possible to measure or "survey" something without asking other people to fill out a questionnaire or to complete an interview. We could also use "observation."

There are many advantages for using observation rather than paper-pencil (or electronic) surveys. There are also several disadvantages. The key is to find the type of survey or assessment that best meets your needs. Generally speaking, observations tend to take more time and they are also usually more expensive than surveys; many observations require the purchase of video and audio equipment. Additionally, observations tend to get data from far fewer people than surveys. (For these reasons, surveys are much more common than observations). However, if you are interested collecting *sensitive* information, or are concerned with getting the truth from people (due to social desirability), then observation is a good way to go. Observation also often allows us to get the "larger picture" than what a survey could provide.

Quantitative vs. Qualitative

Observations are often either classified as "**quantitative**" or "**qualitative**." A quantitative observation is designed to find a count, frequency, or number of a particular thing. For example, if you wanted to see how your clothing store varies from one day to the next in how many customers visit the store, you could simply count how many customers enter the store. Similarly, a nutritionist or dietician can count how many of the all-you-can-eat restaurant customers pick a dessert *before* eating a vegetable.

98

Or a parent could count the number of times her young daughter holds her breath (during a temper tantrum) per day, to see if that count or frequency changes from one day to the next.

Although this may sound like a simple process, it definitely isn't in most circumstances. Can you imagine the distractions that may keep a scholar (or anyone) from creating a legitimate count in the examples in the previous paragraph? It gets even more complicated when you may be trying to count more than one behavior for more than one person.

A qualitative observation has more freedom and flexibility in what is observed (than a quantitative observation). For example, you could go to a professional wrestling event, and observe the reactions of young children who are attending that event. The options are much more open, so the researcher is not tied down to looking at a particular thing, but it is much more difficult to summarize. Do you have any friends whose conversations move from one topic to the next (and then to another) very quickly? Similarly, qualitative observations can, at times, be difficult to summarize and be quite time consuming.

Ethological/Natural vs. The Lab

When many people hear the word "observation," they tend to think, "Well, I can do that. I can just watch people." Although observation does including watching, how to watch, interpret, and analyze behaviors is often more complex than most people imagine.

One of the decisions to make is whether the observation will be in the lab or in a "**natural environment**." Years ago, as a

99

graduate student I visited over 200 families, and videotaped fathers and their children playing. The initial idea was that fathers and their children would feel more comfortable being videotaped in their homes (rather than in a laboratory setting), but the opposite was also true; many fathers weren't happy with the idea of being videotaped in their own homes, and felt like we were being critical of how they parented.

But what would have happened if we asked them to be videotaped in a **lab setting**? (A lab setting would often consist of individuals being in a small room, designed by the researchers, to limit outside influences on the family). Would it have been better? We could have limited many of the distractions, including phone calls, people knocking on the doors. There likely would have been some disadvantages; if fathers felt criticized in their homes, I imagine that feeling would have been magnified in a lab setting. There is also the likelihood that many fathers would avoid driving to a lab setting simply to be videotaped and analyzed.

The advantage for using a lab setting can also be its disadvantage. Lab settings "control" for other distractions, but it cannot control for the fact that people behave differently when they know they are being videotaped or observed.

Years ago I saw a minivan go through a drive through at Burger King. Just before getting to the speaker, the driver was yelling at the passenger children. "Shut up! Seriously, shut up! Sit down or you won't get anything!" A moment later, I heard (through the speaker), "Welcome to Burger King. What can I get you today?" There was a bit of a pause, and then the driver of the minivan responded in the kindest, sweetest voice you've ever heard. "Well, hello there. Thank you so much. Yes, let's see

100

what we'll be having today. Children, what would you like to have?"

It took me several minutes to stop laughing. I don't think I had ever seen that kind of turnaround before, and yet it does illustrate how people change their behavior when they realize others are watching or listening to them.

Case Studies

Case studies are used when you want to focus on one person, or perhaps a very small group of people. You may want to observe the life of someone living with Down Syndrome, the eating patterns of an Amish family, or the shopping behaviors of a family living in poverty. The goal of a case study is to get as much information, and especially as much detail and context, as you can. Many may use case studies when they are wanting to write a book about a particular person.

Returning to Validity

Perhaps one of the greatest challenges with observation is being certain that you are seeing what is happening, or even that you are observing what you think you're observing. In my previous example of videotaping fathers and their children, when others would watch the videotape, they would all say how awful, cold, and distant the fathers were with their children. They then considered how terrible the children's experience with their fathers must be even worse when we (the researchers) weren't in the home. As I watched the "coders" examine videotaped recordings of the fathers I recorded, I asked a simple question. "How do you know their frustration is with their children and not the researchers who are videotaping them?" No one could answer that question. And yet that would be a very important question to answer.

Some observers go to great lengths to ensure their data is valid. John Gottman, who has studied marital interactions for decades, invites couples into a lab setting. There the couples are videotaped, but they also have other measurements, including heart monitoring, to assess stress levels.

Summary

There are many options for how, where, and when to observe people. Whether you want to observe people or give them a paper-pencil (or electronic) questionnaire depends largely on your goals, your resources, and your limitations (such as time). Although questionnaires tend to be more convenient than observations, observations tend to provide more context and depth of a topic. Questionnaires and observations also have the burden of being valid; assessments that are not valid will not provide valid (i.e. accurate) responses.

Review Questions

1. On a separate piece of paper, or by using the space below, compare traditional surveys with observations (with regard to strengths and challenges). As this chapter is relatively short, it may be a good idea to skim through the chapter to find these answers.

Advantages for using observations

provide more context and depth of a topic

Challenges for using observation

time consuming ; expensive

2. Identify some reasons why you would use "quantitative observation."

to see how much time I spend on my phone
how much water I drink

3. Identify some reasons why you would use "qualitative observation."

attend a place & observe the reactions of ppl.
like children at a park

4. What is "validity"? Why is it important to have "valid" observations?

    accurate ; so they can provide accurate responses

Personal Application

1. When (or why) do you think you would use "observation" in your career? List some ideas below.

    How many ppl. are buying this certain style clothing.
    What days do more ppl. come to shop.

2. Practice observing a group of people, or perhaps even only one person (preferably with their permission first!). What are you going to observe? Would this be qualitative or quantitative? What challenges did you find with observation?

Chapter 7: Statistics

Few words emit as much disdain as the word "statistics." It is much like asking everyone how much they like liver. For most of us, just the idea of liver is enough to gross us out.

Or perhaps you are on the other end of the spectrum. You like liver. Or at least you like statistics. You've memorized every statistical test and term and spend your weekends performing t-tests and ANOVAs.

Wherever you are on that spectrum, this chapter just might have something that you can use, learn, and master. Chances are also high that, if you have learned about statistics before, what I will share with you will seem a bit different than what you have heard. There is a reason for that: Our goal is to actually understand statistics, not just compute them or spew out some gobbly-gook nobody in their right mind understands. Statistics should be used to actually help us in our professions, but somewhere down the road, statistics has become a source of painful magic; we watch it and repeat what we're hypnotized to remember, but we don't understand it.

After years of teaching basic statistics, I want to share a few things that work for students (and a few things that don't work). First, if you are doubtful that you can learn statistics, I simply ask for a chance. I was a math major in college, and yet when I took a statistics course for the first time, I felt hopelessly lost. I remember how it made me feel: stupid. So as my southern friend once told me, I ask of you as well: "Hang in there like a hair in a biscuit." *How* statistics are taught can make a huge difference with whether or not we understand the concepts.

Second, even if you have taken a statistics course before, please be patient. Perhaps you know the lingo and have confidence intervals for breakfast, but by the end of this chapter you will likely see statistics in a completely different light. Don't discard everything you learned from your statistics course, but please do not discard what you learn from this book. Again, you will be able to understand statistics in a meaningful way, and if nothing else, you can use these strategies when you want to explain a complex statistical test or procedure to someone who may not have the background in statistics that you do.

Finally, I am going to try to trick you. I will try to trick you into understanding statistics without you knowing it. We'll see how I do. I have seen hundreds of students use these techniques, patiently, and successfully. Most have come from these strategies and end up saying these words, "I finally get it." Perhaps you will be one of them. Please be patient with me (and yourself), as we will be going through a bit of tedious work that we need to understand before working on the more difficult (and fun?) stuff.

Central Tendency and Variation

I hear what you're saying. . .

"Dr. Cook. You said you were going to help us understand statistics, and then you throw *these* words out. Central tendency and variation? What's up with that?"

Fine. We'll skip it. Let's look at something else. Let's look at . . . averages.

Averages are important because they give us a rough snapshot about what is going on. The average temperature. The average height. The average income level.

Averages can come in handy with your future occupation. Knowing what the average amount of salt consumption is for a particular racial group before it increases the likelihood of hypertension, or the average amount of income your customers are generally willing or able to spend at your store in January (to help you price your products or service) can be valuable pieces of information to have. But what does it really mean when we talk about "averages"?

An **average** is used as an estimate, or middle ground, that is designed to give us one image for a larger, much more diverse, group. To help us do that, there are three "averages" to keep in mind.

The first average, or the one that is most commonly cited, is the "**mean**." The mean is the arithmetic average. But let's move past definitions and see how this actually works.

Below is a list of numbers, where each number represents how often one person has eaten out in the last month. The two zeros mean that two different people did not eat out last month; one person ate out once, another person ate out twice, and another person ate out 12 times.

0

0

1

2

12

To find the mean, you add up all the numbers (i.e. 0+0+1+2+12=15) and divide by the number of people who answered that question (5). Your mean is 3 (15 divided by 5). Your mean tells you that the average amount of times that people eat out is 3 times for last month.

The next average we can find is called the "mode." The **mode** is simply the most common number. Look below and see what the mode would be.

0

0

1

2

12

If your answer was "zero," you are correct. So far, we have looked at two different types of "averages," and each has given us a different answer.

Let's look at one last one: the median. The **median** can be found by putting the numbers in order (which I already did for you) and then selecting the number that is in the middle. When driving down the road, the median is what divides two halves of the road, and the same is true for the statistic known as the median. When we look at the numbers again (below), there are five responses: two zeros, a one, a two, and a twelve. If you had to find the middle of all of those numbers, where would it be? If your answer was 1, because it is literally the middle or falls in the middle of all the numbers, you are correct.

0

0

1

2

12

So now we have learned about three different ways of saying "average," and so the next time you read about "averages," ask yourself which one they are using. Before moving one, here are few more things about these averages.

First, it is possible to have more than one mode. Look below at a slightly different list of numbers, and you see there are two zeros and two ones; both zero and 1 are considered "modes." Having more than one mode can confusing, and researchers will seldom report the mode(s) when that happens.

0

0

1

1

2

12

Second, the mode works well for any level of data (i.e. nominal, ordinal, interval, or ratio), but is usually best for nominal level data. For example, if I asked 30 people what their favorite ice cream flavor was, by the end of their responses the most commonly cited ice cream flavor would be the mode. Third, the mean works well with interval and ratio (but not nominal) data, and the median is also best for interval and ratio level data, but I have seen it used with ordinal data.

Type of statistic	Definition	How to find it	Levels of measurement it works well with
Mean	The arithmetic average	Sum all the responses and divide by the number of responses	Interval and ratio; does not work well with nominal data
Median	The number in the middle	Sort the numbers/data from least to greatest; the number in the	Interval and ratio; can work for ordinal at times. Does not work with

		middle	nominal data
Mode	The most common number/ response	Find the most common response	Works well with all levels of measurement; this is the only "average" that works well with nominal data

I imagine I have not tricked you at all, and you have discovered my devious plan; you have realized that averages are central tendency statistics. **Central tendency** simply looks at where the center is, and for that we look at averages. But what is variation?

Variation looks at how far the responses, as a whole, are from the mean. Perhaps an example would make more sense. Let's look again at how often individuals eat out (below). You can see that the responses vary or range from zero to 12; the "**range**" is a statistic that looks at the difference between the smallest number (referred to as the minimum) and the largest number (also known as the maximum). The range is a measure or statistic for variance.

0

0

1

2

12

The other statistic that is commonly used to describe variance, or variation from the mean, is **standard deviation**. Although we certainly could learn how to calculate a standard deviation, what I want you to remember for now is that the standard deviation is another tool or measure of variability from the mean. (The standard deviation is used in several statistical tests, and although I agree it is important, there are other things I think you will find more useful for now. Perhaps we will revisit it at a later time).

Revisiting Relationships

Recall from a previous chapter that relationships look at links between two or more variables. Rather than bore you with new (or even more) statistics, let's look at what these patterns or links actually look like and practice what you have already learned.

Imagine we give a survey to five people: Abe, Brody, Cody, Eli, and Fred. Each of them is asked the following questions:

A. How many hours do you spend on video games each day?

B. How happy are you, on a scale of 1-5?

C. What is your energy level today on a scale of 1-5?

D. Are you a parent or a child?

E. What is your employment status?

Below is a table with their answers. For example, we see that Abe reported playing video games one hour per day, is very happy, but has low energy; he is a child and yet is somehow working full-time. Take a moment to review the table below before moving on to the next paragraph.

Name	Hrs on video games per day	Happiness level on a scale of 1-5 (1= low; 5 = high)	Energy level (1= low, 5 = high)	Is this a child or a parent? (Child = 1, Parent = 2)	What is your employment status? (1= unemployed, 2 = part-time, 3= full-time)
Abe	1	5	1	1	3
Brody	2	4	2	1	2
Cody	3	3	3	2	2
Eli	4	2	4	2	1
Fred	5	1	5	2	1

Next, let's look at the pattern or link between "Hrs on video games per day" and "Happiness level." Notice that as the numbers increase by one in the "Hrs on video games per day" column, that the numbers in the "Happiness level" decrease or decline by one. Are there any exceptions to that rule? When one column's numbers go in the opposite direction as the other column's numbers, that is called a negative relationship. Whenever there are no exceptions to that pattern (i.e. as one variable increases by one, the other variable decreases by one), we call it a *perfect* negative relationship.

Now take a look at how the numbers in the "Hrs on video games per day" and the numbers in the "Energy level" column are linked. What do you notice?

If you answered that "As one column's numbers increase by one, the other column's numbers increase by one as well," then you are correct. Are there any exceptions to this rule? If not, then we call this a *perfect* positive relationship, meaning as one variable's numbers increase the other variable's numbers increase as well.

Often researchers will use a number or statistic to represent the pattern or link you see in the numbers above. A **Pearson's Correlation Coefficient**, a common statistic (often referred to as "r" or *Pearson's r*), is simply a number to reflect the direction and strength of a pattern between two variables. It ranges from -1.0 to +1.0, where a positive number reflects a positive correlation and a negative number reflects a negative correlation.

Let's look again at the pattern or link between "Hrs on video games per day" and "Happiness level." Again, notice that as the numbers increase by one in the "Hrs on video games per day" column, that the numbers in the "Happiness level" decrease or decline by one. Are there any exceptions to that rule? When one column's numbers go in the opposite direction as the other column's numbers, that is called a negative relationship. Whenever there are no exceptions to that pattern (i.e. as one variable increases by one, the other variable decreases by one), we call it a *perfect* negative relationship. A perfect negative relationship when using a Pearson's Correlation Coefficient is -1.0. You did it!

Name	Hrs on video games per day	Happiness level on a scale of 1-5 (1= low; 5 = high)	Energy level (1= low, 5 = high)	Is this a child or a parent? (Child = 1, Parent = 2)	What is your employment status? (1= unemployed, 2 = part-time, 3= full-time)
Abe	1	5	1	1	3
Brody	2	4	2	1	2
Cody	3	3	3	2	2
Eli	4	2	4	2	1
Fred	5	1	5	2	1

Now let's take a second look at how the numbers in the "Hrs on video games per day" and the numbers in the "Energy level" column can be expressed with a Pearson's Correlation Coefficient.

Do you see that again that, as one column's numbers increase by one, so do the other column's numbers? Are there any exceptions to this rule? If not, then we call this a perfect positive relationship, meaning as one variable's numbers increase the other variable's numbers increase as well. A perfect positive relationship is expressed with a Pearson's Correlation Coefficient of +1.0.

Whenever you hear about a Pearson's Correlation Coefficient, that is all it is looking at---patterns or links between two variables. The more perfect the pattern, the closer it will be to

+1.0 or -1.0, depending on whether it is a positive relationship or a negative relationship.

Let's look at one more example when calculating a Pearson's Correlation Coefficient with one minor change. Look again at the pattern or link between the numbers in the "Hrs on video games per day" and "Energy level" (below). What do you see?

Name	Hrs on video games per day	Energy level (1= low, 5 = high)
Abe	1	1
Brody	2	2
Cody	3	3
Eli	4	4
Fred	5	1

Again, we *tend* to see that as video game time increases, so does energy level, but with one exception to that rule. Fred's experience does not fit with the overall pattern. That means the Pearson's Correlation is definitely positive, because the relationship is positive, but it is definitely going to be less than +1.0; because there *is* a pattern between the columns (or variables), we know that the Pearson's Correlation Coefficient is going to be more than 0.

Many times researchers will look at the effect size, also known as the true effect size. The **effect size** is a method for looking at the true strength of the relationship, and it is done by squaring the statistic. For example, if I had a Pearson's Correlation Coefficient of .20, I would multiply .20 by .20 and get .04. On a scale of 0 to 1, .04 is very weak, and yet researchers often tout correlations of .20 (and less) as being important or meaningful

Next, let's look at whether there is a relationship between "Is this a child or parent?" and "Hrs on video games per day." We are interested in knowing if parents or children spend more time on video games each day. Whereas we can still look at patterns, like we did with the Pearson's Correlation Coefficient, our second variable ("Is this a child or parent?") is a nominal variable, and Pearson's Correlation Coefficients only work well with interval and ratio level data.

But we could try something else. We can look at the means, something we learned how to calculate earlier in this chapter. This time we are going to look at how the means compare based on whether they are children or parents. To do this, we add up all of the "Hrs on video games per day" for those who said they were a child (1+2=3) and divide by the number of responses; 3 divided by 2 equals 1.5 (which is the mean).

Let's find the mean "Hrs on video games per day" for parents. Cody (a parent) reported 3 hours, Eli (also a parent) reported 4 hours, and Fred (also a parent) reported 5 hours. Add them together (3+4+5=12) and divide by the number of responses (or parents), which is 3, and you get the mean (4). We just found that parents average 4 hours of video game time per day, and their children average 1.5 hours per day.

Name	Hrs on video games per day	Is this a child or a parent? (Child = 1, Parent = 2)
Abe	1	1
Brody	2	1
Cody	3	2
Eli	4	2
Fred	5	2

Do you know that you pretty much just calculated a *t*-test? A *t*-test looks at relationships (or links) based on whether there are differences between the means for two different groups (i.e. parent video game time vs. child video game time); when there are only two groups of people and you want to compare their means, that is when you use a *t*-test.

But what if you have more than two groups of people? Then you would use an **ANOVA (Analysis of Variance)**, but the process is very similar to the *t*-test. For example, let's look at how "energy level" differs based on one's employment status.

Those who are unemployed (i.e. Eli and Fred) have the highest energy levels of 4 and 5 (or a mean of 4.5); those who are part-time (i.e. Brody and Cody) have energy levels of 2 and 3 (or a mean of 2.5), and Abe, the only person who is working full-time, has an energy level of 1. When comparing the means for each group (i.e. unemployed, working part-time, and working full-time), what can you infer from these results?

Name	Energy level (1= low, 5 = high)	What is your employment status? (1= unemployed, 2 = part-time, 3= full-time)
Abe	1	3
Brody	2	2
Cody	3	2
Eli	4	1
Fred	5	1

Statistical Significance

Perhaps one of the most cited (and overhyped) statistic in the social sciences is the p value. The **p value** can be defined as:

> The likelihood you would receive as big of a statistic (examples: r, t) as you did BY CHANCE if you were to randomly draw an infinite number of samples (and tested them on the same research question).

The idea is to obtain a result that you can have confidence in, and that is large enough to mean something, and the p value has long been used as that standard. Researchers are typically looking for results that have a p value of less than .05, which they refer to as being "statistically significant."

Let's look at an example. Suppose a Pearson's Correlation Coefficient was .50 (on a scale of -1.0 to +1.0) with $p < .05$. This would mean, using the definition listed above, that "the likelihood for receiving a Pearson's Correlation of .50, by chance (or error), is less than 5% (or 5 times out of a 100); the lower the chance or p value, the greater one's confidence there typically is in the results. Some struggle with the definition and simply

119

interpret "statistical significance" to mean that the result was not a fluke, or that there *really* is a relationship there. However, it really means the likelihood one would receive that large of statistic by chance if one were to randomly draw an infinite number of samples (and test them on the same research question).

If there is a legitimate purpose for the p value, it has more to do with sampling issues than with determining how strong a relationship is between two variables. The p value is really supposed to *infer* whether the sample accurately reflects a (larger) population, and not whether what you found was important or not. (That is why the p value is used as an **inferential statistic**, to infer whether one group's characteristics accurately reflect the larger population. Another way to say this is it is measuring the **external validity** or **generalizability** of a study's results). Unfortunately, few interpret the p value correctly and the p value has become the Gold Standard for whether a study should be published or not.

The p value also assumes that our sample was randomly drawn, which as we learned before, is very rare. In short, whether you are looking to make decisions as a business or as an individual, I encourage you to place greater weight on the differences between means (like we did with the t-test and the ANOVA examples) or the effect size than on the p value.

Common Illustrations for Basic Statistics

You have likely heard the expression, "A picture is worth a thousand words." In research, pictures and/or illustrations (including graphs and charts) are meant to replace or at least summarize words. Illustrations should simplify and condense what the researchers have found. Illustrations are often used to describe averages or frequencies for one variable, and sometimes illustrations are also used to look at the relationship between two variables.

Although illustrations can help put things into perspective, sometimes they can also distort our perspective of the results; sometimes the tiniest of results can appear to be huge. Perhaps you have seen marketing commercials (for cell phones or health products) where the graphs or charts appear to claim one thing and you have to read the fine print to recognize that the chart is not representative of the truth. (Similarly, my son often gets angry that the hamburgers he orders at restaurants do not look like the products advertised in commercials).

Pie Chart

Speaking of food, a **pie chart** is often used to show the size of a particular response compared to the size or frequencies of other responses. Sometimes pie charts use frequencies and sometimes they show percentages, but the focus is always on how big each slice of the pie is, compared to other slices of pie. Pie charts are best used for nominal and ordinal variables, and they can sometimes be confusing or overwhelming if you use a pie chart to describe results from interval or ratio level variables. For example, a pie chart may be used to illustrate which, of five stores, each person prefers to shop at; however, if you wanted to use a pie chart to illustrate the weight, for each of those individuals, it can get very confusing and overwhelming. Below is a pie chart indicated how many people prefer to shop at each store (a nominal level variable).

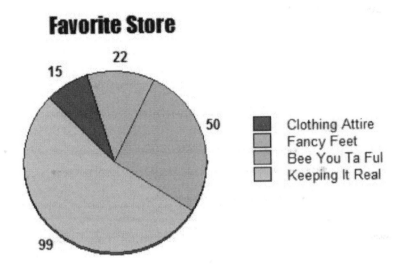

Favorite Store

- Clothing Attire
- Fancy Feet
- Bee You Ta Ful
- Keeping It Real

Bar Graph

Similar to a pie chart, a **bar graph** illustrates the relative size, proportion, or frequency of a response (compared to other responses). It is also most commonly used with nominal and ordinal data. In our earlier example with the pie chart, perhaps 29% of the respondents preferred to shop at Macy's and 30% preferred to shop at JC Penny's. If you were to compare the size of the pie slices, it may not be easy to see a 1% difference, but that difference may be more noticeable if you present it as a bar graph.

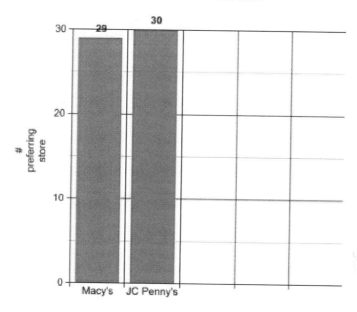

Histogram

Whereas the pie chart and bar graph are best used for nominal and perhaps ordinal data, a **histogram** is used for interval and ratio level data. In reality, a histogram looks very similar to a bar graph (and many people will still call it a bar graph), but either way, when we are referring to a histogram we are specifically looking at interval or ratio level data. Another advantage that a histogram has over a bar graph and pie chart is that a histogram allows you to see the variability from the mean (including the range). For example, if you were interested in looking at the weight for a thousand people, you could see the mean (average) weight, as well as the minimum and maximum (range or variability).

Look at the following histogram (below) about "age." The histogram shows there are 4 people between the ages of 33 and 35, 1 person between the ages of 36 and 38, 1 people between the ages of 39 and 41, and 11 people between the ages of 42 and 45. As you can see, this looks similar to a bar chart, but remember that it's probably a histogram if the variable is interval or ratio level.

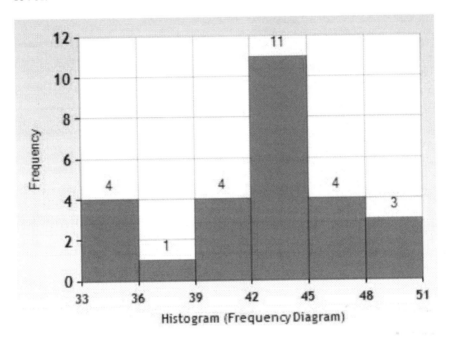

Histogram (Frequency Diagram)

Summary

There are a large number of statistics, and each statistic is designed for a particular reason. Envision statistics as tools, and the overall objective is to find the right statistic for the right job. By the end of this chapter, you have learned about many of the most basic (and in my opinion, the most useful) statistics there is to know for your particular career options.

However, I also recognize that knowing which statistic to use can be a difficult thing to do, especially when learning about these statistics for the first time. Below is a summary of when to use the Pearson's Correlation Coefficient, the *t*-test (or one type of t-test, known as an "independent sample *t*-test"), and an ANOVA.

The Statistic's Name	Level of Measurement for the Independent Variable	Level of Measurement for the Dependent Variable
(Independent Sample) *t*-test	Nominal (2 groups)	Interval or Ratio
ANOVA (Analysis of Variance)	Nominal (3 or more groups)	Interval or Ratio
Pearson's Correlation Coefficient	Interval or Ratio	Interval or Ratio

Review Questions

1. What does "central tendency" refer to?

averages

2. How can you identify the mode, median, and mean? What are some advantages for each?

3. What is "variance"?

4. What "patterns" are you likely to look for when considering how to interpret a Pearson's Correlation Coefficient?

5. What is the primary difference between a *t*-test and an ANOVA?

↑ 2 groups

t 3 or more

6. What is a *p* value?

7. What are some of the differences between a pie chart, a bar chart, and a histogram?

Personal Application

Below are three different examples, from three different fields of study, to help you see why interpreting statistics—in the right way—can be so important.

Example #1. Earlier in the book, I referenced a presentation given by a dietician who touted the importance of a particular nutrition program. She reported a statistically significant ($p <$ .05) Pearson's Correlation Coefficient of .08 between the amount

126

of time one spends in her nutrition program and how good one feels; she reported that those who spent more time in her nutrition program tend to feel better. Knowing what you know now, how would YOU interpret these results?

Example #2. A clothing store surveyed its first 100 customers on Thursday and found, from a statistically significant *t*-test result, that women over the age of 40 tend to spend more than women age 40 and under. In response, the business wants to pour an additional $20,000 into a marketing campaign designed to get those 40 and younger to spend more at their store. If you were an owner or manager of that store, what information would YOU want to see (from the *t*-test) that hasn't yet been shared with you?

Example #3. Research in the social sciences often points to differences between groups. What if you would see that, within a particular school district, there were statistically significant differences in high school GPA among three different racial/ethnic groups? What statistic would have been used to find these differences, and what information would you want to see to determine how meaningful these differences are?

Chapter 8: Building and Evaluating Programs

Chances are you will want to do at least one of the following in your career: improve the well-being of individuals and families, help promote change in a society or community, or increase sales (for your company or your own product/service). In order to do those things, you need to build a program that serves your clientele or customers. And for many people, there is the mistaken assumption that "If I build it, they will show up." In other words, because we feel so passionate about what we do or create, we often (mistakenly) assume others will feel the same way.

Although many of you will not become full-time researchers, being able to understand, interpret, and discuss research principles will be critical aspects of what you will do for your career. You might not compute standard deviations for a living, but most FACS students will find themselves in a career where they will be asked to build a program or intervention that works and is based on science. They will also need to be able to review how effective the program was and how to improve upon it the next time it is offered.

Needs Based Assessment

In nearly every professional career, you will participate (or lead) a Needs Based Assessment, also often known as a Needs Assessment. **A Needs Based Assessment** consists of identifying the needs of a program or organization, specifically by identifying the gaps between where your organization is and where you want it to be. Those "gaps" are the needs that should be addressed. A Needs Based Assessment is conducted for the purpose of being more effective and more efficient in the things your organization does.

In my graduate school years, I worked with an organization that served individuals with disabilities. It was a comprehensive organization, including parent education, physical therapy, speech therapy, nutrition, and many other careers were represented as well. One of the things I liked about this organization was that it was heavily invested in listening to the ideas and recommendations of those they served; patients and their families were viewed as "*stakeholders*," meaning they had an investment in how things ought to be done in that organization. However, sometimes science or professional ideologies do not always match up well with what others will see as commonsense, and so one of the "gaps" in this organization was trying to increasingly balance their services (to their patients) in a way that met professional standards and was sympathetic and compassionate to the voices of those they served.

You may have seen that Needs Based Assessment has some similarities with goal setting. But Needs Based Assessment comes before goal setting; it is establishing what the need is before decisions are made as to what should be done to meet those needs. A Needs Based Assessment is very similar to the Scientific Method, and it is a very systematic (vs. knee-jerk) reaction to what needs your company or organization has. (On a personal level, which person is more likely to keep exercising: The person who systematically, logically determines exactly how much exercise and what kind of exercises would be best for their body, or the person who wakes up on New Year's Eve and quickly decides to pay for a gym membership?)

Sometimes scholars like to separate "Needs Based Assessment" with "Learner Based Assessment." A Needs Based Assessment is based on the organization or company's needs, and a Learner Based Assessment is based on what the learner, student, customer, or patient needs.

Evidenced Based Research/Practice/Programs

Once you know what your organization or institution needs, now what do you do? *"That is a very silly question, Dr. Cook. The answer is clear: You do everything you need to in order to meet those needs."* That is a good response, but keep in mind that most organizations, companies, and institutions have extremely limited budgets: Doing everything possible is both time consuming and budget draining. It is important to be efficient and effective, not only for your organization's benefit, but also to ensure that you keep your job! (If your organization's budget falters, who will they need to lay off?)

The dependency on doing so much with so little is both frustrating and heartbreaking. One of the local non-profit organizations I had been volunteering with, and who taken several of my students as interns, had to shut down because they were unable to meet their budget. More important than me losing my opportunity to work with them was the fact that so many of those employees lost their jobs, as well as many of the families they had worked with would no longer have that resource.

In order to be effective and efficient, you look to see what others have done. You learn from their strengths and challenges. When you conduct research on your needs or gaps, that is referred to as "evidence based research." In reality, "research" should (probably) always be evidence based, but the focus of **evidence based research** is to gather information (about your topic, need, or gap) from credible resources.

Evidence based research, then, will affect your practice. For example, let's say you are a home-based educator for low income families. One of the parents lets you know that her child, who is three years old, isn't eating. Before deciding what to say or do for that parent, it would be important to know, from research:

1.   How much do three year olds usually eat? How much should they eat to remain healthy? Are there gender differences?

2.   What parenting strategies have been used to help their children eat, or to eat more nutritiously?

3.   What organizational strategies have been used to help parents help their children eat, or to eat more nutritiously?

4.   What foods are the best—and worst—choices for three year olds to eat? Which ones will they be more likely---or less likely—to eat?

As mentioned earlier in this book, simply asking Google or Siri for this information has its advantages and disadvantages. You want to make sure that the information and advice you provide is consistent with research guidelines because you want to help the child, you want to help the parent, and you want to avoid you (and your organization) being held liable for bad or dangerous advice. The way to determine what is good advice and practice is through research, to see what others have done in your same situation.

This is why evidence based research and evidence based practice go hand-in-hand. Clinicians and many other professionals, however, are more likely to refer to **evidence based practice** because it involves what they do, not just what they read about.

For example, when I was diagnosed with cancer in 2015, I visited with a radiation oncologist, who told me what was needed in order to beat the cancer diagnosis. How did he know? He could rely on intuition or even his own experience. Instead, he shared with me the odds and likelihoods of beating cancer based on hundreds of other patients who had my type of cancer and had gone into different types of treatment. My doctor was engaging in evidence based practice.

You do not need to battle a life-or-death diagnosis to understand that evidence based practice will be more likely to yield effective and efficient results (that "going with our gut") because we are simply replicating what has already been done. For example, assume you are helping families with their nutritional needs; relying on previous lectures and your education are important, but they often become out-of-date once you get into the field. Knowing how to research will yield the most effective and efficient results.

Program Evaluation

Ideally, the services you provide to others should be evaluated for their effectiveness. There is a certain level of accountability for what we do and what we provide, but there is also the goal for improving the services we already provide to individuals and families. Whether it is your boss, funding individuals or groups (including the government), or your clients, completing a program evaluation helps you stay accountable and it helps you increase your chances for improving what your organization does.

A Program Evaluation is a systematic method for reviewing the practices and policies to determine (1) how effective those practices and policies are, and (2) whether certain practices and policies need to be updated or revised in order to better meet the program's goals. It can also be used to explain why a particular program, intervention, or prevention is not as effective as it should be.

Note: Programs are usually considered a piece or part of an organization, company, or institution. An organization, company, or institution represent who they are, and a program is what they do. For example, Head Start is an organization but they also have several programs or methods for helping individuals and families.

The good news is that you have already learned what it will take to evaluate a program, service, or product. Using the Scientific Method as a guide, you first create your objective or research question. You then collect data. Afterward, you analyze that data. Finally, you interpret and disseminate the results. You definitely can do all of those things!

What I have noticed about evidence based research, evidence based practice, and evidence based evaluation is that each is typically expressed in the form of a map. It will tell you what steps have been used in each process, and it will also describe the pathways used for making decisions about each. I like that these maps or symbols represent a systematic and logical pathway for learning, implementing, or evaluating something.

Summary

There are many tools for increasing your program's chances to be effective and efficient. Which one to use depends on the goals and stage your program is in, and where it wants to go. Evidence Based Research should impact your practice, and your practice or program ought to be evaluated. More specifics about systematically reviewing a program, intervention, or experiment will be given in the next chapter.

Review Questions

1. Define Needs Based Assessment, Evidence Based Research, Evidence Based Practice, and Program Evaluation.

2. Why is each (of the above) important?

3. What does it mean to be "systematic" in research, practice, or with evaluation?

Personal Application

1. Which terms (in this chapter) best reflect what you have done most frequently as a student: Needs Based Assessment, Evidence Based Research, Evidence Based Practice, or Program Evaluation?

2. Which terms (in this chapter) do you feel you will use the most in your career (and why): Needs Based Assessment, Evidence Based Research, Evidence Based Practice, or Program Evaluation? If you want to take it to the next level, interview someone in your field, perhaps a faculty member, and ask them which one(s) they feel are most important to learn about.

Chapter 9: Experimental Design and Evaluating Programs

With most programs, and when we are referring to "program evaluation," we are usually hoping for a specific result (see chapter 7)—improve nutrition, repair relationships, etc.—but when we refer to **"experimental design"** we are interested in a serious analysis of whether the program/experiment was actually the cause of change. We are also interested in plausible *alternatives* for why the experiment worked; we are more skeptical of the program's effectiveness. However, understanding experimental design can be important in a variety of situations, even if you don't think that you'll ever conduct a formal "experiment." (Some scholars actually use the terms "experimental design" and "program evaluation" synonymously, but I think understanding them as separate things makes more sense).

For example, let's consider a retail company who has $20,000 in sales within a two month period (i.e. September-October). Because they want to increase their sales, they spend $10,000 on advertising over the next two months (i.e. November-December). During November and December, their sales are $31,000, and they conclude that the advertising campaign was successful; after all, they sold more than they spent on advertising, right?

In the retail example, would you encourage the company to spend *another* $10,000 to increase sales for the following two months (i.e. January-February)? I imagine you have some doubts, and for good reason. Would the company have increased their sales by $1000 (i.e. $31,000 of sales - $10,000 spent on advertising - $20,000 of sales in their first two months) or more *without* the advertising? Are retail companies likely to sell more in the months of November and December than they are in September and October? If either of these answers is "yes," the money spent toward advertising was essentially money *lost* from the business.

When we move from the academic world into our future occupations, saving money, time, and energy are incredibly important, and there is the need to determine whether we should continue to put these resources into further experiments (especially if we can get the same results without the experiments). Let's look at one more (hypothetical) example. As a parent, you are very discouraged about the amount of conflict you experience with your 14-year-old son. You decide to meet with a counselor, once per month, or a period of two years. At the end of those two years, you find that the conflict with your son has dramatically decreased, and you thank your counselor for helping you and your son. But would that conflict had likely decreased, even without the help from your counselor? (Research shows that most parent-child conflict decreases between the ages of 14-16 as the child matures). Being able to consider alternative explanations for why something works can save a great deal of time and money.

Internal Validity

Do you remember, from a previous chapter, what "validity" is? When we refer to "validity," we are usually referring how "valid" or accurate a survey is. Although both "validity" and "internal validity" are looking at how confident we can be in something, **Internal validity** refers to the following: "the extent or degree the results can be attributed to the treatment/intervention/program and not other factors." In other words, it is the confidence that our treatment/intervention/program worked because of our treatment/intervention/program, and not because of other reasons. When we have confidence that the results from the study are from the experiment (and the experiment alone), we have high internal validity; when we have little confidence that the results from the study are from the experiment alone, we have low internal validity for the study.

A silly example I often provide for my classes involves a driver's safety course my wife enrolled me in. (I have only received one ticket in 30 years of driving, but we were told that we would save money on our car insurance if we took this course). When we arrived at the class, we were given a test to assess our knowledge of safe driving; after we took the test, we held onto our tests and were given the answers along with a workshop about safe driving. After the class, we were again given the same test we had at the beginning. By the end of their workshop or class, every participant had increased their test scores, and were able to "prove" to their insurance companies that they were now safe drivers.

Do you have any confidence that the results from this class and study were due to the actual class, or that we really learned how to be safe drivers, or were there other issues? Like you, I have serious doubts that the class made us better drivers. I suggest there is low internal validity in this instance.

Although it was nice for our pocketbooks (i.e. we got the discount on our insurance rates), the reality is the workshop did nothing to improve our driving abilities or to keep us (or others) safe when we drove. If we had taken the test then retaken the test (without having listened to a lecture or workshop about safe driving), chances are we could have gotten the same results. Did we become safer drivers or did we simply have to recall what the right answers were to do well on the test?

Let's look at another real life example, but this time involving an educational program to help increase vegetable intake among 4-th graders in Pennsylvania. In this study (Wall, Least, & Lohse, 2012), the researchers *randomly* selected which schools would receive their educational program (and which would not). However, for those schools that had more than one 4th-grade class (which was most of them), they only selected one of those classes to participate; deciding which 4th grade class would participate in these schools was left to the discretion of those who were offering the intervention.

After the educational program/intervention was complete, the researchers asked all the 4th-graders (whether their schools/classes were chosen to receive the program/intervention or not) to complete a survey. When the data was analyzed, the researchers found that those who participated in the program, or had received the intervention, were likely to eat more vegetables than those who did not receive the program.

Of course, the good news is that many students increased their vegetable intake. Although there are several notable strengths about this study, perhaps the greatest limitation is that it is up to the discretion of the intervention providers as to which 4th-grade classes would participate and which would not. The authors of this study were aware of this issue, but they did not feel it was really that much of an issue. Do you?

139

Those who offered this intervention are clearly invested in making sure that the results from this study would show that the intervention or program was effective. Chances are that jobs were on the line, or that many of those providing the intervention or program were paid to do so; if the study had shown that the program was not effective, what would happen to their jobs? Is it possible that those who were so heavily invested in the results chose certain 4th grade classes to participate, and decided which would not participate, based on which they thought would be most predisposed to improving their diets? The truth is we simply don't know; perhaps the program/intervention is incredibly effective, but because of how the study was conducted, it does cause us to have some reservations or doubts about the effectiveness of the study. Were certain 4th grade classes excluded from receiving the intervention because they (i.e. those administering the program) did not think those children would be successful with the program? Are some 4th graders more likely to listen to and adhere to adult recommendations whereas other 4th graders are not?

When we have the full story, and are able to cautiously consider whether the intervention caused the results, or if there are other factors involved, we are becoming knowledgeable professionals and consumers. If the leaders of this nutritional program came to you to get your approval (and perhaps funds), and touted the effectiveness of the program, would you allow them to give this intervention to your elementary school? Why or why not?

Experimental Design

A **design** is a description or pattern for something, and it is there to help you make or replicate (i.e. recreate) something based on that pattern. Remember that "proving" something is very

140

difficult to do in research, but the more things are repeated (or replicated) with the same results, the more confident we can have in those results.

When an experiment, treatment, or intervention is provided, it is important to know what the design consists of for two reasons: (1) Other scholars may want to replicate that study, and will need as much information as possible to do so, and (2) To help us evaluate the internal validity of that study or experiment. The design of an experiment or study is most commonly found in the "Methods" section of a peer review journal article, where the authors explain what the experiment consists of and what processes were involved. For example, the study's authors may say something like this: "For our experiment, we enrolled 100 young adults (from the ages of 18-35), and spent five hours detailing the dangers of texting while driving. The class consisted of PowerPoint presentations, guest speakers, and journaling (to help with self-reflection)."

Although having the design or pattern completely explained is incredibly helpful, sometimes having shortcuts or a summary is also helpful when researchers want to evaluate the *internal validity* of their experiment's results. These shortcuts include a variety of design symbols, but often include the letters: R, O, and X.

The letter "R" can sometimes be confusing for several reasons. First, many times a capital "R" signifies a "Regression," a statistical process used to predict something based on current results. But when it comes to experimental design, "R" refers to random assignment, also known as **randomization.** Randomization is the process of participants being assigned to a group or condition, usually either a treatment group or to a control group. A treatment group is the group that receives the intervention (usually signified with an "X"), and a control group does not receive the intervention (usually shown with an absence of an "X"). A control group is designed to help the researchers compare how effective their intervention or experiment was; if the treatment group shows improvement, and the control group does not, the assumption is that the reason one group improved (and the other did not) was because of whether they had the treatment. An "O" represents when a survey had been completed. Let's look at a few examples.

Example #1
R: OXO
R: O O
In this first example (above), there are two groups. One is randomly assigned to a treatment group (signified with an "X") and the other, or second line, is a control group (because there isn't any "X" in it). Each group was surveyed before the intervention was administered (also known as a **pre-test**), and each group was surveyed after the intervention was completed (also known as a **post-test**, because it follows the intervention).

Example #2
R: XO
R: O
In this second example (above) there are two groups; one is in the treatment group and the other is in the control group. Recall that the way to know is by whether there is an "X." However, this time, there is no pre-test; this means that, although you can compare two groups after the intervention, you cannot measure changes over time.

Example #3
OXO
O O
What do you see differently about this third example (above)?
There is no "R," meaning that groups are *not* randomly assigned.

Threats and Controls

Recall that the strongest experiments will have the highest
internal validity, meaning the greatest confidence that the results
are attributed to the experiment (and not to other factors). The
inverse is also true; when there is the least or lowest internal
validity, it is because there are factors that make it that way.
These factors are more commonly referred to as "**threats to
internal validity**," or sometimes simply referred to as "threats."

Although there are many different or possible threats to internal
validity, we will cover the most common ones. History is one of
the more common threats to internal validity, because, well, time
pretty much changes everything. **History** refers to "extraneous
effects that occur outside of the research setting that may affect
the outcome."

Earlier in this chapter, I shared an example where sales increased
between October and January; was it because there was a new
marketing campaign, or is it possible that you would have seen
an increase in sales regardless of the marketing campaign?
When we suspect that things *outside* of the participant may be
responsible for the results, rather than the intervention (or in this
case, the marketing campaign), we say there is a threat to internal
validity known as "history."

Another common threat to internal validity is "Maturation." Similar to History, Maturation looks at changes over time; however, History looks at changes outside of the participants, and **Maturation** looks at changes (over time) within the participant. A silly example of this includes parents who are trying to potty train their toddlers; they may praise/reward or punish their child based on their child's effectiveness with using the toilet correctly. After six months, nearly every child has become potty trained, and parents attribute this remarkable success to their parenting methods. However, is it reasonable that most of these toddlers would have become potty trained, regardless of any parenting intervention, by their third birthdays? Most research shows that 95% (or more) of children are potty trained by their third birthdays.

Another threat to internal validity is Testing, also known as Pre-Test Sensitization. **Pre-test Sensitization** occurs when a pre-test may disturb what is being measured or act as its own intervention. My earlier example of a driver's safety class is an excellent example of pre-test sensitization; I took a pre-test, then I listened to an instructor teaching the class, and then I took the exact same test again. (Hint: When a test/survey occurs after an intervention, even if it is the same test/survey as the pre-test, it is now referred to as a *post-test*). The class instruction cannot fully describe why my post-test was so much higher than my pre-test; chances are the pre-test sensitized me to get the right answers on the post-test more than the instruction.

Statistical Regression is another common threat to internal validity, particularly when groups are formed on the basis of extreme scores. For example, imagine you have developed an 8-week self-esteem workshop for teenage boys who have recently

144

been "dumped" by their girlfriends. Of course, at the time of enrollment, their self-esteem is quite low, but by the end of your 8-week self-esteem workshop, their self-esteem has miraculously increased by 20%. Can we confidently say this increase in self-esteem is because of the workshop? In Statistical Regression, there is an event known as "regression toward the mean." It simply means that things tend to go back to what they most commonly are. In our workshop example, the effectiveness of that intervention is somewhat exaggerated because (1) there was nowhere to go but up with their self-esteem, and (2) we would have expected their self-esteem to go up, to where it had normally been, after a period of time, with or without the intervention.

The last threat is **mortality**, also often known as *attrition*. Mortality refers to when subjects drop out of the experiment and that affects the results. For example, imagine I am a therapist and work with 100 couples; 90 couples quit meeting with me, but the 10 who continue to work with me report that I am a very effective therapist. If the other 90 couples had evaluated me, would they have evaluated me differently than the 10 couples? Because we don't know how their evaluations would affect the "mean" score or evaluation score for how effective I was as a therapist, we refer to it as *mortality*.

When a "threat" is not an issue or problem, or perhaps when we can adequately explain how it affects our results, we say that that threat is "controlled" or "controlled for." Although the word "control" often has a negative connotation or meaning, in the social sciences the word "control" simply means to take care of something or make it so that it is not a problem. Again, keep in mind that the goal is to have confidence that the results we've obtained were because of the experiment, and not other factors (known as "threats to internal validity").

True Experiments and Quasi-Experiments

There are two categories for which we can assess threats to internal validity. These include "True Experiments" and "Quasi-Experiments." True experiments are the gold standard for experiments because they control for all of the threats to internal validity. A big reason for this is "randomization," where there is at least one treatment group and at least one control group.

Quasi-experiments are essentially all experiments that don't meet the level or rigor of a "true experiment." Quasi-experiments include any experiments where there is one or more threats to internal validity. Most experiments, programs, and treatments are considered quasi-experiments.

Despite the advantage of a true experiment, quasi-experiments also have several advantages. They are more convenient and sometimes they can be morally necessary. For example, if you have a nutritional intervention that you know will benefit the lives of people, are you going to randomly assign some to a control group "in the name of science"?

Sometimes, researchers will try to address both scientific and moral issues. For example, in one study (Lam-Cassettari, Wadnerkar-Kamble, & James, 2015), 14 "hearing" parents and their deaf children were invited to participate in a study to see if a series of videos improved the sensitivity of parents to their hearing-impaired or deaf children. Half of the families were assigned to a treatment group, and the other half would receive the treatment *after* the first treatment was done; this allowed the researchers to compare each group as well as to ensure that each family received the program.

Summary

Whether you are interested in a true experiment or a quasi-experiment depends on your goals, your resources, and your limitations. Remember that experiments, no matter their form, an attempt to change behavior.

Review Questions

1. Why would you want to consider the "design" of your experiment, program, or intervention?

2. What does "design" refer to?

3. Define "internal validity."

4. What is randomization, and what is its purpose?

5. Identify each threat to internal validity.

6. What does it mean to "control" for threats to internal validity?

7. What differences are there between a "true experiment" and a "quasi-experiment"?

Personal Application

Design your own experiment, program, or intervention. Write the words/text for what will be done, and then use the symbols (R O X) to draw your design. Finally, consider what threats to internal validity exist for your design or experiment.

References to Chapter 8

Quick Note: Can you remember how to put these references in APA format?

(1) By: Denise E Wall ; Christine Least ; Judy Gromis ; Barbara Lohse (2012). Nutrition Education Intervention Improves Vegetable-Related Attitude, Self-Efficacy, Preference, and Knowledge of Fourth-Grade Students . Published in: Journal of School Health, volume 82 issue 1 (2012), pages 37-43

(2) Christa Lam-Cassettari ; Meghana B Wadnerkar-Kamble ; Deborah M James. (2015). Enhancing Parent-Child Communication and Parental Self-Esteem with a Video-Feedback Intervention : Outcomes with Prelingual Deaf and Hard-of-Hearing Children. Journal of deaf studies and deaf education. , 2015, Vol.20(3), p.266-274.

① Wall, D.E., Least, C., Gromis, J., & Lohse, B. (2012). Nutrition Education Intervention . . . . "Journal of School Health", "82" (1)", 37-43.

② Lam-Cassettari, C., Wadnerkar-Kamble, M.B., James, D.M. (2015). Enhancing Parent-Child . . . . "Journal of deaf studies and education", "20" (3)", 266-274.

Chapter 10: Evaluating Peer Reviewed Journal Articles and the Media

One of the biggest tests to determine whether you understand research is by evaluating a peer review journal article. It can be pretty intimidating at first, but I think you will be pretty surprised with what you already know. In reality, everything in this book has prepared you to review most of the journal articles in your field.

Just because an article is published, and just because most scholars have degrees that exceed your own, it does not mean that you have to accept what they say (or write) at face value. As we have learned already, there are several myths in research, and understanding these myths gives you a great head start.

Because of copyright issues, I am unable to copy and paste journal articles into this book. However, I have created some short, fictitious articles you can practice with. I recommend you read through each article, looking to identify the questions or concerns you may have for each study. At the end of each article, I will test your knowledge. Hint: Don't try to memorize every little detail of this (fictitious) studies; it is more important to apply what you have learned. For example, you should now be able to interpret statistics, experimental design, reliability, validity, sampling, and more! You may want to consider highlighting the phrases or sentences that catch your attention.

Ready?

Study #1

Abstract

In this study, 50 participants enrolled in a 5-month class designed to help parents help their toddlers eat healthier. At the end of the program, the results (p < .05) indicate that the class helped improve eating habits of toddlers.

Introduction

Eating healthy is a critical aspect of human development, especially within the first five years. Research has shown that children from homes where they either do not eat as frequently as they should or when they consistently eat high-fat foods tend to have more health issues within their adult years (Do, Ritos, and Crunch, 2016).

Methods

Design, Sample, and Procedures

We solicited participants from a large "Nutrition" college course; 50 students were parents of toddlers and were invited to participate in our study in exchange for extra credit if their toddler's eating habits improved over the duration of the study. The student-parents attended a 30 minute video workshop, once per month, over a period of five months. At the end of the five months, 20 students had completed the entire series.

Measures

The following information was collected from the participants: their age, gender, and a five-question measure about the eating habits of their toddler children. This measure was given at the

151

beginning of the 5-month duration, as well as at the end (or when participants were done with the program).

Results

The results indicate a positive correlation (r = .11, p < .05) with the amount of time participants spent in our program and their child's healthy eating behaviors. Additionally, paired t-test results show statistically significant improvements from their pre-test to their post-test (p < .05).

Discussion

Our program, the video workshops, was very effective in helping their children eat healthier. Future research and government funding should place more efforts on the VWP (video workshops for parents) programs.

How did you do? Let's look at some of the issues with this first study. The first thing you'll want to do is consider what the research question is. The research question was not clear, but it does appear to be something like this: "Does the video workshop program help toddlers eat better?" And what did they find out? Did the results support their hypothesis or assumptions about the program?

If you read the study, you'll see that the study's authors think that their program is the best thing since sliced bread, but you know better. What were some of the issues with this study?

Let's look first at "measurement precision," also known as validity and reliability. What validity and reliability were cited for this study's measures or survey? If none was cited, what does that mean?

As we learned already, validity and reliability are perhaps two of the most important aspects of research. If there isn't any evidence of validity and reliability, how much confidence can we place in their survey, or in their survey's results? (There is also the issue that the student-parents are motivated to report healthier eating habits in order to get their extra credit!)

And what about sampling issues? How well do parent-students majoring in Nutrition reflect or represent the larger population? In this study, we actually know very little about the sample, but it is clearly not random. What does this mean with regard to generalizability?

Next, let's look at the internal validity of this program. What threats to internal validity are likely relevant to this study? Did you catch pre-test sensitization, mortality/attrition, and perhaps history and/or maturation? With less than half of the sample completing the survey, even with the extra credit incentive, what would have happened with the results if everyone completed the survey? Would they say something different about the program? And what do you remember about the design of this study? We do know there was a pre-test and a post-test, as well as an intervention. The design would look like this: OXO

Finally, what can you say about the results or the statistics? Hopefully you caught that the Pearson's Correlation Coefficient is incredibly weak; don't get fooled by the "statistical significance" phrase.

Are you ready for the second study?

Study #2

Abstract

Eighty-four participants completed a "life happiness" survey. Results demonstrate that most adults are "somewhat" happy with life, and that parents tend to be the least happy of all adults.

Introduction

"Happiness" is a construct often discussed in self-improvement circles (Jones, 2016). However, there is little empirical evidence as to what "happiness" actually is. In our study, we examine happiness, and particularly, how it varies across the life stages.

Methods

A sample of 84 adults (with a range of 18-72 years old) was obtained through an organization that provides counseling to adults. A hundred adults were asked to participate in this study; 16 adults declined.

Participants completed the "Happiness with Life Measure" (HLM). The HLM consists of five items, each measuring happiness with their lives. Questions consist of the following:

(1) How happy are you with the time you spend alone?

(2) How content are you with your "free time"?

(3) How satisfied are you with your leisure time?

154

(4) How happy are you with the time you get to spend with friends?

(5) How satisfied are you with "just me" time?

The Cronbach's alpha (.90) demonstrates evidence and support for this survey. In another part of the survey, participants were asked what life stage they were in (i.e. not a parent, parent, empty-nest).

Results

An ANOVA was used to calculate mean differences between the groups. The results indicate a statistically significant relationship (p < .05), with parents experiencing the least happiness and "not a parent" individuals experiencing the greatest happiness.

the means
(the #'s)

Discussion

These results are surprising, particularly because so many first-time parents tend to have more children. If having children makes them less happy, then why would they have more children? Research should examine why parents tend to be unhappy.

What did you notice about this study?

Let's start by looking at the research question. Again, the research question is quite vague. In the Introduction, the authors made it sound like they were going to operationalize happiness, but the real goal was to determine how happiness varied across individuals.

What did they find out?

They found that parents were the least happy, and that nonparents were the most happy. Can we be confident in these results? How confident?

To determine how confident we can be in the results, we first need to look at the measurement precision of the survey. The authors did cite a high level of reliability for this measure, but what about validity? The lack of validity is important to understand here, because they were consistently measuring something, but without validity we aren't sure what that "something" is. For example, when you look at the survey questions, did you think this measured "happiness" or "happiness as a single or nonparent"? How would this affect the results?

Sampling is another huge issue. The sample is relatively small, and we have very little information about them. All we know is that these individuals are receiving counseling; whether they reflect the larger population is uncertain.

And what about the ANOVA? Was it the correct statistical analysis to use? To determine that, we first need to look at the levels of the independent and dependent variables. That's why it is so important to know what the research question is:

Is there a relationship between parent status and happiness (with life)?

The independent variable is parent status, and the level of measurement is likely nominal. The dependent variable is happiness or happiness with life, and the level of measurement is likely interval or ratio, assuming they used the ANOVA correctly. (We don't have any information about the scale of measurement for the Happiness with Life Measure, so it's difficult to know, exactly, if they used the right test or not).

Let's try one more (fictional) study. This time, see how much you can critique without my help.

Study #3

Abstract

A study with "skinny jeans" was conducted to determine whether skinny jeans makes people feel better about themselves. A sample of 100 teens participated in an experiment conducted by a retail store; participants tried on regular-size clothing (or clothing that fit but was not tight) and then they tried on the skinny jeans. Participants then reported how they felt. The results showed that nearly 100% of the teens reported feeling better about themselves after trying on the skinny jeans.

Introduction

Clothing is an important aspect of how we present ourselves, our identities, and our value (Macey, 2015). Despite the rave of skinny jeans in the last few years, there is very little empiricism about its psychological effects upon the wearer.

Methods

A hundred teens agreed to participate in a "marketing study" about skinny jeans. When the teens entered the store, they were instructed to try on any pair of regular fitting jeans, and then they were told to try on any pair of "skinny jeans." After trying on both pairs of jeans, those who reported preferring the skinny jeans were able to take them home.

Results

Ninety-nine of the 100 participants reported feeling better about themselves after trying on the skinny jeans (compared to the other jeans). The one who did not prefer the skinny jeans explained that he already felt too skinny, and did not want to look thinner.

Discussion

This study proves that skinny jeans improves the well-being of the wearers. It does show that parents who are struggling with depressed teens should get them skinny jeans.

does not

Write your critique of the most recent article (i.e. study #3) here:

- Sample of 100 teens (where did they get them, don't know much about them & 100 is a low # for the population of all teens)
- they got to take the jeans if they said they preferred them
- got to try any jeans maybe only one style
- no clear stats or #

Where the Media Gets It Wrong

Now that you are efficient with critiquing research, you can also critique the media when they try to report research findings. Near the beginning of this book, you learned a little about the myths of research. The myths covered include: (1) all research is scientific, (2) numbers and statistics don't lie, and (3) "they said it was significant."

In all fairness, there is a great deal of good that the media does. The media does a great job with disseminating information that may be useful or of interest to the general public. But they also present information that is either blatantly wrong, or because they do not understand the myths of research, they can completely miss the main points of the research.

Years ago, I was called by a local TV news organization, and they asked if I would share some ideas about "boomerang adults." (Boomerang adults are those who, often because of finances, return home to live with their parents). I had been interviewed over the phone before, and admit I thought that's all it would consist of; I was surprised when they showed up at my office with a camera crew! After about 30 minutes of talking with the interviewer, the interview was done; later that night I watched my 10 seconds of fame on the news, but saw myself seemingly to say something I definitely did not *really* say. They completely took my comments out of context so they could justify one of the points they wanted to make. So yes, there are times when "reporting" the news is more than just sharing the news, but is rather an attempt to sway your opinion or beliefs about something. (I have to give a quick shout-out to the *Wall Street Journal*, however, because it provided a very fair and accurate representation of the things I shared with them about marital boundaries).

When I read or watch the news, and particularly when they are sharing a brief segment from an expert or scholar, my mind reverts back to the time when I was interviewed by a local news organization. I ask myself, "Did they report things accurately?"

More common than distortion of research is simply not understanding research. News organizations want you to trust them, and so they will present information they think you'll believe. They will throw around words like "significant results" and "science" as if they are the ultimate authorities in the universe.

Summary

By the end of this chapter, you should have more confidence with evaluating peer review journal articles. Just because "peer review journal articles" are often thought to be the gold (or highest) standard of research, that doesn't mean it IS the highest standard of research. Similarly, you are encouraged to be a "cautious consumer" when it comes to what the media is sharing with you.

Review Questions

1. What portions or sections of peer review journal article are most important to read? Why?

2. What are some of the differences between the Results and Discussion sections?

3. What are some "media myths"?

Personal Application

1. Find a peer review journal article in your field of study and evaluate it.

2. Go through the three fictional studies provided in this chapter. Can you find any other flaws or concerns with the studies (that weren't brought up earlier in the chapter)?

3. Listen to or read the news to find where they are sharing information about research. Critique what they have to say based

on what you've learned in this textbook. Write down a few of your thoughts below.

_____

_____

_____

_____

Chapter 11: Statistical Programs (SPSS vs. Excel)

Thus far we have learned how to interpret basic statistics, and we have also learned how to calculate some statistics (e.g. mean). But all of these have been done with small datasets, or with very small samples and just a few variables at a time. A *dataset* is a file with data, usually for the purpose of being able to analyze that data. When you enter data, or numbers that represent a variable's characteristics into a spreadsheet, like you may use for Excel or when you work on a spreadsheet in GoogleDocs, you are working with a "dataset." A "statistical program" is a computer program you would use to enter and analyze (i.e. run statistics on) data; statistical programs are used to summarize and describe large datasets.

Two of the most common statistical programs are Excel and SPSS. Each has its advantages and disadvantages.

An Introduction to Excel and SPSS

Outside of academia, Excel is likely the most popular program to use to enter and analyze data. Excel often is part of a bundle of Microsoft programs, and so it is often cheaper than buying SPSS. Because of the familiarity of Microsoft-based programs, learning how to use Excel usually takes less time than learning how to use SPSS. Personally, I prefer Excel over SPSS when entering data, summing up numbers, or when adding different variables to each other. I also think that building charts is sometimes easier in Excel than it is in SPSS; the image quality of tables and charts is much better (especially if you want to copy/paste them into another program) in Excel than it is with SPSS.

Although Excel and SPSS can calculate a massive amount of statistics, when you are working with large datasets are or going beyond calculating summing data or calculating means, I prefer to use SPSS. As mentioned, there is a bit of a learning curve for learning how to use SPSS, but once you learn how to use some of the basic tools, there are some additional advantages, particularly with the things discussed in this textbook.

For example, calculating a Pearson's Correlation Coefficient, reliability (e.g. Cronbach's alpha), *t*-tests, and an ANOVA are much simpler to do in SPSS than with Excel. Of course, deciding which program to use will depend on your needs, your familiarity with each of the programs, your budget, and how much time you are willing to invest in learning each program. The good news is that transferring or copying your data from one program to the next is relatively simple to do. There are also statistical programs available over the Internet, but for the most part, they are used for very small datasets (i.e. small sample size and/or two or three variables).

First Things to Know

All spreadsheets contain "cells," or areas where you can enter numbers. It is a little like the children's game, "Battleship," where you call out a letter and a number to represent a particular area on the board. In the spreadsheet below, A1 says "Exp. Group" and B1 shows "Control Group." Everything under the "Exp. Group" shows data from individuals who are in that group. For example, let's assume that individuals were randomly assigned to one of two groups, an Experimental Group and a

Control Group; the Experimental Group received an intervention to increase how many "pull up" exercises they could do. After the experiment or intervention was done, everyone (including those in the Control Group) were asked to do pull ups.

In this spreadsheet (below), each cell represents how many pull ups a person in that group could do. For example, the first person in the "Exp.Group," A2, could do 10 pull ups. The first person in the "Control Group," B2, could do 12 pull ups. But let's say you are interested in how effective the experiment is, on average, compared to those in the Control Group (or those who are not receiving the treatment or extra help).

	A	B	C	D	E
1	Exp. Grou	Control Group			
2	10	12			
3	12	11			
4	15	10			
5	20	9			
6	15	12			
7	14	15			
8	15	14			
9	18	12			
10	19	13			
11	20	19			
12	21	20			
13	22	15			
14	23	18			
15	24	17			
16	25	14			
17	22	13			
18	20	20			
19					
20	315	244	TOTALS FOR EACH GROUP		
21	18.52941	13.55556	MEANS FOR EACH GROUP		
22					

Recall from our earlier chapter, that the way to look at a numerical average is to calculate the mean. It is quite simple in Excel once you are familiar with the steps, but it does take some practice. You will see, in A20, the number 315. This is the sum of all the numbers in column A, or "Exp. Group." This number represents all the push up's that the Experimental Group was able to do. The sum or total was found by selecting the "Autosum" feature, which looks like a sideways "M," and then highlighting all of the cells you want Excel to add up for you. Now look at

166

A21, or 18.52941, meaning that the average person in that group can do a little over 18 push up's. This is the mean, and it is calculated by selecting a cell (A21), typing in an equals sign (i.e. =), clicking the sum in A20, typing a division sign (i.e. /), then entering the number of those in that group (i.e. 17).

Another thing I really like about Excel is that it is useful for looking at averages over a period of time. In column "I" (below), I typed in May 17, 2016. I then placed cursor at the bottom right of that cell, and dragged it downward; as I moved my mouse downward, Excel generated each new day for me (which saves a great deal of time typing)!

Now it's your time, look at the spreadsheet (below) and imagine that the numbers in the "J" and "K" columns represent dollars spent on expenses for that particular day. For example, Store 1 spent $550 on May 17, 2016, whereas Store 2 spent $600 on that day. Using a calculator, or Excel, go through the steps to sum or total each column, then divide that sum by the number of responses.

	I	J	K	L	M	N
		Store1	Store2			
	17-May-16	550	600			
	18-May-16	525	725			
	19-May-16	435	773			
	20-May-16	599	299			
	21-May-16	575	455			
	22-May-16	233	199			
		2,917	3,051	TOTALS FOR EACH GROUP		
		486.16667	508.5	MEANS FOR EACH GROUP		

If your mean (or amount spent on expenses per day) for Store 1 was $486.17 (rounded up to the nearest penny), then you are correct. If you did not get the correct mean, try it again and make sure you only enter the numbers from that row, and when you divide the sum by the number of responses, you'll want to make sure you have the right number of responses.

If you want flexibility with how to enter data from your survey, Excel is definitely the best way to go (over SPSS). You will want to make certain, however, that you know what you will do with the data after you entered it. A little bit of planning will save a great deal of headaches.

SPSS is very strict, however, with how data is to be entered. The downside is that it can sometimes be confusing (initially), but once you get familiar with it, you will be very happy you used SPSS over Excel.

The example image (below) is a screenshot of some of my data in an SPSS format. You will see that the variable names are listed at the top, from left to right. "PhoneSurveyID" is a number that is given to each participant, and each of the variables to the right of PhoneSurveyID asks spouses how satisfied they are, on a scale of 1 to 7, with their marriage, partner, and relationship. Data is always entered from left to right. For example, on the left side you will see the number "1." That row, "4.0, 6.0, 6.0, 6.0" represents all of the responses given by one person. In short, if you ever use SPSS, make certain you enter data from left to right for each person; doing it any other way will make your statistics uninterpretable.

	PhoneSurveyID	PA1SatisfiedMarriage	PA2SatisfiedPart...	PA3SatisfiedRelationship
1	4.0	6.0	6.0	6.0
2	14.0	7.0	7.0	7.0
3	22.0	6.0	7.0	7.0
4	26.0	7.0	7.0	7.0
5	32.0	7.0	7.0	6.0
6	34.0	7.0	7.0	7.0
7	74.0	7.0	7.0	6.0
8	76.0	7.0	7.0	7.0
9	84.0	6.0	7.0	6.0
10	88.0	7.0	7.0	6.0
11	91.0	7.0	7.0	6.0
12	94.0	7.0	7.0	7.0
13	21.0	6.0	7.0	6.0
14	44.0	7.0	7.0	6.0
15	35.0	6.0	7.0	6.0
16	18.0	7.0	7.0	6.0
17	62.0	7.0	7.0	7.0

Over 90% of the basic functions for calculating statistics in SPSS can be found in the "Analyze" option in the toolbar area (located directly above the spreadsheet). The most common statistics can be found by clicking the following sequences:

Analyze->Descriptive Statistics (including the mean, median, and mode)

Analyze->Compare Means (then selecting which t-test or ANOVA you want to use)

Analyze->Correlate->Bivariate (or Pearson's Correlation Coefficient)

Analyze->Scale->Reliability Analysis (to calculate the Cronbach's alpha)

One of the aspects that can be confusing the first time you run an analysis (or statistical test) in SPSS is that the results are shown in a separate "output" area. If you want to save your data and your output, you will need to do so as two separate files; with Excel, you place graphs and statistics within the same file as your data.

Admittedly, much of this will probably make more sense once you either see a video of these options, or better yet, try them on your own. My hope is that you will have the chance to use each of these statistical programs to help you see which program you may prefer to use in the future.

Summary

Chances are quite good that you will use a spreadsheet in your career. Knowing what is available, as well as the advantages and disadvantages, will save your organization time and other challenges. Remember that most spreadsheets are used to (1) enter information and (2) analyze/summarize large amounts of data. Excel is useful for many of the most basic statistics, but if you are very serious about analyzing large amounts of data, I recommend SPSS.

Review Questions

1. What are some of the advantages and disadvantages for using Excel?

2. What are some of the advantages and disadvantages for using SPSS?

Personal Application

1. Hopefully you have already had the opportunity of developing a survey. If so, practice typing some of that data into a spreadsheet of your choice. In what way are you going to enter the data and why?

2. Search for some tutorial videos for entering and analyzing survey data in Excel and SPSS. Which program makes more sense to you?

3. Using Microsoft Excel or GoogleDocs (Spreadsheet), keep track of a daily goal. For example, keep track of how often you compliment someone. At the end of a week or two weeks, calculate the mean for your "average." What does that average represent?

Chapter 12: Scholarship and Professional Development

Learning about research, including the process of research and how to interpret research, isn't simply for the purpose of learning more about a particular topic. As explained earlier in this book, how well you understand research affects your career and even your personal life.

There is a great need for employees who understand the process of research, whether it involves analyzing social problems, parenting strategies, nutritional programs, or trends and sales in the fashion industry. Many people think research and statistics are too complicated and even mystical, but now you know better. Now that you have an understanding of research, others will want you to help them. This makes you more valuable to your employers.

Your goal should be to use the tools of research, as well as some of the tricks in research, to set yourself apart. You will want to show potential employers what sets you apart (and above) other prospective candidates. Some of these things are available in the next chapter, but for this chapter my goal is to help you get to the point where you can set yourself apart. To do that, there are six strategies.

The first strategy involves taking control of your education. It may sound harsh, but you should not rely on the piece of paper you will be given when you graduate. It is really your responsibility to make it worth something to prospective employers. Most employers will require that you have more than a college education; most will expect that you have experience in the field.

The second strategy involves deciding what you want to do. There may be a lot of choices for careers, but if you limit those choices down to just a few options, your chances for ending up in those careers is greatly magnified. A lot of students say, "I don't want to limit my options." Limiting or narrowing your *choices* does not limit your options, it highlights them. My recommendation is to do your research; find out how much you would make, what it will take to get into the career, and what a real day in the career will look like. Google is helpful, but interviewing actual people in that field is even more helpful.

The third strategy is to get experience, as early and often as possible. Volunteer if you have to. It may seem unreasonable to spend time volunteering while you are also taking school, but you can either volunteer now or once you're out of school; it's better to do so now so that once you are out of school you can apply for a paying job. This experience will be helpful for many reasons; it will give you references and many employers want to know how you react to real-life, stressful situations.

The fourth strategy involves documentation. Building a resume is an art and a science. Potential employers want to see what skills you have, and how you would fit within that organization. Show them what leadership skills you have developed and why they should trust you enough to hire you. It's important to use "positive words" in your resume; show prospective employers what you learned and gained, not just what you did at your former employment place.

The fifth strategy is networking. In my opinion, "social networking" has been one of the worst things for *actual* networking. Shaking a hand, visiting with a person, talking with them and showing them you are interested in them and their accomplishments will take you further than "liking" someone's post. However, social networking sites such as LinkedIn is a start if you need one. Remember that many jobs are taken by those who know someone; again, organizations want to know who they can trust, and if someone in that organization knows them, chances are good they feel they can trust them.

The sixth strategy takes us full circle: Consider/evaluate your education. Throughout your educational experience, ask yourself how well you are doing with the previous five strategies. Just like the scientific method, where it starts with a question, then collects data and interprets those results, you will want to do the same things. Develop your own (personal) Needs Based Assessment, and periodically do a review of what you have completed and what you still need.

Review Questions

1. What is a resume and what is its purpose?

2. Based on this chapter, what needs or "gaps" do you still
   have in your education? When and how are you going to
   meet those needs?

3. What is the advantage of getting experience now, rather
   than waiting until after you graduate?

Personal Application

1. Identify the strategies you are doing well with.

2. Identify the strategies you still need help with.

3. Develop a plan of action for meeting the strategies you
   need help with.

Chapter 13: Conclusion

My hope is that you are able to come away from this book with the recognition that you have learned a great deal. Admittedly, and regrettably, many students think, "Wow, research is harder than I thought it would be!" The goal of this book was not to intimidate or overwhelm you, but rather to give you the tools you need to make the best decisions possible, no matter the direction of your career and personal goals.

My objective is to help you become the expert in your field, and to help you interpret the steady streams of research we are constantly fed in academia, advertising, media, and self-help books. Research is incredibly valuable and useful, but it is also often used to convince people rather than educate individuals. As an employee, a store owner, an educator, or as a consumer, I have every confidence that the tools within the book will help you interpret what others are claiming are "facts."

This does not mean that we need to doubt everything and everyone. It does mean that we should check things out, and learn for ourselves, as to what we read or are taught is true.

Let's take just a brief look at what you have learned:

1. Everyone is a researcher, whether we admit to it or not. We all have questions and are looking for answers. The better we understand research, the better we will be with finding accurate answers.

2. There are a set of professional guidelines and ethics we are expected to abide by, and how we live up to these guidelines reflects how trustworthy we are.

3. Developing a really good survey can be hard work, but at least we know what a good survey must consist of: validity and reliability. If a survey does not have these things, we cannot have confidence in that survey's results.

4. The type and size of a "sample" largely determines how much confidence we can have in whether those results can apply (or generalize) to a larger population. Just because a study is conducted with one group of people, it does not prove that those results will apply to another group of people.

5. Statistics are symbols or representations of relationships and trends. Knowing how to interpret these statistics, everything from a Pearson's Correlation Coefficient to a p value, can help us gauge the meaningfulness of a study and its results.

6. When making decisions, it is essential we follow or use Evidence Based Research and Evidence Based Practices.

7. The concept of "experiments," and how to evaluate them, applies to any time we are trying to change behavior, attitudes, or the health of others. Understanding how to evaluate experiments, interventions, and workshops can save us a lot of time and resources.

I wish you the best of success in your future goals and careers!

--Dr. Jerry Cook

Appendix A: Sample Survey

1. Which of the following type of alcohol drinker are you?

      1. Only on days that end in y (3+ drinks per day) 2. Weekender (3+ drinks per weekend [Friday-Sunday])
      3. Social (2+ drinks only at special events/outings) 4. Occasional (1+ drink per mos) 5. Non-Drinker (0   drinks/mos)

2. How likely are you to consume sweets when you are stressed?
      1. Very likely 2. Somewhat likely 3. Not likely 4. Never

3. The amount of hours I sleep effects my level of concentration at school. Three categories for the hours, such as:
      1. less than 6 hours 2. 6-8 hours 3. more than 8 hours

4. What beverage do you prefer? (1) Soda (2) Water (3) Juice (4) Tea/coffee (5) Decaf tea/coffee

5. How frequent do you go online retail shopping? (1) Daily? (2) Weekly? (3) Monthly?

6. What would you categorize your relationship status to be?
      1.Single, 2.it's complicated, 3. dating, 4. in a relationship, or 5. Married

7. What is your college enrollment status?
      1. Part-time(1-6 units) 2. ¾ time (7-11 units) 3. full-time (12-14 units) 4. super full-time (15 units or more)

8. What is your employment status? 1. unemployed, 2.part time , 3. full time

9. What is your class/student rank?

1. Freshman (0-30 units) 2. Sophomore (30-60 units) 3. Jr (60-90 units) 4. Sr (90-120 units)

10. What time do you typically go to the gym?
    1. Morning. 2. Afternoon. 3. Night. 4. I don't work out.

11. What is your diet preference?
    1. omnivorous 2. vegetarian (some animal products, no meat) 3. vegan (no meat or meat products)
    4. gluten-free 5. pescatarian (eats fish but no meat) 6. Other (specify)_____

5=SA 4=A 3=N 2=D 1=SD
1. I think I am an outgoing person. 5 4 3 2 1
2. My friends think I am an outgoing person. 5 4 3 2 1
3. I consider myself an extrovert. 5 4 3 2 1
4. After a stressful event, my craving for sweets increases. 5 4 3 2 1
5. After consuming sweets, my mood improves 5 4 3 2 1
6. My stress level is low around the holidays because of my sweet consumption 5 4 3 2 1
7. I am able to focus well in class. 5 4 3 2 1
8. I am able to focus well while studying outside of class. 5 4 3 2 1
9. It's easy to comprehend/retain material covered in class. 5 4 3 2 1
10. I make healthy choices. 5 4 3 2 1
11. I exercise often. 5 4 3 2 1
12. I buy organic foods. 5 4 3 2 1
13. I retail shop online daily? 5 4 3 2 1
14. I retail shop online weekly? 5 4 3 2 1
15. I retail shop online monthly? 5 4 3 2 1
16. I am a happy person 5 4 3 2 1
17. I'm usually more happier than sad 5 4 3 2 1
18. I believe I can be happier. 5 4 3 2 1
19. Based on my college enrollment status, 5 4 3 2 1

I do not have enough time to be employed full-time (32+ hours per week).

20. I think college students who are enrolled in 12 units 5 4 3 2 1 or more should be employed less than 30 hours per week.

21. I work or would consider no more than 25 hours of 5 4 3 2 1 employment per week because I want to spend more time on studying and school work.

22. I drink water throughout my shift at work. 5 4 3 2 1

23. I drink 64 ounces of water or more a day. 5 4 3 2 1

24. I drink water during my break(s) at work. 5 4 3 2 1

25. I prefer to grab a caffeinated beverage to drink while I study. 5 4 3 2 1

26. It is more likely for me to choose caffeinated beverages over a non-caffeinated beverage. 5 4 3 2 1

27. I feel I need to drink caffeinated beverages to keep my energy level up. 5 4 3 2 1

28. After I go the gym I feel less stressed 5 4 3 2 1

29..I experience stress 5 4 3 2 1

30. I go to the gym to relieve stress 5 4 3 2 1

31. In general, I feel good about myself 5 4 3 2 1

32. My happiness level declines throughout the day 5 4 3 2 1

33. I consider myself a happy person 5 4 3 2 1

Appendix B: Silly Survey

1. Thank you for taking the time to complete this (silly) survey for our class. It will be used to cover concepts in a fun way, and your name will not be collected. If possible, please try to answer each item.

1.1   What is your GPA? (Please enter 3.20, and Not 320)

3.6

1.2   What is your class rank?   ☐ freshman   ☐ sophomore   ☑ junior
                                          ☐ senior   ☐ it's complicated

1.3   What is your gender?

       ☑ Female   ☐ Male   ☐ Prefer not to answer
1.4   Are you married?   ☐ Yes   ☑ No   ☐ It's complicated
1.5   Are you a parent?   ☐ Yes   ☑ No
1.6   Are your parents   ☑ married   ☐ single   ☐ divorced
                                          ☐ remarried
1.7   What is your gender?   ☐ male   ☑ female   ☐ prefer not to
                                                                            answer

2. For the next set of questions, please just give the number and not the label. For example, if I ask how many feet you have, please mark "2" and NOT "2 feet".

2.1   How many hours per week do you study?

2. For the next set of questions, please just give the number and not the label. For example, if I ask how many feet you have, please mark "2" and NOT "2 feet". [Continue]

2.3   How many times per week do you text while driving?

2.4   How many people have you ever kissed?

2.5   How much money do you spend per week on food?

2.6   How many times per day do you take a shower?

182

2. For the next set of questions, please just give the number and not the label. For example, if I ask how many feet you have, please mark "2" and NOT "2 feet". [Continue]

2.9   How many times per week do you floss?

2.10 How many hours per week do you watch TV?

2.11 How many times per week do you do something embarrassing?

2.12 How many times per week do you call your grandparents?

2.22 What is your concentration in FACS?

☐ Family Studies   ☐ Fashion Merchandising   ☐ Nutrition

☐ Dietetics   ☐ Teaching Credential

3. Please answer the following using the scale below:
1 strongly disagree, 2 disagree, 3 neutral, 4 agree, 5 strongly agree

3.1	I have a poor image of myself.	Strongly Disagree	☐ ☐ ☐ ☐ ☐	Strongly Agree
3.2	My parents are rich.	Strongly Disagree	☐ ☐ ☐ ☐ ☐	Strongly Agree
3.3	Most of my instructors at Sac State are good-looking.	Strongly Disagree	☐ ☐ ☐ ☐ ☐	Strongly Agree
3.4	I had a happy childhood.	Strongly Disagree	☐ ☐ ☐ ☐ ☐	Strongly Agree
3.5	My parents were strict.	Strongly Disagree	☐ ☐ ☐ ☐ ☐	Strongly Agree
3.6	It's impossible for marriages to last a lifetime.	Strongly Disagree	☐ ☐ ☐ ☐ ☐	Strongly Agree
3.7	I enjoy country music.	Strongly Disagree	☐ ☐ ☐ ☐ ☐	Strongly Agree
3.8	I think about the nutritional content of the foods I eat.	Strongly Disagree	☐ ☐ ☐ ☐ ☐	Strongly Agree
3.9	I worry how others will perceive me when I put on a new outfit.	Strongly Disagree	☐ ☐ ☐ ☐ ☐	Strongly Agree
3.10	I enjoy shopping for clothes.	Strongly Disagree	☐ ☐ ☐ ☐ ☐	Strongly Agree
3.11	I expect to have an awesome career when I'm done with school.	Strongly Disagree	☐ ☐ ☐ ☐ ☐	Strongly Agree

183

4. Finally, please answer the following questions with either a "yes" or "no."

4.1   Are you currently "in love"?   ☐ Yes   ☐ No

4.2   Do you have any memories of yourself before the age of 2 ½ years old?   ☐ Yes   ☐ No

4.3   Can you play the piano?   ☐ Yes   ☐ No

4.4   Do you prefer Macs over PC's?   ☐ Yes   ☐ No

4.5   Do you prefer Pepsi over Coca Cola?   ☐ Yes   ☐ No

4.6   Do you ever talk with your mouth full?   ☐ Yes   ☐ No

4.7   Have you ever Googled yourself?   ☐ Yes   ☐ No

4.8   Do you ever get upset with how others squeeze the toothpaste?   ☐ Yes   ☐ No

4.9   Do you ever get frustrated with how the toilet paper roll rolls out?   ☐ Yes   ☐ No

4.10 Do you usually watch or read the news?   ☐ Yes   ☐ No

4.11 How old are you?

Made in the USA
San Bernardino, CA
15 January 2020

will happen again (and again . . .). You have come to the right place. This book is the map you need to get you from kidney stone to treatment to prevention.

Think about this: If your doctor diagnosed you with another medical condition other than kidney stones, such as diabetes or heart disease, you would probably do what you could to learn about it and, hopefully, make lifestyle changes to stay healthy and avoid any setbacks. If your doctor told you that you needed to lose weight because you were at risk of suffering a massive heart attack, you would hopefully learn what you needed to do to drop a few pounds. Being diagnosed with chronic kidney stones is no different. You have been diagnosed with a lifelong—yes, lifelong—condition that you now have to learn live with.

This book not only shows you what you need to know about having kidney stones, from diagnosis to treatment, it also shows you various lifestyle changes you can make to reduce your risk of going through this hell again. This is, extremely, important because the more kidney stones you have, the higher the risk of developing kidney disease, so reducing your chances of kidney stones, also, reduces your chances of developing chronic kidney disease later in life.

If you really, truly do not want to experience this pain again, it is important that you review the guidelines and information in this book. I will show you the difference between the four major types of kidney stones, why they happen, how they can be removed and what to eat and drink to prevent them from forming again. Please understand that this book is not intended to be a scientific reference for clinicians, but rather a guide for patients, and is not intended to be a substitute for a consultation with a physician with an expertise in kidney stone disease.

Interestingly, kidney stones are even mentioned in the Hippocratic Oath that we, as doctors, take. It states: "I will not cut for the stone, but leave that to the practitioners of the craft."

Evan R. Goldfischer, MD, MBA
Pleasant Valley, New York
November 2017

The scientific name for a kidney stone is renal calculus or nephrolith. You may hear health care professionals call this condition nephrolithiasis or urolithiasis.

CHAPTER 01

WHY DO I GET KIDNEY STONES?

You may be wondering why is this horrible thing happening to you and is there anything you can do to prevent the kidney stones from forming in the first place? First, kidney stones start forming in the kidneys, obviously, which are two bean-shaped organs that are located in your flank region. Every day, the kidneys are responsible for filtering approximately 120 to 150 quarts of blood and producing about one to two quarts of urine. The kidneys also regulate the levels of fluids, minerals, salts, and other substances in your body. Your risk for kidney stones increases when these levels change – whether you are dehydrated and not putting out enough urine, taking certain medications that affect your levels, or have an excessive amount of certain substances in your urine that can form stones.

Kidney stones also form if you have certain diseases or medical conditions that are conducive to stone formation, such as:

》 Primary Hyperparathyroidism: when your body produces an abnormally high concentration of parathyroid hormone in the blood, which causes bone weakness through the loss of calcium and can also lead to kidney stones.

》 Renal tubular acidosis: a medical condition where acid accumulates in the body because the kidneys cannot acidify the urine.

You're Not Alone

The incidence of kidney stones in the United States is on the rise. According to the National Kidney Foundation, the amount of Americans who have had kidney stones has increased from 3.8 percent in the late 1970s to 8.8 percent in the late 2000s. This increase was seen in both men and women.

One reason the amount of kidney stones is rising is because the American diet has changed, dramatically, in the past three or four decades. Americans are now eating more animal protein-based foods, such as red meat, poultry, eggs, and seafood than ever before. These foods reduce the level of citrate in your urine that you need to help prevent the stones from forming. They also increase the amount of calcium in the urine, and high calcium levels can cause kidney stone formation.

Another reason that the incidence of kidney stones has increased particularly in women is because women are exercising more. That might sound crazy, because exercise is good for you, but when you exercise and you sweat, which means you lose water. The more you sweat, the more water you lose. If you do not replenish the water your body has lost, you can become dehydrated, which can lead to the formation of kidney stones.

Remember what I went through?

) Hyperoxaluria: when your kidneys have to eliminate high levels of oxalate in the urine, either because you eat or produce too much of it. This can lead to calcium oxalate stones.

) Cystinuria: a rare condition where kidney stones are made from an amino acid called cystine that form in the kidney, ureter, and bladder.

) Urinary tract infection: otherwise known as a UTI, a urinary tract infection can introduce bacteria into the kidneys, ureters, bladder, or urethra. This bacteria can lead to bladder and/or kidney stones. Symptoms of a UTI include a strong, persistent urge to urinate; a burning sensation when urinating; passing frequent, small amounts of urine; urine that appears cloudy, red, bright pink or brownish (a sign of blood in the urine); strong-smelling urine; pelvic pain in women — especially in the center of the pelvis and around the pubic bone area.

) Gout: a form of arthritis that is characterized by severe pain, redness, and tenderness in the joints. Gout is caused by an increase in uric acid levels, which can lead to an increased risk for uric acid stones.

For example, if you consume a diet rich in substances that are found in animal protein, such as meats, fish, and shellfish, it may increase the uric acid in your urine, which can lead to the formation of a stone. Beware, if you consume a diet that is full of salami and other processed foods and that are laden with salt, or you and your salt shaker are on a first name basis, as too much sodium in your diet can cause your kidneys to excrete more calcium into the urine, which may cause stones to form.

Taking certain medications can also lead to the formation of kidney stones, including decongestants, diuretics, anticonvulsants, steroids and chemotherapy medications. Your diet may, even, be the offender because you may be eating certain foods that can increase your risk of stones.

If you're looking for someone to blame for your kidney stones, you may want to look on your family tree. You may have these little buggers simply because of your genetics. Say Aunt Jane or Uncle Brian have a genetic medical condition that leaves them at risk for stones. You might be one of the lucky ones who will inherit that condition. Later, we'll talk about how knowing your family history might actually help you to avoid stones.

Kidney Stones and Metabolic Syndrome

In 2014, research from the National Kidney Foundation showed that the terrible pain of kidney stone disease may be more common in people with metabolic syndrome, which is a

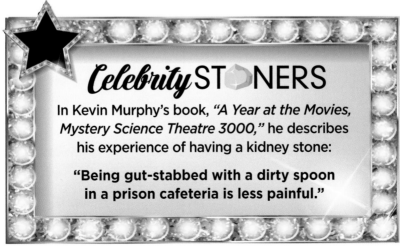

Celebrity ST◯NERS

In Kevin Murphy's book, *"A Year at the Movies, Mystery Science Theatre 3000,"* he describes his experience of having a kidney stone:

"Being gut-stabbed with a dirty spoon in a prison cafeteria is less painful."

cluster of five traits that also sets the stage for heart disease and stroke. A report in the American Journal of Kidney Diseases, the official publication of the National Kidney Foundation, showed that the prevalence of kidney stone disease tripled among individuals who had all five traits of metabolic syndrome.

The study showed that being overweight was a central factor in this syndrome, so maintaining a healthy weight was important to lowering the risk of kidney stones. Excess weight also leads to diabetes and hypertension. The study made the parallel that the incidence of kidney stones has risen with the incidence of obesity.

The report also showed that almost one person in 20 reported a history of kidney stones (4.7 percent).

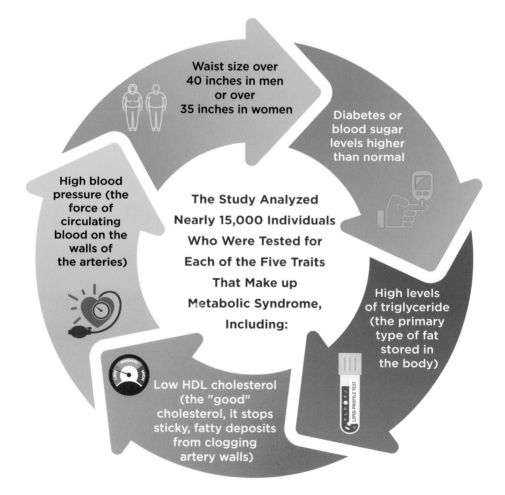

Waist size over 40 inches in men or over 35 inches in women

Diabetes or blood sugar levels higher than normal

High blood pressure (the force of circulating blood on the walls of the arteries)

The Study Analyzed Nearly 15,000 Individuals Who Were Tested for Each of the Five Traits That Make up Metabolic Syndrome, Including:

High levels of triglyceride (the primary type of fat stored in the body)

Low HDL cholesterol (the "good" cholesterol, it stops sticky, fatty deposits from clogging artery walls)

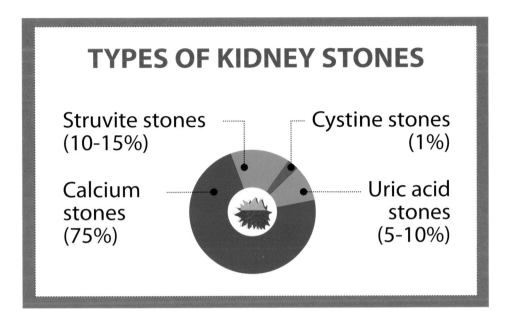

TYPES OF KIDNEY STONES

Struvite stones
(10-15%)

Cystine stones
(1%)

Calcium
stones
(75%)

Uric acid
stones
(5-10%)

The proportion of people with kidney stone disease grew along with the number of metabolic syndrome traits, from 3 percent with zero traits, to 7.5 percent with three traits and 9.8 percent with all five traits.

When researchers took into account other factors that would affect risk, such as age and gender, they estimated that individuals with four or five traits were twice as likely to have kidney stone disease as those without the syndrome.

What Kind of Stones Do I Have?

Not all kidney stones are alike. They do not all look alike, nor are they the same size or shape. They also are not all composed of the same materials. When categorizing kidney stones, they fall into four major categories. Once it is determined that you, indeed, have a stone, it will either be classified as calcium-based; infection or struvite; uric acid; or cystine stone.

Eighty percent of all kidney stones are diagnosed as calcium-oxalate stones, while calcium phosphate kidney stones make up between 8 and 10 percent of all attacks. Ten percent of all stones are diagnosed as uric acid stones and rounding out the list are the least common of all types, cystine kidney stones.

I will get into the differences between each of these stones in more detail later, but the good news is that, no matter what type of stone you

SIGNS & SYMPTOMS

Now I know when I get kidney stones because the pain is excruciating and easily memorable, but here are all of the symptoms that a kidney stone has taken residence in your body:

- Severe pain in your side and back, below the ribs
- Pain that spreads to your lower abdomen and groin
- Pain that comes in waves
- Pain that fluctuates
- Pain when you urinate
- Urine that is pink, red or brown
- Cloudy or foul-smelling urine
- Persistent need to urinate
- Urinating more often than usual
- Urinating small amounts
- Nausea and vomiting
- Fever and chills, if an infection is present

It's important to note that not everyone will experience all of these symptoms.

have, they can be prevented! Even if you are at risk for a stone, but are lucky to have not had one yet, you can still follow a prevention plan of medication, diet and an ample amount of fluids to make sure they never form.

There is even better news for you if you are currently going through a kidney stone attack and have turned to this book for advice and support to get through it. More often than not, small kidney stones that are less than 5 mm will pass through you without any need for surgical intervention. You will need to stay well hydrated, and be able to take pain relievers, such as ibuprofen (Motrin®, Advil®) or acetaminophen (Tylenol®), or perhaps a narcotic such as Percocet® to reduce your discomfort during your ordeal. If necessary, your doctor can also prescribe medications, such as an alpha blocker or a calcium channel blocker that will help to relax the ureter muscles. Relaxing these muscles will relieve some of the pain and allow some of the urine to flow, which will relieve the pressure.

It's All in the Numbers

Most likely, you are reading this book because like me, you are one of a half a million of Americans who have ended up in the emergency room this year, writhing in pain and wondering what is causing it. You may also be one of the estimated 177,496 Americans, 20 years or older, who were admitted to the hospital in a one-year period and diagnosed with "calculus of kidney and ureters," otherwise known as kidney stones. Statistics also show that in that same one-year period, there were approximately 2 million adult visits to primary care or specialty doctors' offices with, again, a diagnosis of calculus of kidney and ureters. In that same year, there were approximately 2.7 million adult visits with "urolithiasis" listed as their diagnosis. Urolithiasis is the process of forming the stones in the kidney, ureter, or bladder.

Here is a more somber statistic for you: it is estimated that one in 10 people, or approximately 30 million Americans, will experience a kidney stone at some point in their life. Out of these, white Americans are more prone to developing kidney stones with white men at a much higher risk than white women. Although women's risk has increased during the past few years. Another study, published in 2016 in the Clinical Journal of the American Society of Nephrology, showed that not only are kidney stones increasing in women, but are also rising in adolescents and African-Americans. The team analyzed data from nearly 153,000 child and adult kidney stone patients from a total population of 4.6 million. Overall, the annual incidence of kidney stones increased 16 percent between 1997 and 2012. The greatest rates of increase were among adolescents (4.7 percent per year), females (3 percent per year), and African-Americans (2.9 percent per year). Between 1997 and 2012, the risk of kidney stones doubled during childhood for both boys and girls, while there was a 45 percent increase in the lifetime risk for women.

Interestingly, a 2014 study showed a link between higher daily temperatures and an increase in patients seeking treatment for kidney stones in five U.S. cities. What this means is that patients in these climates are, as we've seen with women, sweating more, but not drinking enough.

I, also, regret to share even more bad news, but if you have already suffered through one kidney stone episode — painful or not — you will likely suffer through another and maybe even another, sorry. Statistics show that it's almost a 50 percent chance that it will happen again.

Kidney stones do not only cause

The highest rate of increase in kidney stones was among **adolescent females**, and in any given year, stones were more common among females than males ages 10 to 24 years. Among **African-Americans**, the incidence of kidney stones **increased 15 percent** more than in whites within each five-year period covered by the study. This study cited possible factors for the rise, including **poor water intake and dietary habits**.

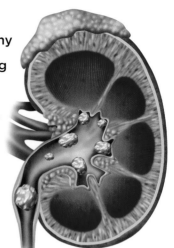

physical pain, they cause financial agony too. It is estimated that more than $2 billion was expended in the United States for the evaluation and treatment of kidney stone patients in just one year. Isn't it amazing that these little stones can cause such huge problems?

Going Forward

New research on the treatment and prevention of kidney stones is being done all the time. For example, one study conducted by researchers from the Clinic of Ankara Training and Research Hospital in Ankara, Turkey, suggested that having sex at least three to four times per week can help with the spontaneous passage of small kidney stones (hey, whatever works for you).

At this point, though, you are probably not concerned about any future, or even current research. If you are currently in what's called the acute phase of kidney stones, it means that you are, unfortunately, still in the pain portion of the program. Your kidney stone has obviously presented itself with symptoms and you want immediate information, relief and support, while you are either waiting to pass the stone or waiting for the next stage of treatment.

CLINICAL TRIALS

Want to be part of a clinical trial?
The National Institute of Diabetes and Digestive and Kidney Diseases (NIDDK) and other components of the National Institutes of Health (NIH) conduct and support research into many diseases and conditions.

What are clinical trials, and are they right for you?
Clinical trials are part of clinical research and at the heart of all medical advances. Clinical trials look at new ways to prevent, detect, or treat disease. Researchers also use clinical trials to look at other aspects of care, such as improving the quality of life for people with chronic illnesses.

What clinical trials are open?

Clinical trials that are currently open and are recruiting can be viewed at **www.ClinicalTrials.gov**.

This content is provided as a service of the National Institute of Diabetes and Digestive and Kidney Diseases (NIDDK), part of the National Institutes of Health. The NIDDK translates and disseminates research findings through its clearinghouses and education programs to increase knowledge and understanding about health and disease among patients, health professionals, and the public. Content produced by the NIDDK is carefully reviewed by NIDDK scientists and other experts.

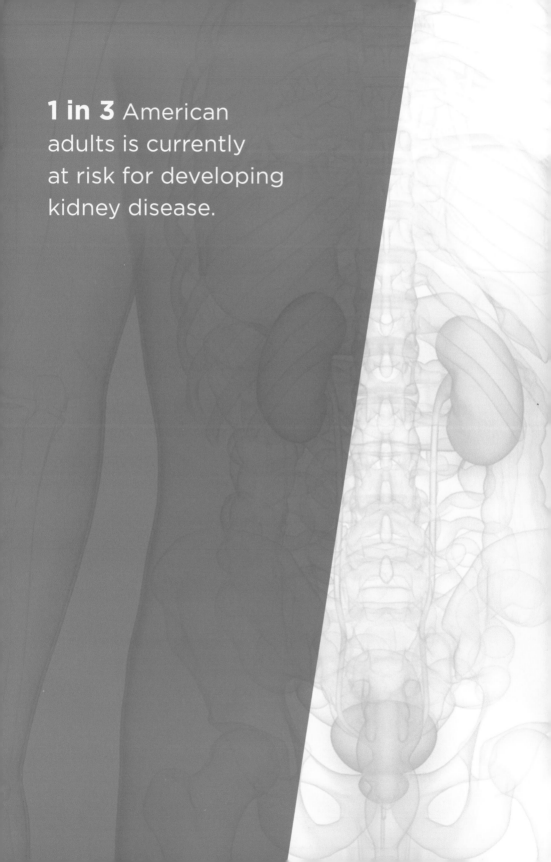

1 in 3 American adults is currently at risk for developing kidney disease.

CHAPTER 02

SYSTEM CHECK

To better understand why your body is producing kidney stones and how to prevent them, you should first have some basic knowledge of your urinary system, how it works, and how things can go wrong.

Your urinary system, is comprised of two kidneys, two ureters, a bladder and a urethra. Each kidney is attached to the bladder via the ureters, which are made of muscle fibers that push urine toward the bladder where the urine is stored. When the bladder, a pear-shaped sac in the pelvis, is full, it sends a signal to your brain that it is time to go to the bathroom. When you urinate, the bladder contracts, which opens two sphincters that allow the urine to flow into the urethra and out of your body. A man and a woman have the same urinary system until you get to the urethra—that's when the big differences begin. Not only is the man's urethra longer, but it has a prostate and all of its associated structures.

Every day, an average of one to two liters of urine are produced by the kidneys, but this amounts also fluctuates depending on how hydrated and active you are, your weight, and your overall health.

Your kidneys are responsible for eliminating waste, regulating electrolytes (sodium, potassium and calcium), controlling blood volume and maintaining blood pressure.

There are several problems that can occur with your urinary system and some are simply due to age:

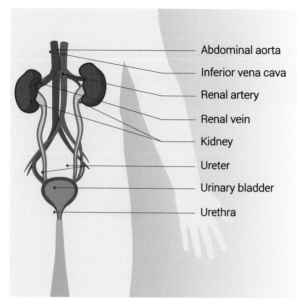

Abdominal aorta

Inferior vena cava

Renal artery

Renal vein

Kidney

Ureter

Urinary bladder

Urethra

Urinary Tract Infections: The older you get, the more all of your muscles start to lose strength and, in similar fashion, the kidneys lose some ability to remove waste. This muscle weakness then allows bacteria to stay behind in the kidneys, which causes an increased risk of urinary tract infections (UTIs). In addition, the vaginal flora and vaginal pH can change making a woman more prone to infections, particularly after intercourse. Making sure to wipe front to back instead of back to front; urinating after intercourse; and avoiding public hot tubs and public pools are measures women can take to decrease the chances of acquiring a UTI. While UTIs are more common in women, they can also occur in men. UTIs can be treated with antibiotics.

UTIs are caused by protozoa, fungi, viruses, or bacteria, with bacteria being the biggest culprits. Typically, the bacteria is removed through urination before it causes any symptoms, but sometimes it stays behind and causes an infection. If the infection is in the urethra, it is called urethritis. A bladder infection is called cystitis. Bacteria may travel up the ureters to multiply and infect the kidneys. A kidney infection is called pyelonephritis.

Incontinence: Weakness in the pelvic floor muscles or urinary sphincter may also cause a condition called incontinence, which is the uncontrollable, and often embarrassing, leaking of urine. Incontinence affects one quarter to one-third of all men and women. You can be at an increased risk of incontinence as you age, or if you have been pregnant or delivered a baby either by C-section or vaginal birth. Post-menopausal women, men with prostate issues and those who take certain medications that may cause bladder weakness can also become incontinent as well.

There are several types of urinary incontinence, including stress-induced, which is when your bladder leaks because you are bending during exercise or simply because you sneeze. This is different than an overactive bladder, which is an urgency to pee, even if you do not have to.

Interstitial Cystitis: This is a very uncomfortable condition that causes chronic pain for women between the vagina and the anus, pain during sex, as well as a constant need to urinate (up to dozens of times during the day). Interstitial cystitis is not the same as a urinary tract infection.

Chronic kidney disease: When kidney disease is chronic it means there is damage to the kidneys and decreased kidney function that has lasted for longer than three months. Chronic kidney disease is caused most commonly by diabetes.

Kidney failure: There are two types of kidney failure: Chronic kidney disease and acute renal failure (also called acute kidney injury). Acute renal failure is sudden and can be caused by a variety of reasons, including a lack of blood flow or damage to the kidneys, a blockage of urine, traumatic injury, dehydration, sepsis, or damage from certain medications or toxins. This can be reversible. Chronic kidney disease develops over several years, and often leads to dialysis or a kidney transplant being required. According to the National Kidney Foundation, more than 661,000 Americans have kidney failure. Of these, 468,000 individuals are on dialysis and approximately 193,000 live with a functioning kidney transplant.

Bladder cancer: According to the American Cancer Society, about 74,000 people were diagnosed with cancer of the bladder in 2015 (about 56,320 men and 17,680 women), and there were nearly 16,000 deaths (about 11,510 men and 4,490 women). The symptoms of bladder cancer include back or pelvic pain, difficulty urinating, blood in the urine, and urgent and/or frequent urination.

Pyelonephritis: Inflammation of one or both kidneys due to a urinary tract infection that moves to the kidneys from the bladder or an infection that is carried through the bloodstream from other parts of the body. You are at risk for pyelonephritis if you have a defect in your urinary system and it is blocked by a kidney stone or even an enlarged prostate which can cause urine to back up into the kidneys.

The Numbers Tell the Story

1 in 3 American adults is currently at risk for developing kidney disease.

High blood pressure and **diabetes** are the two leading causes of kidney disease.

Kidney disease is the **9th LEADING CAUSE** of death in the United States.

Major risk factors for kidney disease include **diabetes, high blood pressure, family history of kidney failure** and **being age 60 or older**. Additional risk factors include **kidney stones, smoking, obesity** and **cardiovascular disease**.

26 MILLION American adults have kidney disease—and most don't know it.

Those at risk should have **simple blood** and **urine tests** to check if their kidneys are working properly.

Men with kidney disease are more likely than women to progress to kidney failure.

Every year, kidney disease kills more people than breast or prostate cancer.

In **2013**, more than **47,000** Americans died from kidney disease.

3X The number of African Americans are more likely to experience kidney failure.

Every day, 13 people die waiting for a kidney.

Once the kidneys fail, dialysis or a kidney transplant is required.

Of more than **121,000** people waiting for lifesaving organ transplants in the U.S., **100,791** await kidney transplants (as of 1/11/16). Fewer than **17,000** people receive one each year.

More than **661,000** Americans have kidney failure. Of these, **468,000** individuals are on dialysis, & approximately **193,000** live with a functioning kidney transplant.

Hispanics are 1½ times more likely to experience **kidney failure.**

Benign prostatic hyperplasia (BPH): A condition in men that affects the prostate gland, which is part of the male reproductive system. The prostate is located at the bottom of the bladder and surrounds the urethra. BPH is an enlargement of the prostate gland that can interfere with urinary function in older men. It causes a blockage by squeezing the urethra, which can make it difficult to urinate. Men with BPH frequently have other bladder symptoms, including an increase in frequency to empty the bladder day and night. Most men over age 60 have some BPH, but not all have problems with blockage.

Prostatitis: inflammation of the prostate glands. The symptoms include frequent and urgent urinating, burning or painful urination and pain in the lower back and genital area. Many urologic disease experts feel that between 5 and 10 percent of males in the U.S. will experience prostatitis, making it one of the most common urologic diseases in the U.S.

Proteinuria: a condition where there is a high amount of protein in the urine. People who have diabetes, hypertension, and certain family backgrounds are at risk for proteinuria. African Americans are more likely than whites to have high blood pressure and to develop proteinuria. Other groups at risk for proteinuria are American Indians, Hispanics/Latinos, Pacific Islander Americans, older adults, and those who are overweight. These at-risk groups and people who may have a family history of kidney disease should have their urine tested regularly.

Urinary retention: this is the inability to urinate or empty your bladder, which can result in pain and discomfort from whatever is causing the obstruction. People with acute urinary retention cannot urinate at all, even though they have a full bladder. Acute urinary retention, which can cause great discomfort, is a potentially life-threatening medical condition and requires immediate emergency treatment.

Primary Doctor or Urologist?

While your primary doctor can treat some of these urinary issues, it is important to develop an ongoing relationship with a urologist, who specializes in treating problems with the entire urinary system, especially kidney stones. Typically a urologist, like myself, treats the male reproductive organs and both male and female urinary systems, while a gynecologist treats reproductive disorders in females, although some gynecologists are comfortable with the female urinary system, as well.

If you don't already have a urologist, now is the time to find one. If you are a young man in his 20s and are reading this book because you have had a kidney stone, or are at risk for one, and don't think that you need a urologist because that's for the old guys and their prostate problems, think again. In addition to treating your kidney stones, a urologist treats any problems you may have with your penis, including sex and conception, prostate and testicular cancers, premature ejaculation, and issues with erections. Start a relationship with a urologist now, who will already know your medical history when you aren't feeling your best.

Finding a Urologist

To find a urologist, you should first contact your insurance company to see which local urologists are on your plan, or you can visit the Urology Care Foundation website at www.urologyhealth.org to locate one near you.

You can also seek recommendations from your family physician, local hospital, or, if you do not feel it's too personal, ask family and friends. Do not be surprised that more than 90 percent of urologists in the United States are men and that there is currently a great shortage of female urologists.

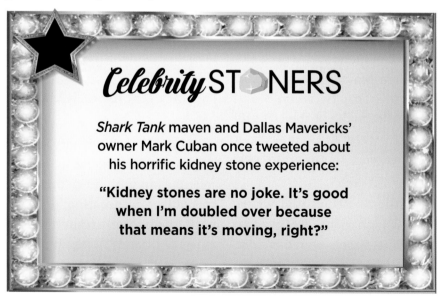

Celebrity STONERS

Shark Tank maven and Dallas Mavericks' owner Mark Cuban once tweeted about his horrific kidney stone experience:

"Kidney stones are no joke. It's good when I'm doubled over because that means it's moving, right?"

Once you find a few potential candidates that you might want as your physician, make an appointment for a consultation and talk to each doctor about his training and area of specialization. During this meeting, you should take time to get to know the doctor and his practice. At the same time, the doctor will get to know you and what kind of doctor you need. Ask several questions about the urologist's background and about the practice, including:

▶ **Can you tell me about your training and specialty and if you are board certified?**
To become a urologist, an individual needs to graduate from four years of college and four years of medical school and then complete a five- or six-year residency. Some graduates will open their own practice or join an existing one. Other graduates will continue their education and subspecialize in stone disease, pediatrics, cancer, or female incontinence, to name a few examples. They will spend an extra one to three years in training to complete a fellowship. All urologists are trained surgeons, although some will forgo the operating room for a career in academic research or teaching.
Why it is important for you to know this: Knowing your doctor is board certified tells you that they completed a level of education approved by the medical board.

▶ **How long have you been in practice?** Do you want to see a young doctor who is new to medicine or an older, more experienced physician? A younger doctor might have different ideas and approaches.

▶ **Is this a group or single practice?** Note: If it is a single practice, who will see you if your doctor is unavailable? If it is a group practice, will you get to meet the other doctors, and who you will see if your doctor is not in?

▶ **What medical equipment and testing do you have in the office?** (Note: This is especially important when you are in pain and do not want to go to the emergency room.) In my practice, we can perform several tests right in our office, including CT scans, blood tests, biopsies, and urinalysis.

Your Medical History

Once you find one you are happy with, make an appointment for a consultation so the doctor can get a basic medical history from you. This will benefit you when you have kidney stone symptoms, or symptoms of other diseases or conditions that affect your reproductive or urinary system.

At your first visit or physical, you will be asked to fill out medical history forms. A family medical history is a record of your health, as well as the health of your closest relatives, which includes your parents, brothers and sisters, aunts and uncles, nieces and nephews, grandparents and cousins. If you do not know your family medical history, ask your relatives about any medical conditions, especially kidney stones, that they've had and when they had them. You should know if your Grandma Patty on your mother's side or your Grandpa Joe on your father's side was ever diagnosed with cancer—and if so, what kind—or whether your brother or sister suffer from conditions such as irritable bowel syndrome, heart disease or, of course, kidney stones. Also, try to find out the medical history of any deceased relatives. Keep this information as up-to-date as possible.

Of course, this might be difficult if you are adopted and do not have any background on your birth parents or if you are estranged from your family, but do the best you can. Every little bit helps.

Putting your personal medical history together with your family's medical history will give your doctor a clearer picture of your overall health and future health issues. It can also help to determine if you are at risk for certain medical conditions, such as the gout that your Uncle Chris has or the cancer that your Grandpa Joe has. Keep in mind that just because they have these illnesses doesn't mean you will too. It just helps us to understand what medical conditions run in your family and what your risks are.

If you do not know your family medical history, that's okay. Do not let that stop you from seeking medical attention or having a physical. We can still work with your personal medical history, so make sure you keep an updated list of any conditions that you might have had in your own life as well any symptoms you currently have.

You should also bring the following to your doctor's appointment:

- A list of dates of any past surgeries you have had
- A list of current medications that you are taking
- A list of your current doctors' names and contact information
- Next of kin and contact information
- Your health insurance card and a picture ID
- A list of any drug allergies you have
- A list of your current symptoms

If you have already had a stone and are seeing a new doctor, make sure to bring your history of stones, which would include the dates of your first and last kidney stone attack. In addition, make a list with the answers to these questions:

- How many stones have you already had?
- What procedures have you had and when did you have them?
- Did you have any complications from these procedures?
- What prevention treatments and medications have you tried?

If you have caught any kidney stones you have already passed, make sure to bring them with you, so the doctor can send them to the lab for analysis. You should also bring copies of any previous test results, such as your bloodwork, CT scans, ultrasounds, and urinalysis. This includes:

- CDs of most recent CT scans, or other radiographs or ultrasound images for stones
- Reports of recent blood work— especially any parathyroid hormone measurements, or serum calcium, phosphate, creatinine, potassium, chloride or total CO_2 test results
- All 24-hour urine kidney stone tests to date — bring actual reports not summaries

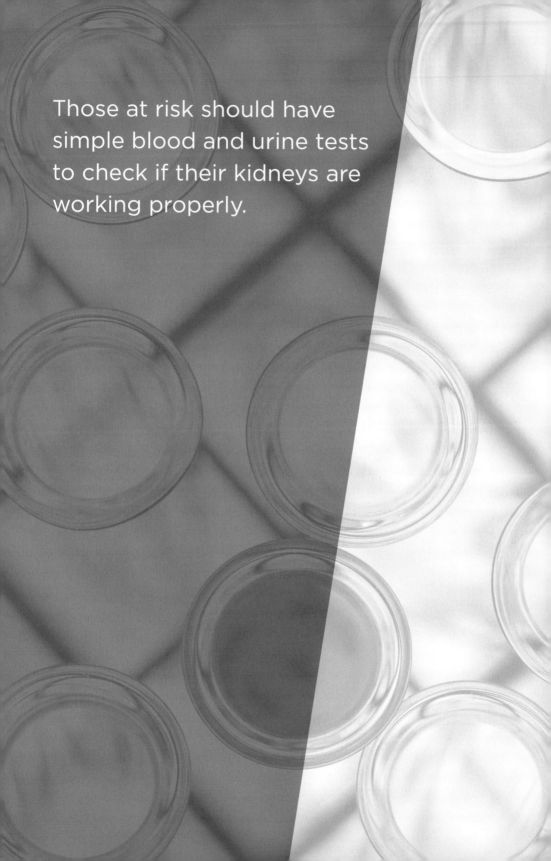

Those at risk should have simple blood and urine tests to check if their kidneys are working properly.

CHAPTER 03

INITIAL TESTS

At your first visit, there will be several tests you may undergo. For men who might have prostate issues, the doctor may perform a digital rectal exam. This allows the doctor to physically examine the prostate. The doctor may also perform other tests such blood work, including a PSA (Prostate Specific Antigen) level.

Women may undergo a pelvic exam, especially if you have any recurring urinary tract infections (UTIs) or incontinence.

Urinalysis

At your first visit, both men and women will be asked to provide a urine sample for a urinalysis, which is a test that examines the urine's color, concentration, and content. It also tests the urine's level of bilirubin, blood, sugars, pH levels and looks for any leukocytes, nitrates, and other signs of infection.

Urinalysis, also referred to as a routine urine test, is used to check for abnormalities in the urine. There are a number of diseases and conditions which can result in abnormalities in the urine and can often be detected through physical, chemical, and microscopic examination.

The urinalysis is usually done by a dipstick test. The dipstick test involves placing papers that contain small pads of chemicals into the urine sample. The papers will change colors depending on what substances are in the urine. The color will tell you what the problem may be. However, this type of urine testing can result in false-positive or false-negative results.

Timing is Everything

Urinalysis should be performed soon after the collecting the urine sample. If that is not possible, the urine should be refrigerated. If you can't hold your urine until you arrive at your doctor's office, arrive a bit earlier than your scheduled appointment time. Bring a bottle of water (or juice) with you and drink it while you sit in the waiting room. When you feel your bladder is full and you can provide your sample, let the medical staff know and they will either give you a plastic cup or a jar with a lid.

It is vital to collect a clean urine sample, which means catching the urine midstream in a sterile jar with unsoiled hands. At your consultation appointment, the doctor may give you a kit so you can collect the urine sample at home and bring it to your appointment.

Before doing a clean catch, you should wash your genital area. Girls and women need to wash the area between the vagina "lips" (labia). You may be given a special clean-catch kit that contains sterile wipes. Sit on the toilet with your legs spread apart. Use two fingers to spread open your labia. Use the first wipe to clean the inner folds of the labia. Wipe from the front to the back. Use a second wipe to clean over the opening where urine comes out (urethra), just above the opening of the vagina.

Men should clean the tip of the penis before urinating. Clean the head of the penis with a sterile wipe. If you are not circumcised, you will need to pull back (retract) the foreskin first.

If possible, collect the sample when urine has been in your bladder for at least 2 to 3 hours. Hold the urine cup a few inches from the urethra and urinate until the cup is about half full. Most importantly, do not touch the inside of the rim of the jar at any time during the catch; otherwise you can contaminate the sample. When you have collected enough of urine, wash your hands with soap and warm water, close the lid, and give it to the nurse on duty.

If you collect the urine at home and you are not going to your appointment immediately, store the urine sample in a sealed bag, label it and refrigerate it until it is time to leave.

A urinalysis involves checking the appearance and color of urine. For example, infections may cause urine to appear cloudy. But it also gets lighter and darker depending on a variety of factors, including what you drink and eat, how much or little you drink every day, and by laxatives, medications and supplements you take.

The color of urine can vary from pale yellow to dark yellow, and even red, green, or blue For example, urine can be affected by food coloring and certain foods, such as beets, asparagus, blackberries and yellow vegetables. The presence of bilirubin in the urine can make the urine dark in color, even olive green. Hemoglobin, which may indicate injury to the urinary tract, can make the urine pink or red. Here is a breakdown of the tints and what they mean:

CLEAR URINE: Clear urine might seem like a perfectly healthy urine sample, but it could also mean you are drinking too much water. If you are chugging a few gallons, it's too much.

NEON YELLOW: Vitamin B2, or Riboflavin, is common in vitamins, but can give off a bright yellowish color to your urine.

DARK YELLOW: Slightly yellow urine is normal, but if your urine is a darker yellow, it could be that you aren't drinking enough of water or you may be taking certain vitamin supplements that change the urine color. If you are a heavy drinker, darker urine might even be an indicator of alcoholic hepatitis or liver disease. If your urine has always been a light yellow, but is now getting darker, increase your water intake and stop taking your vitamin supplements. If this does not lighten the color of your urine, talk to your doctor.

RED: It is an unsettling experience to urinate and see streaks of blood, also called hematuria, in the toilet or when you wipe, as it could be an indication of several medical issues, such as a urinary tract infection, kidney stones or something more serious, such as bladder or kidney cancer. The blood, which can be pink, red or even brown can come from the kidneys, ureters, bladder, or urethra. If you have blood in your urine, please see your urologist as soon as possible. A sample can also have microscopic hematuria, which is blood that is present, even though you do not see it.

SMELL: Urine has an odor, but it's not usually a very strong smell. However, if your urine has a foul odor, don't worry about it just yet. It could be a temporary situation that has been caused by certain vitamins or other supplements you are taking or it could be from something you ate, such as asparagus. A foul urine odor

Urine Dipstick

should only last a short period of time, but if it lingers or if you have other symptoms or you are concerned about the odor for whatever reason, make an appointment with your primary care doctor or your urologist. Foul smelling urine that doesn't go away could be a sign of dehydration or a bladder or urinary tract infection.

Acidic or Basic

The urine's pH can also tell you a lot about your health, depending on how acidic or basic it is. A neutral pH is 7.0 so the higher the number the more basic the urine. The lower the number, the more acidic the urine is. Urine that has a low pH is the perfect environment for the formation of kidney stones. It may also mean that you may have one of a variety of conditions, such as diarrhea, dehydration, or acidosis, which is a higher amount of acid in your blood.

Many factors, including what you eat and drink as well as medications and supplements, can change the acidity or alkalinity of your urine. Because of this, your doctor may have you stop taking certain medications, supplements or vitamins prior to the test, including acetazolamide, ammonium chloride, methenamine mandelate, potassium citrate, sodium bicarbonate, and thiazide diuretics.

However, your urologist will also want your urine's pH to be as close to what it normally is as possible, and may tell you to continuing eating the way you have been up to that point. Keep in mind, however, that if you eat

CAN'T URINATE? Tell Your Doctor

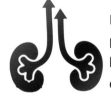 If your kidney stone is causing you to have problems urinating, you can help the doctor by keeping a diary of how many times you urinate day and night, as well as how much and what you drank. Doctors can use this information to help evaluate your symptoms and diagnose your condition. If you have a problem urinating, but do not have a kidney stone in the way, your doctor may use a catheter, which is a flexible tube, to collect the urine by inserting it through the urethra and into the bladder.

a lot of meat, your urine is probably going to be more acidic than if you eat a healthier diet of fruits and vegetables.

If you have other tests done at the same time as the urinalysis, you may need to fast. Fasting means not eating or drinking for a certain number of hours prior to your test. The results of the urinalysis may take several days to come back and, if they come back abnormal, it may require additional testing to determine what the problem may be, if it's something other than your kidney stones.

In addition to a urinalysis, the urologist might also run a variety of other tests, including blood, testosterone, PSA (prostate-specific antigen) levels and more.

Blood Tests

As part of your initial examination, the urologist may take a blood sample and run a comprehensive metabolic panel. Blood tests can be used to diagnose and observe a variety of urologic conditions. Often, blood work results can help doctors determine if further lab tests, such a parathyroid level, or treatments are necessary.

Blood testing is a routine procedure. A blood test involves using a needle to collect blood, usually from a vein in the arm. This blood sample is then sent to a laboratory for analysis.

Here are some common blood tests that health care providers use to help diagnose urologic conditions:

Blood urea nitrogen (BUN) test: Used to evaluate kidney function, diagnose kidney problems, and monitor dialysis results.

Creatinine test: A high level of creatinine in the blood may indicate kidney damage caused by kidney infection, kidney stones, or decreased blood flow to the kidneys.

Estimated glomerular filtration rate (eGER): Will test how well the kidneys are working.

Prostate-specific antigen (PSA) tests: Used in men to screen for prostate cancer and to monitor prostate cancer treatment. PSA is a protein produced by the prostate gland. The PSA test also may be used to diagnose benign prostatic hyperplasia (BPH, enlarged prostate) and or prostate infection (prostatitis) in men.

Calcium test: Measures the level of calcium in the blood and can be used to screen for parathyroid disease.

Phosphate test: Measures for phosphate levels in the blood and used to diagnose kidney problems and monitor dialysis.

Uric Acid Test

A uric acid blood test, also known as a serum uric acid measurement, determines how much uric acid is present in your blood and how well your body produces and removes the acid. Uric acid is a chemical produced when your body breaks down foods that contain organic compounds called purines. Too much uric acid in your blood can lead to uric acid stones.

When your doctor has ordered a uric acid test, it's important to know that there are several things that might affect the results, including alcohol; certain medications, such as aspirin and ibuprofen (Motrin®); dyes used in x-rays; and high levels of vitamin C. Be sure to tell your doctor if you are taking any prescription or over-the-counter medications so they can determine if you need to stop taking them until the test is over.

Once collected, the blood is sent to a laboratory for analysis.

According to the Clinical Reference Laboratory, normal values

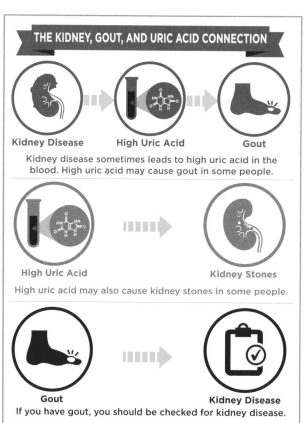

THE KIDNEY, GOUT, AND URIC ACID CONNECTION

Kidney Disease → High Uric Acid → Gout

Kidney disease sometimes leads to high uric acid in the blood. High uric acid may cause gout in some people.

High Uric Acid → Kidney Stones

High uric acid may also cause kidney stones in some people.

Gout → Kidney Disease

If you have gout, you should be checked for kidney disease.

A URIC ACID TEST IS ORDERED FOR SEVERAL REASONS:

1. To find the cause of your kidney stones.

2. To monitor patients with gout.

3. To monitor patients who are undergoing chemotherapy.

4. To check your kidney function find the cause of kidney stones.

5. Another option for uric acid testing is to test your urine over a 24-hour period.

for women are 2.5 to 7.5 milligrams/deciliter (mg/dL), and 4.0 to 8.5 mg/dL for men. However, the values may vary based on the lab doing the testing.

If you have gout, your target blood uric acid level is less than 6 mg/dL, according to the American College of Rheumatology. Low levels of uric acid are less common than high levels and are less of a health concern.

If your test results come back with a high level of uric acid in your blood, it means that your kidneys aren't removing the waste adequately. Recent studies state that people with a uric acid level of 10 mg/dL or higher are at a greater risk for kidney stones. There are several reasons why your uric acid levels can be high. You may have:

- Cancer or are going through chemotherapy

- Diabetes

- Gout, which involves recurring attacks of acute arthritis

- Bone marrow disorders

- A diet high in purines, which are in proteins

- Kidney disorders, such as acute kidney failure

The blood uric acid test isn't considered a definitive test for gout. The only test that can absolutely confirm the presence of gout is testing a person's joint fluid for monosodium urate.

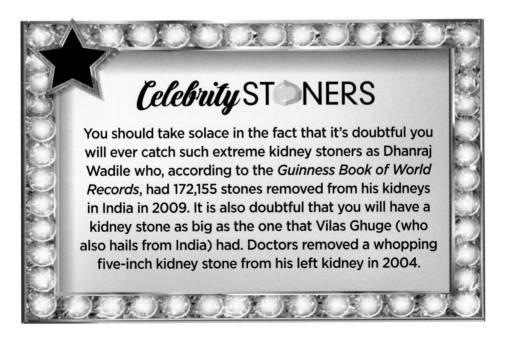

Celebrity STONERS

You should take solace in the fact that it's doubtful you will ever catch such extreme kidney stoners as Dhanraj Wadile who, according to the *Guinness Book of World Records*, had 172,155 stones removed from his kidneys in India in 2009. It is also doubtful that you will have a kidney stone as big as the one that Vilas Ghuge (who also hails from India) had. Doctors removed a whopping five-inch kidney stone from his left kidney in 2004.

However, your doctor can make an educated guess based on high blood levels and your gout symptoms. Also, it's possible to have high uric acid levels without the symptoms of gout. This is known as asymptomatic hyperuricemia.

Comprehensive Metabolic Panel

A Comprehensive Metabolic Panel (CMP) may be ordered, which is a group of blood tests that provide information on your body's chemical balance and metabolism.

During a routine first examination, a urologist will also check your genitals and, if you are male, conduct a complete rectal examination to examine your prostate. Depending on your complaint and symptoms, you may also have tests that give a better picture of your reproductive and urinary systems. These tests may include a sonography, ultrasound, and CT scan. If you are already suffering from kidney stones, you might undergo other tests as well, but I will get into those in more detail later.

During your initial examination, your urologist should also discuss your lifestyle, including your dietary habits, which have direct connections between what you eat and drink and any urinary issues you may have. For example, if you are on the Atkins diet, you might think you are doing your body good, but this high-protein, low-carb diet

The CMP includes the following tests.

- **Sodium (Na) Potassium (K), Chloride (C) and Carbon Dioxide (CO2)**
  These tests check the electrolytes in your body. These numbers can be too low or too high because you might have been dehydrated, vomiting, taking medications that affect these numbers or have kidney problems that can cause problems.

- **Albumin (Alb), Alkaline Phosphatase (ALP), Total Aspartate Transaminase (AST); Alanine Transaminase (ALT), and Bilirubin**
  These tests check liver function, liver injury or liver disease.

- **Blood Urea Nitrogen (BUN), Calcium (Ca), Creatinine (Cr), and Glucose Testing**
  These tests check for a range of problems that affect the kidneys, including kidney disease. These also measure the waste in the blood that may affect kidney filtration.

It will take a few days for your test results to come back.

program might be the reason you have, or are at risk for kidney stones. Or perhaps you drink a lot of high-protein shakes. Protein contains amino acids that break down into uric acid. Too much protein equals too much uric acid in your system, which can lead to the formation of uric acid kidney stones.

I have a 44-year-old patient who is a vegetarian and is suffering from kidney stones. Since she does not eat any meat or eggs, I had to do a little digging into her dietary habits to pinpoint the problem. Later, I discovered that while she drank a lot of water, she also drank protein shakes to satisfy her daily protein requirement. This led her straight to the formation of kidney stones.

Your urologist will also want to know how much water you drink every day and what medications and supplements you take. All of this information will help determine your diagnosis.

Now that you understand the basic workings of your urinary system and understand the importance of a good relationship with a urologist, it is important to understand how and why these kidney stones are formed.

How Stones Are Formed

Now you understand your urinary system, but how the heck do these stones form? In order for a kidney stone to form, the right atmosphere needs to be present. First, your urine needs to be concentrated. If it's diluted – in other words, if you do the right thing and drink enough of water so the toxins are flushed out of your system – there is less opportunity for crystals to form. However, if certain levels in your body are off, or you have an infection, such as a urinary tract infection, or an anatomic anomaly in one or both kidneys or ureters, the stone can start to form and, without treatment, get bigger and bigger.

However, even if your body forms crystals or tiny kidney stones, you may not even realize you have them if you drink enough water to wash everything away. But sometimes a stone gets so big it can get stuck in the kidney and you will have trouble draining your urine. Every time the urine is concentrated the crystals can get bigger and bigger and bigger.

And that is how the stone is formed, but what is your risk of getting one (or two, or three . . .)?

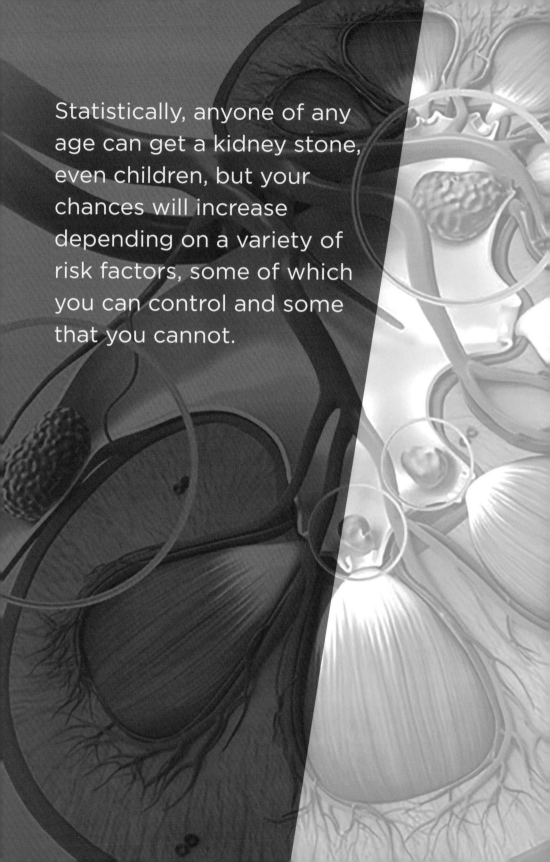

Statistically, anyone of any age can get a kidney stone, even children, but your chances will increase depending on a variety of risk factors, some of which you can control and some that you cannot.

CHAPTER 04

WHAT ARE YOUR ODDS?

If statistics say that one in 10 Americans will get a kidney stone at some time in their life, what puts you at a greater chance of getting one than say, your friend, cousin, or coworker? Of course, if you already had a kidney stone, you know by now that the odds are, unfortunately, in your favor that you are going to have another one at some point in your life.

If you have not had a kidney stone up until now, it is important to know exactly what might increase your odds of getting one. By the time you are done reading this chapter, you may discover that you have one, two, or maybe more risk factors for forming kidney stones. However, this still does not mean that you will ultimately get one, but it does mean you need to be cognizant of the signs and symptoms of kidney stones

and take care of yourself to reduce your chances.

Statistically, anyone of any age can get a kidney stone, even children, but your chances will increase depending on a variety of risk factors, some of which you can control and some that you cannot. For example, you really cannot do anything about your age, your gender and your genetic makeup.

Age

Studies show that up to one-third of all children are born with a possible genetic defect that can change the flow of urine, putting them at risk for kidney stones. Other medical conditions, including urinary tract infections and metabolic disorders, such as hypercalciuria and hyperoxaluria that may make them a higher risk.

As they get older, children may drink too little water or, on the other hand, too much juice, caffeinated beverages, or soft drinks. As a result, their urine can become concentrated too, which is a hotbed for kidney stone formation. They may also have issues with their diet and eat too many salt-laden processed foods. This too, can lead to stone formation. Children experience the same symptoms of kidney stones and are diagnosed and treated the same way as adults.

Men between the ages of 30 and 50 are at the highest risk of getting kidney stones, with white men at the top of the ladder. White people are more likely to experience them than African-Americans or Asian-Americans.

Genetics

If you are at risk for kidney stones due to your DNA, you cannot change that either. Approximately 40 percent of people who form kidney stones have a family history of stones. If you have a genetic condition, such as hypercalciuria, it means there is an increased level of calcium in your urine that may be caused by defects in your family genes that were passed on to you.

As I mentioned before, other hereditary conditions can cause kidney stones, such as distal renal tubular acidosis; disease; Bartter syndrome, types III and IV; autosomal dominant hypocalcemic hypercalciuria; familial hypomagnesemia; and hypocitraturia. Another condition, cystinuria, causes the kidneys to excrete excess cystine into the urine, which may lead to the formation of cystine stones.

The Female Factor

Until recently, women had a much lower risk of getting kidney stones than men. But, sorry ladies, the odds of landing a stone are now almost equal to men. One reason women are getting stones is the obesity epidemic. The impact of obesity on stone risk appears to be greater in women than in men.

As crazy as it sounds, another reason is because women are taking better care of themselves. Over the last decade or so, women began exercising more, but unfortunately some forget one very important component to an exercise routine: water. The more you sweat, the less you urinate. And because you are lacking fluids,

CLOUDY URINE CAUSES

DEHYDRATION
Cloudy urine may be a sign of dehydration, and when it occurs without symptoms and goes away rapidly, there are usually few consequences

INFECTION
Infections in the urinary tract can cause blood and pus to appear in the urine, giving it a cloudy appearance

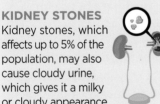

PREGNANCY
It's important that pregnant women seek medical attention if they notice cloudy pee or other UTI symptoms because risk factors, such as preterm delivery and low infant weight, are most commonly associated with bacterial infections during pregnancy

KIDNEY STONES
Kidney stones, which affects up to 5% of the population, may also cause cloudy urine, which gives it a milky or cloudy appearance

DISEASES
Some diseases, such as diabetes, preeclampsia and heart disease, affect other body systems in addition to the urinary tract and may cause your pee to appear cloudy

toxins that aren't flushed out start to form inside the kidneys. This, as you learned in the last chapter, can ultimately lead to stones. Bottom line: You need to drink water to replace what you lose through sweat.

Expectant Mothers

Pregnant women are also at a higher risk for stones, although pregnancy itself is not what causes them. The stones may form because, again, either a pregnant woman may have a genetic predisposition to stones or because she is not drinking enough of water during the gestation.

In addition, if you are pregnant, the physiology of your body changes during those nine months. Your kidneys increase their filtration – in other words, you pee a lot more. Your heart and cardiovascular system is also working overtime, pumping enough blood for two. In the meantime, your body absorbs more calcium into the intestine, which is then released into the urine.

This can also increase your risk for urinary tract infections (another risk factor for kidney stones) and the need for added nutrients, including calcium.

Also, your kidneys and ureters become compressed because of your growing uterus which can cause a higher risk of urinary tract infections.

So, can you pass a stone during pregnancy? Well, first, treatment is a little harder when you are expecting, because you should not be exposed to large amounts of radiation from x-rays and other treatments. It is too risky for you and the baby, especially during the first trimester. For an expectant woman, a low-dose CT scan, plain x-rays, or ultrasound may be safer in the diagnosis of kidney stones.

Whether or not you can pass it or have to be treated will depend on a variety of factors, including how big the stone is, if there is an infection or if you are in a tremendous amount of pain. Some options for treatment include placement of a ureteral stent with or without a ureteroscopy or nephrostomy tube.

If a stent is chosen and the stone cannot be safely removed, it may need to be changed every three months or more frequently because of the faster development of stent encrustation (stone particles forming on a stent) that occurs in pregnant women. A nephrostomy tube, placed through the skin and directly into the kidney, avoids this issue but is associated with the inconvenience of requiring an external drainage bag. Treatment during pregnancy is usually limited to ureteroscopy with laser lithotripsy.

Shockwave lithotripsy is not performed because of risks from the shockwaves on the developing fetus. Percutaneous nephrolithotomy is also, usually avoided because the belly down position is necessary for surgery. Both procedures also require a moderate amount of undesirable x-rays.

Is Genetic Testing for Me?

Want to delve deeper into your DNA? Genetic testing can tell you a lot about your family medical history passed on to you by your mother and father. Genetic testing can help diagnose a disease, its severity, and help your doctor determine the best course of treatment. It can also pinpoint gene changes responsible for a health issue you already have diagnosed, and those that may be passed on to your children.

The Institute also says that genetic tests can help to:

▶ Determine the severity of a disease

▶ Guide doctors in deciding on the best medicine or treatment to use for certain individuals

▶ Identify gene changes that may increase the risk to develop a disease

▶ Identify gene changes that could be passed on to children

▶ Screen newborn babies for certain treatable conditions

Genetic test results can be hard to understand, however specialists like geneticists and genetic counselors can help explain what results might mean to you and your family.

As genetic testing tells you information about your DNA, which is shared with other family members, sometimes a genetic test result may have implications for blood relatives of the person who had testing.

Diagnostic testing is used to precisely identify the disease that is making a person ill. The results of a diagnostic test may help you make choices about how to treat or manage your health.

Predictive and pre-symptomatic genetic tests are used to find gene changes that increase a person's likelihood of developing diseases. The results of these tests provide you with information about your risk of developing a specific disease. Such information maybe useful in decisions about your lifestyle and healthcare.

Carrier testing is used to find people who "carry" a change in a gene that is linked to disease. Carriers may show no signs of the disease; however, they have the ability to pass on the gene change to their children, who may develop the disease or become carriers themselves. Some diseases require a gene change to be inherited from both parents for the disease to occur. This type of testing usually is offered to people who have a family history of a specific inherited disease or who belong to certain ethnic groups that have a higher risk of specific inherited diseases.

Emotional: Learning that you or someone in your family has or is at risk for a disease can be scary. Some people can also feel guilty, angry, anxious, or depressed when they find out their results. Although there are familial traits, most people inherit stone disease from genetic abnormalities that are not yet well defined. Genetic testing can cost anywhere from less than $100 to more than $2,000. Health insurance companies may cover part or all of the cost of testing.

There are many reasons that people might get genetic testing. Doctors might suggest a genetic test if patients or their families have certain patterns of disease. Genetic testing is voluntary and the decision about whether to have genetic testing is complex.

A geneticist or genetic counselor can help families think about the benefits and limitations of a particular genetic test. Genetic counselors help individuals and families understand the scientific, emotional, and ethical factors surrounding the decision to have genetic testing and how to deal with the results of those tests.

For more information, visit the National Human Genome Project website at www.genome.gov.

To prevent your risk of a kidney stone while you are pregnant make sure to drink a lot of water. It will dilute your urine and make it less likely for a stone to form. If you think you are suffering from stone symptoms including nausea, vomiting, blood in your urine, or flank pain, contact your obstetrician immediately.

Sedentary Population

Another high risk group for kidney stones are patients who are either paralyzed or immobile because of an accident or illness, including long-term residents of nursing homes. Even office workers who spend an extended period of time at a desk can be at a higher risk for kidney stones.

Bariatric Surgery and Kidney Stones

There is not yet a complete understanding of the long-term effects of bariatric surgery, but urologists have taken note of a significant short-term effect of the gastric bypass. Within six months of this surgery, a patient's risk of developing kidney stones nearly doubles. That's because the whole digestive process changes for people who have had Roux-en-Y gastric bypass surgery. The planned malabsorption caused by this procedure—which significantly affects the composition of urine— drives most of the stone risk. Bariatric surgery can create the perfect storm for stone disease, especially in patients who experience diarrhea, which results in fluid loss.

The Message in the Urine

Your urine gives you a significant amount of information about your risk of getting kidney stones. Your body as a whole is amazing at giving you signals that something might be wrong, so after you pee, do not be in such a hurry to flush. Take a look at how much urine is in the toilet. For example, the less you urinate each day, the more you are at risk. The ideal range for daily urine output is 70 ounces, if you are drinking approximately 2 liters of fluid per day (you can estimate that as an entire big bottle of soda). However, if you are urinate significantly less than that, you may be increasing your risks of getting a kidney stone. If you are not quite sure how much urine you are excreting, your doctor can order a 24-hour urine test which, collects and measures your output.

Now look at the color. If your urine is the color of a traditional manila folder, it might mean a stone is starting to form. If you have streaks of blood in your urine, you might already have one.

Not only is the volume of your urine important to evaluating your risk of kidney stones, but the content of your urine is important too. For example, if you have one of these conditions, you are at a higher risk of getting a kidney stone:

▸**HYPOCITRATURIA:** A condition when your kidneys are not excreting enough citrate, a known inhibitor of calcium stone disease. Hypocitraturia is a common metabolic abnormality found in 20 percent to 60 percent of stone formers. It can be caused by renal tubular acidosis, which is a disease in which the kidney tubules malfunction and fail to excrete acids in the urine. Hypocitraturia can also be caused by high-protein, low-carbohydrate diets; certain drugs and excessive amounts of sodium, corticosteroids, antacids, diuretics, and vitamin D.

▸**PRIMARY HYPEROXALURIA:** A rare condition that occurs when you are missing an enzyme that prevents the buildup of oxalate. As a result, your kidneys excrete too much oxalate, which can lead to calcium oxalate kidney stones. These stones cause kidney damage, kidney failure, and injury to other organs. This condition often ends in end stage renal disease (ESRD), a life-threatening condition that prevents the kidneys from filtering fluids and waste products from the body. There are three types of primary hyperoxaluria that differ inseverity:

▪**TYPE 1 Primary Hyperoxaluria:** Estimated to occur in 1 to 3 per million people; it is more common in some Mediterranean countries, such as Tunisia. With type 1 primary hyperoxaluria, patients have a shortage of a liver enzyme called alanine-glyoxylate aminotransferase. Kidney stones appear anytime from childhood on.

▪**Type 2 Primary Hyperoxaluria:** Patients are missing a liver enzyme called glyoxylate reductase/hydroxypyruvate reductase. It is similar to Type 1, but ESRD occurs later.

▪**Type 3 Primary Hyperoxaluria:** This type is currently rare. It is not as severe a form of the disease as Type 1, but may eventually become more common than Type 2. Kidney stones develop in early childhood. While it is not known to occur in infancy, it may be possible.

▶**DIETARY HYPEROXALURIA:** This differs from primary hyperoxaluria. Rather than being inherited, it occurs when a patient ingests too much oxalate.

▶**ENTERIC HYPEROXALURIA:** Can occur when there are high levels of oxalate in the urine. It can result as a complication of inflammatory bowel diseases, ileal resection and Roux-en-Y gastric bypass. Enteric hyperoxaluria can cause nephrolithiasis, nephrocalcinosis and contributes to chronic kidney disease.

▶**HYPERURICOSURIA:** A condition where there is too much uric acid in your urine. For men this is at a rate greater than 800 mg/day, and for women, 750 mg/day. This can result in the development of uric acid stones. This may also be a sign of gout.

▶**HYPERCALCIURIA:** A genetic condition where your kidneys are excrete an excessive amount of calcium, which can cause an impairment of renal function, kidney stones, and renal insufficiency. Hypercalciuric stone formers have been demonstrated to have a 5 to 15 percent lower bone mineral density than non–stone formers. Hypercalciuria can still

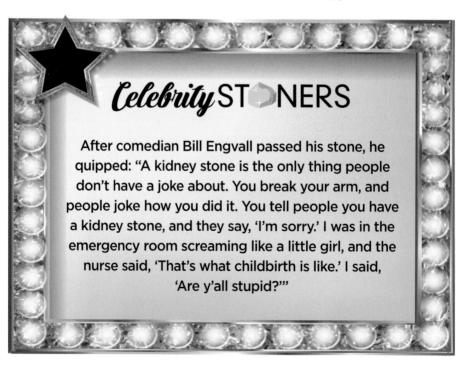

Celebrity ST◆NERS

After comedian Bill Engvall passed his stone, he quipped: "A kidney stone is the only thing people don't have a joke about. You break your arm, and people joke how you did it. You tell people you have a kidney stone, and they say, 'I'm sorry.' I was in the emergency room screaming like a little girl, and the nurse said, 'That's what childbirth is like.' I said, 'Are y'all stupid?'"

be managed by reducing salt intake, increasing fluids and making sure to add citrate into your diet. Citrate can be purchased as a supplement and is also present in fresh lemonade. A diuretic called thiazide is available by prescription and can also reduce the amount of calcium in the urine.

Medical Conditions

If you have been diagnosed with certain medical conditions, you may already have a predisposition for getting kidney stones through no fault of your own. I have already discussed some of those conditions, but others include:

 Gout: Another painful disease that happens when uric acid builds up in your blood and forms crystals in the joints and/or kidneys. The good news is that gout can be controlled with medication and dietary changes. Eliminating foods from your diet that trigger gout attacks, include organ meats (liver, kidney, sweetbreads, and brains); meat gravies and extracts; sardines; anchovies; herring; mackerel; scallops; and most wild game. The following foods are only allowed once per day – meat, fish, poultry, dried beans and peas, asparagus, mushrooms, cauliflower, and spinach. In addition, drinking plenty of water and maintaining a healthy lifestyle is important in your battle against gout attacks and kidney stones.

 Primary Hyperparathyroidism: A condition that creates an abnormally high concentration of parathyroid hormone in the blood, resulting in weakening of the bones through loss of calcium. In most cases, there is no known cause of the condition and symptoms may not always be present.

 Cancer: Some types of cancer, especially any involving the kidneys and urinary tract, increase your risk of getting kidney stones. In addition, chemotherapy medications, that can cause an increase in your uric acid levels and also increase your risk of stones.

Renal Tubular Acidosis (RTA): A condition where your kidneys fail to excrete acids into the urine, which causes your blood to remain acidic. RTA and kidney stones can be caused by anti-epileptic medications, such as topiramate, zonisamide and acetazolamide. Stones can also be caused by the combination of a high urine pH and low citrate. Without proper treatment, chronic acidity of the blood leads to growth retardation, kidney stones, bone disease, chronic kidney disease, and possibly total kidney failure.

 Sarcoidosis: This is a chronic disease caused by the enlargement of lymph nodes in many parts of the body. It can cause excess calcium to form in the blood and urine, which can then lead to kidney stone formation.

 Inflammatory Bowel Disease: If you have been diagnosed with this disease of the small intestine, then you need to know that oxalate stones are the most common complication you will have. Crohn's patients are at risk for oxalate kidney stones because of fat malabsorption, which means that calcium in the gut binds to fat instead of oxalate. This leaves oxalate free to be absorbed and sent to the kidneys where it can form a stone. If you have had any bowel resections because of your Crohn's diagnosis, your risk increases. Crohn's disease can be treated by making sure that you follow a low-oxalate diet and drink plenty of water (more on that later).

 Medullary Sponge Kidney: This is a birth defect that causes cysts to form in the kidneys of the fetus, creating a sponge-like appearance and preventing the urine from flowing freely from one or both kidneys. It's also known as Cacchi-Ricci disease, and symptoms do not appear until the child is typically in the teen years. Research shows that medullary sponge kidney affects about one in 5,000 people in the United States.

Urine Reflux: Urine reflux works the same way as acid reflux. When you are diagnosed with acid reflux, it means the acid in your stomach backs into your esophagus, which is not the direction it should go. With urine reflux, you have an anatomical defect where your urine backs up and ends up in your kidneys instead of your bladder. As a result, this increases your risk of forming kidney stones.

 Kidney and Urinary Obstruction: Any medical condition that causes an obstruction in your urine flow can lead to stones.

The ABCs of UTIs

If you are at risk for or prone to urinary tract infections, you have already raised your risk for getting a particular type of kidney stone, called a struvite stone. According to the National Kidney Foundation, urinary tract infections UTIs) are responsible for nearly 10 million doctor visits each year. Although they are more common in women, men can get them too. In addition:

- **1 in 5** women will have at **least 1 UTI** in her lifetime.

- Nearly **20%** of women **who have a UTI** will have another, and **30%** of those will have yet **another**.

Of this last group, 80 percent will have UTI recurrences.

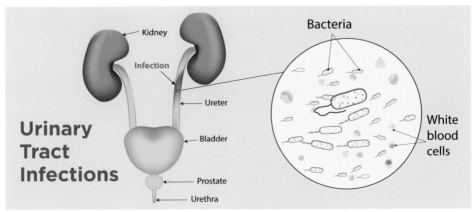

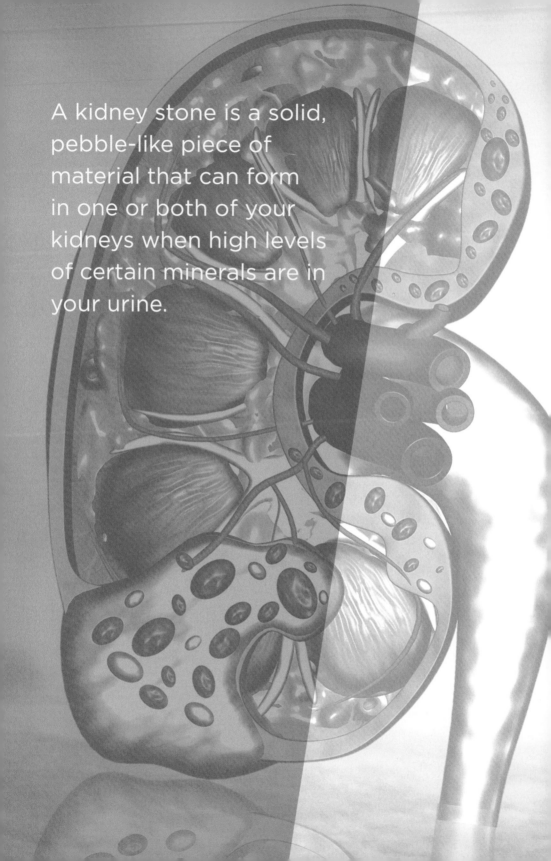

A kidney stone is a solid, pebble-like piece of material that can form in one or both of your kidneys when high levels of certain minerals are in your urine.

CHAPTER 05

MADE OF STONE

The type of kidney stone you have will, most likely, fall into one of these four major categories: calcium-based; infection or struvite; uric acid; or cysteine. However, there other rare types of stones too. For example, patients who have been diagnosed with human immunodeficiency virus (HIV) take high doses of retroviral medications during their treatment, including crixivan (indinavir sulfate), which can lead to what are called crixivan kidney stones.

Keep in mind that no matter what type of kidney stone you are diagnosed with, even if I have not discussed it here, the symptoms are similar but the medical and surgical options can vary.

Cystine Stones

According to the University of Chicago, cystinuria occurs in 1 in 7,000 people worldwide. Cystinuria is a rare condition in which stones made from an amino acid, called cystine, form in the kidney, ureter, and bladder. The University of Chicago states that, "as the disorder is genetic, there is variability in its occurrence based on who your ancestors were. For example, it occurs in 1 in 100,000 people in Sweden, but is far more common in Israeli patients of African origin: 1 in 2,500. In the United States, the incidence is about 1 in 15,000 individuals."

While clearly rare, it is responsible for 1 percent of all kidney stones, and is even more common in children (about 5 percent) as stones are generally less common in the young."

The way it works is this: As your kidneys filter your blood to create urine, the cystine is typically absorbed back into the bloodstream. Patients who have cystinuria cannot reabsorb cystine, so it accumulates in the kidney and begins to form crystals.

The only risk factor for getting cystine stones is that you must have been diagnosed with this condition and, to be diagnosed with it, you must have the gene for cystinuria. No matter what your other risks are for kidney stones, if you do not have the cystinuria gene, you will not get a cystine kidney stone.

Interestingly, how many kidney stones a patient with cystinuria will have is not directly related to the level of cystine that is being excreted in the body. In other words, some patients with very high cystine levels form very few, if any, stones, while others with comparatively low cystine levels are high-volume stone formers. Unfortunately, cystine stones are very hard and extremely difficult to break up compared to other types of kidney stones.

Struvite Stones

Struvite stones are produced by urinary tract infections that are caused by such organisms as Proteus, Pseudomonas and Providencia. These stones can grow to be very large and can block the kidney, ureter, or bladder. However, compared to cystine stones, struvite stones – which are made up mostly of calcium or magnesium, ammonia, and phosphate – are soft and can be broken up very easily.

Patients who are at risk of getting struvite stones are those who have

Ben Franklin's Catheter

Here's an interesting tidbit about catheters. It's uncertain as to who invented the catheter, but it's documented that the earliest American inventor of the flexible catheter was none other than Benjamin Franklin, who also invented the lightening rod. However, Franklin said that someone else did it.

been hospitalized for long periods of time, such as nursing home and rehab patients, as well as patients who are often catheterized, such as paraplegics and quadriplegics. Catheterization means that the patient has a tube inserted into the urethra and up to the bladder to remove the urine.

For a struvite stone, patients first often need to be treated with antibiotics to clear the urinary tract infection before the stone can be removed. Bacteria can live on the struvite stone and, although one round of antibiotics may stop the

fever and chills, the infection may still be present, so multiple rounds may be needed.

One patient of mine, an elderly man who has been the resident of a nursing home for several years, came in for an appointment. After running tests, I diagnosed him with a struvite stone that was so large that it filled up one of his kidneys. Because of his previous urinary issues, he had been catheterized and ended up suffering from repeated urinary tract infections. Unfortunately, struvite stones recur and each time the infection can

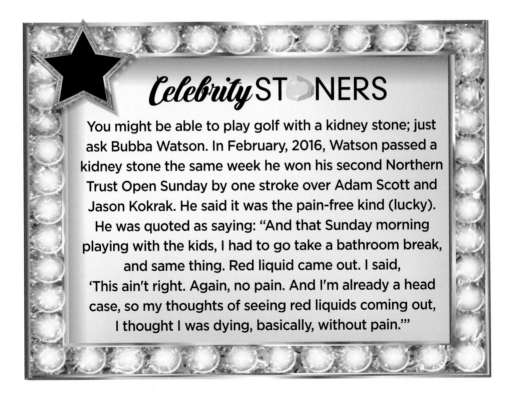

Celebrity ST◇NERS

You might be able to play golf with a kidney stone; just ask Bubba Watson. In February, 2016, Watson passed a kidney stone the same week he won his second Northern Trust Open Sunday by one stroke over Adam Scott and Jason Kokrak. He said it was the pain-free kind (lucky). He was quoted as saying: "And that Sunday morning playing with the kids, I had to go take a bathroom break, and same thing. Red liquid came out. I said, 'This ain't right. Again, no pain. And I'm already a head case, so my thoughts of seeing red liquids coming out, I thought I was dying, basically, without pain.'"

damage your kidney. As a result, by the time the patients are in their 40s or 50s, some have often lost their kidney function and are on dialysis.

Struvite stones can make you sick – septic shock sick. Septic shock, also known as blood poisoning, is a serious condition that occurs when your body suffers from an infection that leads to a dangerous drop in blood pressure. Septic shock can also lead to little or no urine being produced, light-headedness, rapid heart rate, cool arms and legs and skin rash, among other symptoms. It can affect any part of your body, including your heart, brain, kidneys, liver, and intestines. According to World Sepsis Day (world-sepsis-day.org), sepsis claims more lives each year than any form of cancer.

If struvite stones are left untreated for large periods of time, they can develop into a chronic inflammatory disorder called Xanthogranulomatous pyelonephritis (XGP). XGP is rare and serious, and is characterized by a destructive mass. It is four times more common in women than in men and typically affects patients older than 50. XGP affects both kidneys and can make them nonfunctional. Eventually, one or both kidneys may have to be removed. If left untreated even further it can result in death.

FIDO'S KIDNEY STONE

 Did you know that cats and dogs can get kidney stones, especially struvite stones, too? According to dogaware. com, struvite crystals can be found in the urine of an estimated 40 to 44 percent of all healthy dogs and are not a cause for concern unless accompanied by signs of a urinary tract infection. Researchers estimate that more than 98 percent of all struvite stones are associated with infection (although cats can get them through diet alone without having an infection). Struvite crystals in your pets do not require a change in diet. Short-term changes, such as a low-protein diet can speed the dissolution of struvite stones – when accompanied by appropriate antibiotic treatment – but it is not necessary for the prevention of struvite formation in dogs who are prone to this problem. For almost all dogs, controlling infections will prevent more stones from forming. Also, Dalmatians are missing the enzyme xanthine oxidase, which is involved in protein breakdown, so they are more prone to uric acid stones.

Uric Acid Stones

Over time, increased uric acid levels in your blood may lead to deposits of urate crystals in and around your joints. The ultimate form of uric acid excess is a condition called gout that affects more than three million Americans.

Years ago, gout was considered the disease of those who were rich enough to afford luxurious dining and drinking. Today, however, gout is recognized as a distinct medical condition caused by an excess of uric acid in the body. The association of gout with wealth, therefore, wasn't so far off the mark – only the wealthy could afford the rich sauces, fatty foods, meat, fish, and vast quantities of alcohol to wash them down (a prime recipe for the overproduction of uric acid if there ever was one).

Patients with gout are missing an enzyme called Xanthine oxidase, which is one of the final steps of the breakdown products of purine. Gout occurs more often in men, women after menopause, and people with kidney disease. Gout patients and others who suffer from it are encouraged to follow a low-protein/purine diet and decrease uric acid in their system, often by the use of a medication called allopurinol (zyloprim), which lowers the blood uric acid level by preventing uric acid production.

Uric acid stones are formed by crystals in the urine and make up 10 percent of all kidney stones. Uric acid is the second most common cause of stones, especially for the 8.3 million people in the U.S. who have gout. Gout is a condition that is most associated with extremely painful swelling in the big toe that occurs when uric acid deposits in the joints. The most important risk factors for uric acid stones to crystallize is urine with a low pH or an excessively high-protein diet. Patients who are taking certain chemotherapy medications are also at a risk for uric acid stones.

Uric acid stones do not show up on a typical x-ray, so if it is suspected that you may have a uric acid stone, you will undergo a CT scan to make a thorough diagnosis.

What's good about uric acid stones versus other types of kidney stones is they can be dissolved if your urine pH level is kept at a level higher than 6.5. A blood test can determine your serum uric acid level while a 24 hour urine can measure how much you are excreting in your urine per day, and if it does come back high, more tests can be ordered to see if you have gout.

However, if your uric acid level is too high, the doctor will try to alkalinize your urine with several different medications, pills or syrups, which are all derivatives of citrate or bicarbonate. Citrate, which is a derivative of citric acid, helps to dissolve kidney stones and raise your urine pH level. Instead of trying to swallow huge citrate tables, you can also drink Crystal Light Lemonade because of its high levels of citrate, but be careful. Crystal Light Lemonade is artificially sweetened and drinking too much of that is not good for you either.

Calcium Stones

So your work up is complete and your kidney stone test results show that you have a calcium-based kidney stone, the most common stones in the United States and Western Europe. As I have already discussed, there are many different types of calcium-based stones, including calcium oxalate, calcium phosphate and a combination of both. Eighty-five percent of all kidney stones have a calcium oxalate coponent and 8 to 10 percent of all kidney stones are calcium phosphate stones. There are also two types of calcium oxalate stones—monohydrate and dihydrate stones. Monohydrate stones are super hard and very difficult to

break up, while dihydrate stones are softer and easier to fragment.

It's important to remember that calcium-based stones can form, because you have some abnormality, such as primary hyperoxaluria, where calcium is being excreted by your kidney and combining with oxalate or phosphate to form stones, instead of being filtered through the kidneys and back to the bloodstream where it belongs.

There are others who have a condition called primary hyperoxaluria, which means they have a rare condition where there is an overproduction of oxalate thanks to a missing enzyme that normally prevents this buildup. In the kidneys, this excess oxalate combines with calcium to form calcium oxalate, which can lead to stones, kidney damage, kidney failure, and injury to other organs.

Staghorn Calculi

When a kidney stone becomes so large that it takes up more than one branch of your kidney, it's called a staghorn kidney stone. It looks like a staghorn piece of coral or the antlers on a deer. Some of the risk factors for staghorn stone formation include a long history of stones, certain unique metabolic defects, and repeated urinary tract infections with particular types of bacteria. If a staghorn stone occurs in association with infection, there may be a pattern of intermittent and recurrent infection, which may persist until the staghorn stone is removed. Patients with a staghorn stone and infection can become septic and die, so this is a condition which requires immediate medical attention. A patient with a staghorn stone should be treated to avoid loss of kidney function, pain, and infections, as, over time, an untreated staghorn calculus is likely to destroy the kidney and/or cause life-threatening infections (sepsis). Complete removal of the stone is important to eradicate infection, relieve obstruction, prevent further stone growth, and preserve kidney function. A percutaneous nephrostolithotomy is usually the best approach for treating a staghorn stone.

Stones Following Hospitalization

Young or muscular patients who undergo surgery can suffer from a rare side effect of anesthesia, which is called flash pulmonary edema, which pulls fluid into the lungs. If a patient is kept on a ventilator, it's possible that it can metabolize all of the blood and fluid so quickly that it results in gout, which can ultimately lead to kidney stones. Please know this is a rare situation.

Patients can also develop calcium stones if they have prolonged bedrest which can lead to hypercalciuria caused by immobilization.

And, chemotherapy medications can cause kidney stones. It happened to two young female patients of mine who suffered from leukemia. The medications are toxic to the cancer, but they are also toxic to other cells in the blood. As a result, not only do the medications kill the bad cancer cells, they kill the good cells too. This can cause stones to form.

If your doctor suspects you have a kidney stone, you may have diagnostic tests and procedures

CHAPTER 06

MAKING A DIAGNOSIS

Whether you have excruciating pain in your flank, you're vomiting and have chills, or you suddenly found blood in your urine, you want to be diagnosed and treated right away. You might call your family doctor, internist, or urologist or head to the nearest emergency room.

Instead, if it's the first time you are experiencing these symptoms, head directly to the emergency room. Do not pass go, do not collect $200. When you get there, you will either be examined by an emergency room physician, a nurse practitioner, or a physician's assistant (PA). Physician's assistants are wonderfully qualified, but when you're in that much pain and want answers quickly, it's best to be examined by a specialist as the diagnosis is not always straight forward.

Some patients who are in a lot of pain, do not go to the emergency room because they don't realize the pain is related to kidney stones. Instead, they may think it's a pulled muscle in their back and they call a chiropractor or an orthopedist first to rule out any potential muscular, bone or nerve issues. If they have lower abdominal pain they might think they have food poisoning or appendicitis and might make an appointment to see a gastroenterologist, a doctor who handles the stomach, intestines and liver. If they cannot urinate, they may think it's a urinary tract infection and head to their primary care doctor first. I repeat though, if you know the symptoms of a kidney stone and believe you have one for the first time, go to the emergency room!

If you have a kidney stone that has grown to the size of a baseball and completely filled up your kidney, you may be referred to an endourologist and/or a nephrologist. An endourologist has completed a specialized fellowship in kidney stones and minimally invasive surgery after completing a urology residency. They, often, handle complex stone cases. A nephrologist completes a residency in internal medicine and then specializes in nephrology (the study of kidneys and renal disease), and

important

Of course if you are in such extreme pain that you may pass out or you have other accompanying life-threatening symptoms of something else other than possible kidney stones, have someone take you to the ER or call 911 immediately.

Once you are diagnosed with a kidney stone in the ER, you will be treated and advised to follow up with a urologist. If the ER docs tell you that you need surgery, your urologist can always call ahead to the operating room and immediately find out if you can be scheduled for a same day procedure.

A SPECIAL CAUTION: Know what equipment your urologist has and procedures that the urologist is capable of doing in their office before you head there in pain. Not every urologist's office is equipped with the right technology to diagnose you on the spot. For example, some primary care physicians and urologists can do a complete urinalysis in the office, but not much else. They may send you directly to the emergency room anyway because of your symptoms or because the ER has more advanced medical equipment. Some physicians may have ultrasound, CT scan and sophisticated laboratory testing right in their office. That's why it's wise to first go for an initial consultation and ask the right questions. Hopefully, you do this before showing signs of any symptoms.

can often provide counselling as to how to prevent future kidney stones, although some urologists are well versed in this too.

Once the ER physician reviews your symptoms, you will have a physical examination. Most likely, the doctor will press on your

Symptoms of Kidney Stones

To make a diagnosis, the ER physician or the urologist will first review your medical history and then go over your symptoms. This helps to target your diagnosis. Some questions you may be asked about your symptoms include:

1 If you have pain, when did it start?

2 Where is the pain located? Does it spread to your lower abdomen and groin? Does that pain radiate down your side and into your scrotum or labia? (The most traumatic pain you will have from kidney stones will be in what's called your flank area, which is usually down your side and into your back.)

3 Is the pain a sharp stabbing pain or a dull throb? Is it a dull ache that gets worse over a short period of time? Or is it a sharp, stabbing pain that comes and goes quickly?

4 Does the pain come in waves or is it constant?

5 When the pain starts, how long does it last?

6 Have you had a fever?

7 Do you have any chills?

8 Does it hurt when you urinate?

9 When you urinate, is your urine a pink, red or brown color?

10 Is your urine cloudy or does it smell foul?

11 Do you feel a persistent need to urinate more than you usually do?

12 Are you nauseous or vomiting?

Coping with Nausea

Kidney stones can cause an intense bout of nausea that will not lessen or go away with practical or diet changes, but there are anti-nausea medications that can help ease your symptoms. These medications can include Compazine (prochlorperazine) and Zofran (ondansteron). Some anti-nausea medications are available as suppositories if nausea prevents you from taking pills. Depending on the severity of your pain and what medications you can tolerate, your doctor may also prescribe dronabinol (Marinol — which comes from the psychoactive part of marijuana, called THC) or even medicinal marijuana itself.

Before you take any medications, talk to your doctor about the risks and benefits of them and let him know about any medications you are currently taking. While these medications may ease your nausea, they also come with their own side effects. For example, Compazine may cause sleepiness, blurred vision, missed periods, and restlessness. Consider whether adding another prescription to what you may already take is something you can and want to do.

abdomen and flank area and push on your kidney to test your pain level. If you jump toward the lights, the doctor will know something really bad is going on.

Other parts of the physical examination might include:

- Taking your temperature.
- Checking your weight.
- Pressing or tapping on your abdomen (called an abdominal palpation) or back to check for pain or fluid buildup.
- Examining your groin to check for enlarged lymph nodes.

Whether you are visiting the urologist or the ER, you will probably be asked to provide a urine sample (that is, if you can pee). As I mentioned in chapter two, a urinalysis screens for a variety of conditions, including diabetes and urinary tract infections, and the results can tell the doctor if there is any bacteria or blood in your urine, which can be signs of kidney stones. Next, the ER physician or the urologist may order a complete blood count (CBC) test that can also provide clues to your pain. For example, with struvite kidney stones, blood work may show signs of neutrophilia, or an increased neutrophil granulocyte count. It is, also, likely, that your electrolytes and kidney function will be checked by a blood test.

Even though you might suspect that you have a kidney stone, the ER may rule out other diseases or conditions that could be causing your pain. For example, such conditions as diverticulitis, irritable bowel syndrome (IBS), ovarian torsion, appendicitis, gallstones, Crohn's disease, testicle torsion or even an ectopic pregnancy (a pregnancy located outside the inner lining of the uterus), can share similar symptoms and pain to kidney stones.

Collect Your Kidney Stone

If, at any point during your painful episode, you pass a kidney stone and can somehow collect it and bring it into your doctor, do it. A chemical analysis of your stones will be done to determine what the stone is made up of and your best course of treatment and prevention.

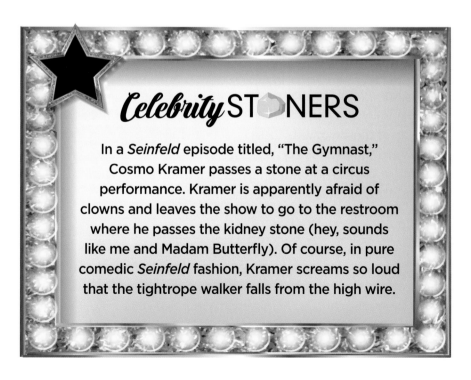

Celebrity ST◆NERS

In a *Seinfeld* episode titled, "The Gymnast," Cosmo Kramer passes a stone at a circus performance. Kramer is apparently afraid of clowns and leaves the show to go to the restroom where he passes the kidney stone (hey, sounds like me and Madam Butterfly). Of course, in pure comedic *Seinfeld* fashion, Kramer screams so loud that the tightrope walker falls from the high wire.

Passing the Test

In addition to the urinalysis and physical exam, the physician may order other tests as well including:

▶**ULTRASOUND:** Also called a sonogram, diagnostic sonography, or ultrasonography, an ultrasound test uses high frequency sound waves to create an image of the inside of the body. Ultrasounds are not nearly as accurate in diagnosing kidney stones as other tests are. It is much more difficult to get a really good ultrasound study compared to a CT scan, but when it comes to a good ultrasound test, it doesn't matter how good the machine is, it matters how good the radiologist is.

▶**NON-CONTRAST CT SCAN:** A non-contrast CT or CAT scan is a computed tomography that's noninvasive (which means there's no injectable dye) and shows detailed images of any part of the body, including the bones, muscles, fat, and organs. It is the preferred test to determine if you have kidney stones. CT scans are more detailed than standard x-rays. A note of caution: if you are pregnant and are suffering from kidney stone symptoms, it may be safe to have a low dose CT scan, but an ultrasound test is preferred. Ask your doctor about the amount of radiation used during the CT procedure and the risks. Let the technician know if you are pregnant or suspect that you may be pregnant. Radiation exposure during pregnancy may lead to birth defects.

Certain factors or conditions may interfere with the accuracy of a CT scan of the abdomen. These factors include but are not limited to the following: metallic objects within the abdomen, such as surgical clips, barium in the intestines from a recent barium study; stool and/or gas in the bowel; or a total hip replacement.

▶**CT SCAN WITH CONTRAST:** If you have a CT scan with contrast, let the technician know if you are allergic to the contrast or if you have ever had a reaction to contrast media or kidney problems. Patients with kidney failure or other kidney problems should notify their doctor. In some cases, the contrast media can cause kidney failure, especially if the person is dehydrated or already has underlying kidney disease.

▶**INTRAVENOUS PYELOGRAM (IVP):** An x-ray that uses a dye to obtain pictures of the kidney, bladder, and ureters and may show if you have a kidney stone. You may be asked to take medicine to clear your bowels before the procedure to provide a better view of the urinary tract. If you can, you will be asked to empty your bladder before the procedure starts. The procedure may take up to an hour and you must lie still. If you are in pain, this can be difficult to do. To begin, your provider will inject an iodine-based contrast (dye) into a vein in your arm. You may feel a burning or flushing sensation in your arm and body. Then, a series of x-ray images are taken. This is to see how the kidneys remove the dye and how it collects in your urine. A compression device (a wide belt containing two balloons that can be inflated) may be used to keep the contrast material in the kidneys. Before the final picture is taken, you will be asked to urinate again. This is to see how well your bladder has emptied. Side effects include a metallic taste in your mouth, headache, nausea, or vomiting after the dye is injected.

▶**RETROGRADE PYELOGRAM:** If the IVP or CT scan does not provide a clear cut diagnosis, a retrograde pyelogram may be the next course of action. You may receive anesthesia prior to the procedure, which involves injecting a dye into the ureter and taking x-rays to better visualize the ureter and kidney.

▶**AN ABDOMINAL X-RAY:** Otherwise known as a KUB, it provides pictures of the kidneys, bladder, and the ureters. Before having the x-ray, tell the provider if you are pregnant, have an IUD inserted, have had a barium contrast x-ray in the last 4 days or have taken any medicines such as Pepto Bismol in the last 4 days (it can interfere with the x-ray). There is no discomfort. The x-rays are taken as you lie on your back, side, and while standing. However, remember that uric acid stones do not show up on an x-ray, so a CT scan is best if there is suspicion that you have uric acid stones. It is also important to note that a CT scan emits more radiation than a KUB.

You may be able to prevent kidney stones by drinking enough water, changing the way you eat, or taking medicines.

CHAPTER 07

TREATING THE STONES

T here are many ways to treat stones that refuse to pass on their own. Some involve roller coasters, sex, and beer, but I recommend treating stones with medication, or if that's not an option, surgery is needed. Surgical treatments can vary depending on the size and type of stone you have.

Surgical options range from non-invasive Shock Wave Lithotripsy to minimally invasive treatments, including Cystoscopy with Ureteroscopy and Laser Treatment, Percutaneous Nephrolithotomy—all of which are explained in great detail in the following pages. And although it's rare, some people may undergo open, invasive surgery to remove the stones. No matter the option, it's helpful to learn all you can so you and

your doctor can make an informed decision on the treatment that is best for you.

Passing the Stone without Surgery

You want that stone out, but what are the odds that you will pass it on your own and not need any intervention? Although it is not scientific, in the least, but based on loose evidence and personal experience, I tell a patient with a 1mm stone – the size of three grains of salt – there is a 90 percent chance of passing it. A 2mm stone has an 80 percent chance of being passed, while a 3mm stone has a 70 percent chance, etc. This is no rule of thumb and will vary patient by patient, but this gives you an idea of what your odds are.

In general, when one of my patients has a kidney stone that is small (under 5mm), and they do not have a fever and the pain can be controlled with medication, I will encourage them to try to pass it. In addition, I will also tell them to drink a lot of water and prescribe an alpha blocker that dilates the ureter so it will relax and allow some of the backed up urine to pass. Examples of alpha blocker medications I may use include tamsulosin (Flomax), alfuzosin (Uroxatral), terazosin (Hytrin), and doxazosin (Cardura).

Tamsulosin and other alpha blockers are typically prescribed to men to treat an enlarged prostate, a condition called benign prostatic hyperplasia (or BPH), by relaxing the prostate and bladder muscles. Studies have shown that tamsulosin also helps kidney stones.

However, recently tamsulosin and the other alpha blockers are being called into question because of their side effects, but, for now, doctors are continuing to use them. I'm still using tamsulosin in my practice, because those recent studies questioning its efficacy are not convincing to me. There are flaws in a lot of those studies.

Like any medication, there are a variety of side effects to using alpha blockers that include dizziness, lightheadedness, drowsiness, runny/stuffy nose, or ejaculation problems. Make sure that you tell your physician if you experience any of these symptoms.

Roller Coaster Stone Buster

 A recent study suggests that kidney stone sufferers may be able to get more than a thrill on a roller coaster. In fact, those jolts and turns could perhaps, help you pass a kidney stone – painlessly – but be sure to sit in the back. Researchers took 60 kidney stones on the Big Thunder Mountain Railroad roller coaster at Walt Disney World in Orlando, Florida. The stones were suspended in urine and placed inside of a dummy at kidney height. Turns out, that if the dummy was placed in the front of the roller coaster, about 17 percent of the stones passed compared to about 64 percent in the back of the coaster. The findings were published in the Journal of the American Osteopathic Association.

Romancing the Stone

 While you are trying to pass a kidney stone, you might also want to think about dimming the lights, putting on some sexy music and getting busy with your partner. One study conducted by researchers from the Clinic of Ankara Training and Research Hospital in Ankara, Turkey suggested that a little amoré at least three to four times per week can help with the spontaneous passage of kidney stones. In this study, 75 participants were split into three groups: one was asked to have sex at least three to four times per week, one group received tamsulosin, and a third received the standard medical treatment for kidney stones. Two weeks later, researchers found that 26 of the 31 sex group participants were able to pass their kidney stones.

Those who have been desperate to get their stone out have also resorted to jumping jacks to try and jostle the stone loose. As I've said before, whatever works. One of my patients, a marine, told me that jumping up and down and jumping rope helped him to pass his stone. I would not bet the farm that one of these methods is going to work, but it can't hurt either.

Beer, Really?

 From the first moment you show your first symptom of a kidney stone attack, it is extremely important to start drinking a lot of water to help pass it. While you are drinking ample amounts of water, you may want to throw in a beer or two (or you can combine the beer and water with some love-making). One Finland study showed that drinking a pint of beer a day can actually help lower the risk for kidney stones by up to 40 percent. That is because alcohol is a natural diuretic, which stimulates your urine flow. As a result, this increase in urination prevents kidney stone crystallization and allows you to excrete the minerals and reduce your risk of kidney stones forming.

These creative attempts at passing your kidney stone are not really going to hurt most people. However, if a month has passed since your pain started and you still have not passed the stone, you probably won't. Besides, after about a month of pain, medications and trying to get that little bugger out of you – especially for stones that are bigger than 5mm – most patients have had enough and want some additional medical intervention.

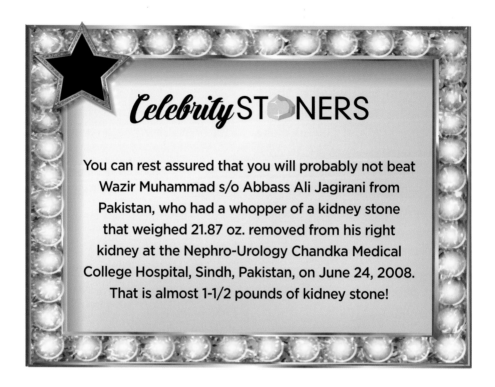

Celebrity STONERS

You can rest assured that you will probably not beat Wazir Muhammad s/o Abbass Ali Jagirani from Pakistan, who had a whopper of a kidney stone that weighed 21.87 oz. removed from his right kidney at the Nephro-Urology Chandka Medical College Hospital, Sindh, Pakistan, on June 24, 2008. That is almost 1-1/2 pounds of kidney stone!

Old School Treatments

You might have been diagnosed with kidney stones, but thankfully, you live in a wonderful time now when it comes to medical advancements. Be grateful that you don't live in Ancient India. According to "The History of Urinary Stones: In Parallel with Civilization," by Ahmet Tefekli and Fatin Cezayirli, if you lived in Ancient India and were suffering from a kidney stone, they recommended a regimen of a vegetarian diet, a urethral syringe of medicated milk, clarified butter, and alkalis. Also, be grateful that you did not live in the European medieval period (1096–1438) when lithotomists would travel from town to town, performing procedures on kidney stoners through the perineum (the area between the genitals and anus) in public and without anesthesia.

Stone Surgery

The only true successful method of kidney stone treatment up until just a few decades ago was surgery. If you had a kidney stone, even in the early 1980s, the doctor would make a large incision across your belly to explore, locate and then remove the stone. Today, just a little over 30 years later, it is very rare that this large, openly invasive surgery is even necessary. In fact, I have performed more than 4,000 kidney stone surgeries in my medical career and have never used that method. If you need to have kidney stone surgery, ask if it can be performed laparoscopically, a minimally invasive procedure that uses a thin, lighted tube that is inserted into a very small incision made in your back to look at your kidney. We've come a long way baby.

Edward Lyon and the Cystoscope

Every kidney stone does not mean you are going to be in a tremendous amount of pain or earn yourself an automatic trip to the operating room. The next steps for treatment will depend on the size, location and composition of your particular kidney stone. The course of treatment will also depend heavily on your disposition. So, if you are a patient who is asymptomatic, which means that you are not exhibiting any kidney stone symptoms right now, you have more options than a patient who is in a tremendous amount of pain and has other symptoms, including a fever.

If you have already had a kidney stone before and were lucky enough to have caught it and brought it in for testing, you should know by now what it was made of. Now, if you suffer another attack you will have a clear idea of how your doctors are going to approach your treatment.

For example, you might be treated with a cystoscopy, which can remove a stone in the bladder or urethra, or with a retrograde pyelography. This is an x-ray where a dye is injected into the ureter to see how your urine is flowing and if there is any obstruction. In fact, it was Dr. Ed Lyon, a urologist at the University of Chicago (and my former mentor), who with several colleagues, first put a pediatric cystoscope into a ureter, which inspired him to develop further minimally invasive techniques for removing stones from the ureter.

Cystoscopy

A cystoscopy is also done to find problems of the urinary tract, such as:

- Urinary tract infections that did not respond to treatment
- Overactive bladder
- Painful urination
- Urinary incontinence
- Urinary frequency or hesitancy
- An inability to pass urine (retention)
- Urinary blockages

Preparing for a Cystoscopy

If you are undergoing a cystoscopy procedure, make sure to tell the doctor if you have any drug allergies and have had bleeding problems, are taking take blood-thinning medicine, such as aspirin or warfarin (Coumadin), or if you could be pregnant.

You should empty your bladder just before the test. You may be given medicine to prevent a urinary tract infection that could be caused by the test.

If regional or general anesthesia is being used, patients are instructed to fast for at least 8 hours before the procedure. If local anesthesia is being used, a topical anesthetic (lidocaine) may be introduced prior to the procedure to numb and lubricate the urethra.

Minimally Invasive Surgery: Ureteroscopy

A ureteroscopy is a surgical procedure in which a small flexible telescope – called a ureteroscope – is inserted into your bladder through your ureter to locate the stone and remove it. If the stone is located in the lower area of your ureter, a rigid ureteroscope is used for direct access to the stone. If the stone is in the upper portion of your ureter, a flexible ureteroscope may be used, which provides the surgeon greater movement to locate the stone. For men, the ureteroscope will go through the opening of your penis, and for women it means it goes through your urethra. There is no surgical incision on the outside of your body.

These scopes continue to evolve with digital versions that provide excellent clarity for the surgeon to locate the stone. When the stone is found, a wire basket is then passed into the ureter to catch the stone. The stone can also be broken up by a holmium laser if it is very large, and smaller pieces can then be removed.

Laser Technology

The laser is a great device because it can break up nearly any kind of stone, even if it is very hard. While, laser technology has been around since the 1990s, it has evolved so that modern lasers are thin and flexible so the surgeon can precisely target the stone. During the laser procedure, the surgeon feeds the laser through a section of the ureteroscope until it reaches the stone. The surgeon then fires the laser using a foot pedal until the entire stone is full of pits and begins to break into tiny pieces.

The entire procedure can take anywhere from 30 minutes to a couple of hours and is done under general anesthesia.

Newsflash

One company has just created the first digital, single-use ureteroscope that, when inserted into the patient's urethra, can find, remove, and destroy kidney stones and then be disposed of. According to reports, the Boston Scientific company said the disposable unit addressed problems of inconsistent performance of reusable devices that break down after multiple uses.

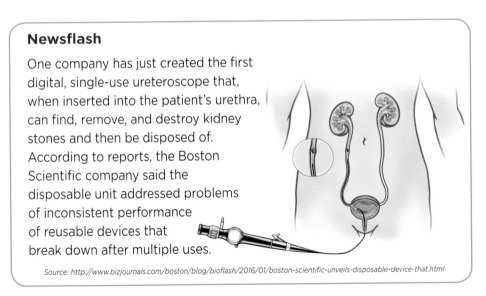

Source: http://www.bizjournals.com/boston/blog/bioflash/2016/01/boston-scientific-unveils-disposable-device-that.html

When the stone has been removed, a ureteral stent is, often, inserted to allow any inflammation in the ureter to settle down. The stent can vary in size depending on anatomy, and remain in place for several days to several months.

What to Expect After Your Ureteroscopy

- You will be monitored in the recovery room to ensure you have no signs of complications and that your vital signs are within the normal range

- You will be sleepy as the anesthesia wears off

- Anesthesia may also cause nausea, which can be treated with medication

- You may have an IV in place for several hours to give you necessary fluids and pain medication

- You will receive support to begin walking before being discharged home

- You may have a burning sensation while urinating, which can be alleviated by drinking plenty of fluids (no alcohol though)

- Stents can result in pain, an urgency to urinate and bladder spasms during urination, which can be treated with medication

- Constipation is common, and can be treated with an over-the-counter stool softener

- Fatigue may continue for several days after the procedure

The Harsh Reality about Stents

Before you rush to your urologist requesting a ureteroscopy, please know that there are some drawbacks caused by the stent placement. Some patients barely feel the stent inside of them, while others have a dull pain in their flank. Still, for other patients, the stent causes excruciating pain that they say is almost as bad as having the stone.

Again, a stent can be painful, not for everyone, but for many. Pain can be caused as the stent rubs against the bladder, which causes a frequent urge to urinate. Discomfort can also be felt because the stent allows urine to flow backward from the bladder to the kidney during urination, which can result in a feeling a mild tingling sensation to intense pain. Some patients have said that the first urination is the worst. These fragments still need to pass, and it may hurt. Remember that a stent is still a foreign body that has been placed inside of you, albeit temporarily, and it can be uncomfortable. It can also cause a urinary tract infection or a kidney infection, and significant bleeding, especially for patients who are taking anticoagulants.

But there is a bright side: most people can (believe it or not) continue their daily activities with a stent, and many remain sexually active.

If you do have a stent, be sure to have it removed at the time your urologist recommends. Leaving in a stent can cause major complications, including kidney failure.

What are the Risks of Ureteroscopy?

Stent pain is one of a few possible side effects that may result from complications after having a ureteroscopy. Other complications include, but are not limited to, a ureteral stricture (an abnormal narrowing of the tube that carries urine out of the body from the bladder) or scarring of the ureter. Today, this is a rare occurrence thanks to smaller ureteroscopes and the extra precautions surgeons make to avoid these issues. Finally, it is possible to make a hole in the ureter (perforation), which could require

prolonged stenting or at worse a more advanced reconstructive procedure.

WHEN TO CALL THE DOCTOR

Call your surgeon immediately if you have:

- Intense back, stomach or flank pain
- Difficulty urinating
- Fever or chills
- Bright red blood or blood clots in your urine (although it is normal to see a pinkish-colored urine for about 24 hours after a stent placement)

A Word on Blood Thinners

Keep in mind that all of the procedures I've talked about have a risk of bleeding and you want to minimize that risk as much as you can. If you are on a blood thinner because of atrial fibrillation or blood clots that could increase the risk of bleeding, your doctor may not do the procedure or may give you a drug to counteract the possibility of bleeding. Remember, never stop taking your blood thinner without being under the guidance of your doctor.

Shocking (Noninvasive) Treatment!

If your kidney stone is located inside your kidney and has not traveled down into the ureter, you might undergo a procedure that will shake you up a bit, but it's meant to get that stone out of there! It's called the Shock Wave Lithotripsy (SWL), a sound wave treatment that was unintentionally invented by the Germans during World War II. After they dropped bombs, they went to assess the damage they caused to their enemies. They discovered that the tanks were intact, but the soldiers inside were dead. The shockwaves from the bombs did not damage to the tank, but instead, permeated the tank and killed the soldiers inside.

That same shockwave concept that killed German enemies was introduced as a medical treatment. Physicians used water bottles placed behind the patient's back to send strong shockwaves into the body, efficiently, and break up kidney stones without causing incident to the patient. In the 1980s, the first SWL machines were approved for use in the United States, but the earlier generation of machines were too expensive and needed to be kept in a dedicated room. In order to be treated, the patient would have to travel to the center where the machine was to have their stones shocked. SWL machines have dramatically improved over the years. Today, they are portable and can be moved between locations on trucks.

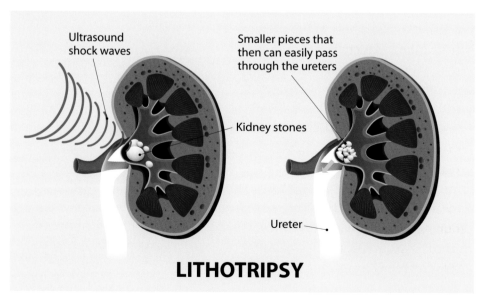

Ultrasound shock waves

Smaller pieces that then can easily pass through the ureters

Kidney stones

Ureter

LITHOTRIPSY

Various factors will determine whether or not the SWL machines will be your method of treatment, including where the stone is lodged. If it is in the upper portion of your ureter, your surgeon may opt for this treatment. Stones in the lower portion of the ureter will likely be treated via ureteroscopy.

This shock therapy procedure takes under an hour to complete and, yes, even though it is a noninvasive treatment, you are sedated. If you were awake you would feel as if boxer Mike Tyson was punching you 3,000 times in 60 minutes. Here's how it works: You lay on an operating table with a soft, water-filled cushion placed on your abdomen or right behind your kidney. Your body is positioned so that the shock waves can target the stone. The physician can see the kidney stone on the x-ray and note if the procedure is successful. Or, the stone breaks up into dust and washes out. Other times the stone does not break up into smaller pieces on the first try. It can take up to 2,500 shocks to loosen the first kidney stone, which may be followed by another procedure to get the job done (A body cannot endure more than about 3,000 shocks in one procedure.).

What to Expect After SWL

Here are some facts that you should know about the SWL procedure and what you can expect after the procedure is over:

- After the procedure, you will usually stay at the facility for about an hour before you are allowed to return home.

- You will be encouraged to drink plenty of liquid and strain your urine through a filter to capture any extra stone pieces for testing.

- You may need to take antibiotics and painkillers because you will be sore.

- When you are fully recovered, you may resume your usual diet and activities unless your doctor advises you differently, but it is important to follow up with your urologist.

- It is normal to have blood in your urine for up to a few days after the procedure.

- There may be some bruising on your back or abdomen from the shocks.

Immediately notify your doctor if you have these side effects: fever and/or chills; burning with urination; urinary frequency or urgency; or extreme lower back pain.

A few weeks after the procedure, you will have a follow-up appointment and, if the doctor has put in a stent during the procedure, it may be removed at that time.

In some cases, the doctor will insert a tube, called a stent, into your bladder and up to the kidney to help any fragments or dust from the stones to pass. The stents are used when the ureter is blocked, when there is a risk of infection, and in patients with intolerable pain or reduced kidney function. Please see "The Harsh Reality about Stents" in this chapter to learn about risks and complications about stents.

The success rate of a SWL depends on the size, location and the type of instrument being used. According to the National Kidney Foundation, in 50-75 percent patients who are thought to be good candidates for this treatment are free of stones within three months of SWL treatment. The highest success rates are in patients with smaller stones (such as less than 1 cm).

Are You a Candidate for SWL?

As I stated before, SWL is used to break up stones that are smaller than 2 centimeter, and ideally less than 1 centimeter so it is not blocking urine flow to the bladder. Even then, multiple treatments may be needed to "blast" all of the stones.

Many other factors also come into play when determining whether SWL is appropriate for a patient. Your surgeon will determine where the stone is lodged in your urinary tract and consider if the stone's size, shape, and type are conducive to treatment. For example, certain types of stones, such as cysteine and some calcium stones, are extremely dense and can be difficult to break up. Therefore, SWL is not usually recommended. If you have a uric acid stone, your surgeon may determine it's not visible on a plain x-ray and may opt for another treatment, or utilize a special technique along with SWL.

And, since x-rays and sound-waves are necessary for SWL, pregnant women are never treated with

WHEN TO CALL THE DOCTOR

If you experience any of the following, call your doctor immediately:

- Intense urgency to urinate, even after emptying bladder

- If you have unbearable pain, even after taking pain medication

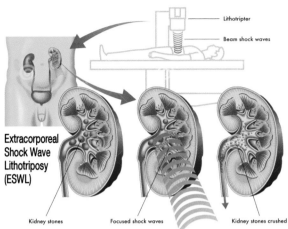

Lithotripter

Beam shock waves

**Extracorporeal
Shock Wave
Lithotriposy
(ESWL)**

Kidney stones   Focused shock waves   Kidney stones crushed

What are the Risks of SWL?

Don't fret, risks and complications of SWL are rare, but I would be amiss if I failed to mention them. They include urinary infection, which is treated with antibiotics either at home, or in few cases, in the hospital. SWL also poses the risk of injury to nearby organs, skin, muscles, nerves, and tissue. These would be minor injuries that typically heal on their own and require no further intervention. And, some patients may have minimal bleeding in the urine and possible around the kidney, which is referred to as a hematoma. Hematomas may require a blood transfusion—but remember, the chance of this happening is less than one percent.

this procedure. It is also not recommended for those who are obese because increased body tissue can make it difficult for the surgeon to see and correctly target the stone for the procedure.

Here are some other reasons why SWL may not be an option if you have:

- Poor health
- Infected urine
- Obstruction of the kidney
- Bleeding disorder
- Unable to take some type of anesthesia
- Narrowing of the urinary tract
- Infection
- Severe skeletal abnormalities
- Cardiac pacemaker
- Certain medical conditions

Rarely, patients may acquire steinstrasse, literally "stone street", which occurs when a large number of unpassable stones accumulate in the ureter, requiring additional treatment. Another potential risk that is being studied is the development of diabetes or hypertension following SWL. While this is currently being debated, it's worth mentioning so you have all the facts.

Finally, few patients may experience stone resistance to SWL therapy, despite several attempts to break up the stone, and another treatment option will be necessary.

Minimally Invasive Surgery: Percutaneous Nephrolithotomy

There are some stones that are just too big, aren't accessible by a ureteroscopy procedure, or do not respond to a SWL procedure. These may need to be treated with a procedure called a percutaneous nephrolithotomy or percutaneous nephrolithotripsy, which are fancy names for that minimally-invasive procedure I talked about earlier.

These are, usually, inpatient procedures that require a short one-to-three-day hospital stay and take from 1-6 hours. You are given general anesthesia and a 1 centimeter incision is made over your flank area. A miniature fiber optic camera called a nephroscope and other small instruments are threaded in through the incision. If it is needed, high frequency ultrasound is used to break up the stone. A vacuum is used to eliminate the stone if it's turned to dust. If the removal of the stone as a whole is successful, the procedure is called a nephrolithotomy, but if the stone is first broken up and then removed, the procedure is then called a nephrolithotripsy.

Once the procedure is complete, you may have a drainage (nephrostomy) tube coming out of your back. It is used to drain urine directly from the kidney and into a drainage bag. Most nephrostomy tubes are removed within 24 to 48 hours but can remain for up to two weeks if your doctor feels it is necessary. You may also have a ureteral stent placed to drain urine from the kidney to the bladder. Some patients will be sent home with a stent in place. Unfortunately, I have

Nephrolithotomy

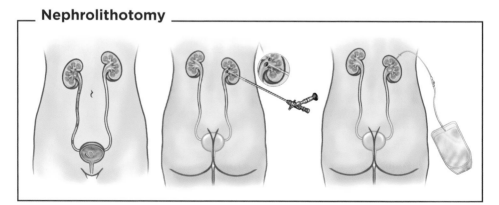

had patients tell me that the stent was harder to deal with than the tube. Please see "the Harsh Reality about Stents" in the Ureteroscopy section. Recovery from a percutaneous nephrolithotomy or percutaneous nephrolithotripsy can take anywhere from two to four weeks to recover from surgery.

What to Expect After Your Percutaneous Nephrolithotomy

During your hospitalization

- You will be monitored in the recovery room to ensure you have no signs of complications and that your vital signs are within the normal range

- You will be sleepy as the anesthesia wears off

- Anesthesia may also cause nausea, which can be treated with medication

- You will be transferred to your hospital room once you are fully awake

- You may experience post-operative pain around your kidney for a few days, which can be controlled with medication

- You may have an IV in place for several hours to give you necessary fluids and pain medication

- A urinary catheter is placed in the operating room and removed before you are sent home.

- Patients with a nephrostomy tube and ureteral stent will have them removed within one-to-two weeks

- You will receive support to begin walking before being discharged home

- Walking can prevent blood clots so it's best to walk as much as you can tolerate

- Fatigue may continue for up to a month after surgery

- Pain medication will be prescribed and then you will be advised to switch to extra strength Tylenol

- You may shower, but not take a bath

- Be sure to clean the area around the nephrostomy tube insertion site with soap and water and pat dry; then clean with hydrogen peroxide and a cotton swab before applying a clean bandage

Risks of Percutaneous Nephrolithotomy or Percutaneous Nephrolithotripsy

Both of these procedures have the highest success rates of removing kidney stones, but like any invasive procedure, even a minimally invasive one, there are a few potential risks, including infection, bleeding, transfusion, embolization of the kidney if an artery is inadvertently injured and other complications. The incision in your kidney will typically heal on its own, but there are risks of injury to your other nearby organs, including the bowel, ureter, liver, or bladder.

A percutaneous nephrolithotomy and percutaneous nephrolithotripsy are not common procedures, and not every urologist is capable of doing them well. The goal for you, as a patient, is to try to minimize the number of procedures you have, so talk to the doctors and find out what your options are.

Open Surgery

Open surgery is the most invasive option for kidney stone removal. Twenty years ago, it was the only option, but is a rare treatment today accounting for less than one percent of all kidney stone removal procedures. It is an inpatient procedure that requires a large incision in your abdomen or side to provide the surgeon access to the ureter and kidney. Once the stone is removed, a catheter is temporarily placed near the kidney to help drain urine. Recovery is longer than other types of treatment and may include a hospital a long hospital stay and four-to-six weeks before returning to normal daily activities.

While open surgery is uncommon, it may be performed if other types of treatment have been unsuccessful in removing the kidney stones. It's also an option if there is

WHEN TO CALL THE DOCTOR

- Pain that intensifies, even after taking pain medication

- Urine with multiple blood clots in it

- Fever and chills

- Nausea and vomiting

- Chest pain

- Difficulty breathing

- Pus forms around the nephrostomy tube insertion site

- Your catheter stops draining or leaking around the tube

an abnormality in the urinary system that has disrupted urine flow in the bladder, kidneys or ureter. And finally, it can be a chosen method if you have kidney stones caused by an infection.

What to Expect After Open Surgery

During your hospitalization

- You will be monitored in the recovery room to ensure you have no signs of complications and that your vital signs are within the normal range

- You will be sleepy as the anesthesia wears off

- Anesthesia may also cause nausea, which can be treated with medication

- You will be transferred to your hospital room once you are fully awake

- You may experience post-operative pain around your kidney for a few days, which can be controlled with medication

- You may have an IV in place for several hours to give you necessary fluids and pain medication

- A urinary catheter is placed in the operating room and removed before you are sent home.

- You will receive support to begin walking before being discharged home

- Walking can prevent blood clots so it's best to walk as much as you can tolerate

- Fatigue may continue for up to a month after surgery

- Pain medication will be prescribed and then you will be advised to switch to extra strength Tylenol

- Bathe per the instructions provided to you when you were discharged from the hospital

- Be sure to schedule your follow-up appointment with your surgeon when recommended

The risks of open surgery to remove a kidney stone include:

▸ Severe bleeding

▸ Infection

▸ Risks associated with anesthesia

▸ An increased risk for hernia at the location of the surgical incision

▸ Damage to the kidney requiring it to be removed

Stone-Specific Treatment

Each stone responds to each method of treatment in a different way. For example, cystine stones usually respond to a ureteroscopy. However, stones that are located in the ureter do not tend to break apart as well as stones that are located in your kidney. So, if the stone is clogging up your ureter, the best first course of treatment is the urteroscopy procedure. On the other hand, if the stone is located higher up in the ureter, you may have to undergo two procedures

to completely remove it. Stones in the kidney can be treated by SWL, ureteroscopy, or a PCNL

Calcium oxalate monohydrate stones also do not break up very well, so the ureteroscopy or PCNL is recommended.

Pure uric acid stones have a reasonable chance of dissolving if the focus is on increasing the pH of your urine to 6.5 mg/dL or higher.

Whether or not you will need surgical intervention for any type of stone will depend on a few factors:

- The stone is too large to pass on its own.
- The stone is still growing.
- The stone is blocking your urine flow and causing an infection or kidney damage.
- Your pain cannot be controlled with medication.

The truth is, more often than not, doctors do not know what type of kidney stone you have until you either pass it or it has been removed by one of these procedures and then sent to the lab for evaluation. There is also a chance that the surgeon will not get the stone out in one procedure, which is why some patients lean toward the ureteroscopy procedure versus the shock therapy. I respect my patients who want the least amount of invasion of their body. Again, however, the final method of treatment will be determined by the size, location and composition of the stone and whether or not you can withstand the pain anymore.

Alternative Therapy

Alternative therapies are another option for ridding yourself of kidney stones. Acupuncture, acupressure and chiropractic care are all methods to consider. Some patients are drawn to alternative methods because of their simplicity. However, it's important to note that the success rate of these treatments are not as high as surgical intervention and the scientific data supporting them is, usually, very weak.

▶ACUPUNCTURE:
Acupuncture can be used for stones smaller than 5 mm. It involves placing tiny needles in various areas of the body, including the legs, abdomen, back, and perhaps in the urinary and bladder channels. These needles are said to be painless, and stay in place for 20 to 30 minutes. Practitioners aim to strengthen the energy of the kidney to break up the

stone. This can be done by needles placed in targeted areas to dilate the ureters so the stone will be released. Needle placement can also change the chemistry of the urine, which can not only help the stone pass, but may also prevent future stones from forming. Acupuncture is a safe procedure and involves using disposable one-time-use needles.

> **A word to the wise:** if you are seeking acupuncture therapy, be sure to do your research and choose a qualified acupuncturist who is licensed and experienced in treating kidney stones.

▶REFLEXOLOGY/
ACUPRESSURE:
Reflexology and acupressure, also called pressure therapy, is similar to acupuncture but no needles are involved. Instead, firm pressure is placed on specific areas of the body, usually the hands and feet to target the energy in the kidney. You can perform acupressure on yourself, or have a friend or family member do it for

you. An internet search will provide several images of pressure points. One point to target kidney stones is in the center of the arch in the foot, just below the instep. Pressure is applied with the thumb or fingers for one to three minutes, or in 10-second intervals 10 times. The pressure should be applied just to the point where pain is felt, but not intense. Pressure should be applied to both the right and left foot at the same time, or one immediately after the other.

▸**CHIROPRACTIC CARE:**

Chiropractors apply force to the joints of the spine to realign them and improve blood flow to those areas.

When manipulating on the lower back, a chiropractor may be able to help release a stone by focusing on the tis-sues around the lumbar and abdomen. Chiropractic care is also proven to relieve pain, and may serve to relieve pain during kidney stone passage.

Easing the Pain with Medication

Speaking of pain, which many of my patients have described as 'worse than giving birth,' you will definitely want something to ease your discomfort while you try to pass the stone (trust me, I know). Some patients rely on such non-medicinal techniques as using a hot water bottle to help relax the kidney spasms, but, in general, kidney stone pain is usually pretty severe and needs medication. Tylenol is a good choice to ease your pain and is typically prescribed in 1,000 mg or more, but there are other more potent options as well, including Toradol and Percocet.

▸**TORADOL**

Toradol (ketorolac) is a nonsteroidal anti-inflam-matory drug (NSAID) that

Remember, alternative therapies can be worth a try, but may only be effective in the initial stages of kidney stone formation, when it is very small. After that, surgical intervention is your option.

is given first by injection and then by pill and used for several days or less to treat moderate or severe pain. Toradol is not recommended if you have any active or recent bleeding; a head injury; stomach ulcer; severe kidney disease; bleeding or blood-clotting disorder; a history of severe allergic reaction to aspirin or an NSAID; scheduled to have surgery; in late pregnancy, or breastfeeding. Toradol may also cause stomach or intestinal bleeding, which can be fatal.

Before using Toradol, tell your doctor if you have any of these conditions: heart disease; high blood pressure; high cholesterol; diabetes; a history of heart attack; stroke or blood clot; a history of stomach ulcers or bleeding; inflammatory bowel disease; ulcerative colitis; Crohn's disease; liver disease; kidney disease; asthma; or fluid retention. Do not use Toradol if you are pregnant or nursing.

▶PERCOCET

Percocet, which is a combination of oxycodone and acetaminophen, is also an alternative for moderate to severe pain. Side effects of Percocet include: abdominal or stomach pain; black, tarry stools; chills; dark urine; dizziness; fever; headache; itching; light-colored stools; loss of appetite; nausea; rash; unpleasant breath odor; unusual tiredness or weakness; vomiting of blood; and yellow eyes or skin.

▶DILAUDID

Dilaudid (hydromorphone) is an opioid pain medication that is also used for moderate to severe pain. You should not take Dilaudid if you have ever had an allergic reaction to hydromorphone or other narcotic medicines, or if you have: severe asthma or breathing problems; a blockage in your stomach or intestines; or a bowel obstruction called paralytic ileus.

Do not use Dilaudid if you have used a monoamine oxidase inhibitor in the 14 days before you take it because of a possible drug interaction. Before you take Dilaudid, tell your doctor if you have any of the following: any type of breathing problem or lung disease; a history of head injury; brain tumor; seizures; a history of drug abuse, alcohol addiction, or mental illness; urination problems; liver or kidney disease; sulfite allergy; Addison's disease or other adrenal gland disorders; or problems with your gallbladder, pancreas, or thyroid.

▶MORPHINE

Finally, we can also prescribe morphine, which is an opiate pain medication used to treat your pain around the clock. Since morphine can slow or stop your breathing, you should not take it if you have severe asthma or breathing problems, a blockage in your stomach or intestines, or a bowel obstruction called paralytic ileus. If it has been prescribed to you, make sure to call your doctor at once if you have: slow heart rate; sighing; weak or shallow breathing; chest pain; fast or pounding heartbeats; extreme drowsiness; or if you feel like you might pass out. Common side effects may include: drowsiness, dizziness; constipation, stomach pain, nausea, vomiting; headache, tired feeling, anxiety, or mild itching.

▶OXYBUTYNIN

In addition to pain medication, I, often, prescribe oxybutynin to reduce muscle spasms of the bladder and urinary tract. You should not use oxybutynin if you have untreated or uncontrolled narrow-angle glaucoma; a blockage in your digestive tract (stomach or intestines); or if you are unable to urinate. Before using oxybutynin, tell your doctor if you have glaucoma; liver or kidney disease; an enlarged prostate; myasthenia gravis; ulcerative colitis; a blockage in your stomach or intestines; or a stomach disorder such as gastroesophageal reflux disease (GERD); or slow digestion.

You should also stop using this medication if you experience hot and dry skin; extreme thirst; severe stomach pain or constipation; pain or burning when you urinate; or if you stop urinating. Get emergency medical help if you have any of these signs of an allergic reaction to oxybutynin: hives; difficult breathing; or swelling of your face, lips, tongue, or throat.

▶PYRIDIUM

 Pyridium is a pill that can be taken to act as an oral anesthetic on the urinary tract. It is not a narcotic and it is non-additictive, but it will turn your urine a bright orange, which can surprise patients, who have not been warned, in advance.

As a final note, it's important to take all pain medication as directed. If you have any concerns about your medication, call your doctor.

You know the old expression, you are what you eat? When it comes to kidney stones, this expression rings very true.

CHAPTER 08

DIETS AND STONES

You know the old expression, you are what you eat? When it comes to kidney stones, this expression rings very true. In fact, your diet is one of those factors that you can control to reduce your risk of kidney stones.

First, the most important diet advice I can give you is avoid fad diets. Ignore any diet that requires you to eat a large amount of one food or completely abstain from something else. I'm not a fan of these diets. For example, I've mentioned it quite a few times already, but the Atkins Diet is just one example of these diets that promote a fairly high protein intake.

I am starting to see more patients who are coming in with uric acid stones because they are following these diets. Any diet that does not allow you to have your favorite foods is a diet that you are not going to comply with. If you love chocolate and were told that you could never have it again, odds are that diet isn't going to work, right? Or what about what you should 'always' have? These words are hard to use. You have to be able to fit your favorite things into your lifestyle. Even diabetics when told they can never have sugar again struggle. There is a nutritional expert who tells diabetics that an entire chocolate bar is not good, but a few Hershey Kisses is okay. It's all about moderation balance and integrating what you like into your lifestyle.

There are some changes though that you should make to improve your health to decrease your risk of another attack. I've already talked

Drop the Weight (And Likely) Your Risk for Kidney Stones

Researchers believe obesity may increase the risk for kidney stones. The reasons suggested for this possible link include the fact that people of a heavier weight may excrete more uric acid and oxalate in their urine, which are risk factors for calcium kidney stones. Furthermore, obesity and type 2 diabetes are associated with a lower urine pH and thus a higher risk of uric acid stones. In fact, research has shown uric acid stones are more common in patients with type 2 diabetes. Another reason is those who are obese are more likely to ingest larger amounts of animal protein and salt, making them more likely to form kidney stones.

What to do? The best bet is to go the old fashioned weight-loss route—lower fat, lower intake and exercise. And stick to the plan. Try to avoid making changes that you can't commit to for life. Simple things, like opting for smaller portions, eating less animal protein and salt, increasing water intake and enjoying a daily walk go a long way. But, please, avoid fad diets. These diets are often proven to be counter-productive as most people gain any lost weight back—and then some.

about how, if you are a meat and potatoes lover, you might want to reconsider putting that next steak on the barbie. A diet that's high in protein can increase your risk of forming kidney stones. Protein is found in beef, pork, poultry, fish and eggs, so you are at risk of a kidney stone if your diet includes a large egg omelet for breakfast, a protein shake or two for lunch, and a steak with a huge kale and spinach salad for dinner (after all, you want to get some greens in there too), you might do your body more harm than good. Dark green leafy foods contain high quantities of oxalate, and as you now know, too much oxalate in your system can lead to the formation of calcium oxalate stones. Check the High Oxalate Food chart for a list of other foods that have a high level of oxalate.

If you opt for foods such as anchovies, liver, and sardines, you're, also, at risk. These foods are high in purines, which break down into uric acid. Too much uric acid in your system increases your risk for uric acid stones. Beware that high-purine foods, such as the ones I've mentioned, can also be high-protein foods so it's a double whammy to your risk level.

High Oxalate Foods

Here are some other examples of foods with high levels of oxalate that could be putting you at risk for kidney stones:

 FRUITS: blackberries, blueberries, raspberries, strawberries, currants, kiwifruit, concord (purple) grapes, figs, tangerines, and plums.

 VEGETABLES: spinach, Swiss chard, beets (root part), beet greens (leaf part), collards, okra, parsley, leeks and quinoa are among the most oxalate-dense vegetables. **Moderately dense in oxalate:** celery, green beans, rutabagas, and summer squash.

 NUTS & SEEDS: almonds, cashews, and peanuts

LEGUMES: soybeans, tofu, and other soy products

GRAINS: wheat bran and wheat germ

 OTHER: cocoa, chocolate, and black tea

See chapter nine for an expanded list of high-oxalate foods, moderate-oxalate foods, and low-oxalate foods.

The Calcium Catch

If you are popping a large amount of antacids to either ward off the heartburn in your life or just because your doctor said it would help increase the amount of calcium in your body, beware. Too many might push your chances of a stone a little higher. The more you take, the higher your risk. Most calcium found in your urine does not come from your diet, it comes from your bones. There are other ways to achieve a higher level of calcium in your body without depending on antacids (see chapter nine).

On the other hand, the more citric acid you have in your system, the less likely you are to form stones. That's because citric acid contains citrate, which is a salt that increases urine pH. Citric acid is naturally found in many fruits and fruit juices, such as lemons and oranges, and it helps to break up baby stones that are just beginning to form. Citric acid is not to be confused with ascorbic acid, otherwise known as Vitamin C.

Salty Stones

Who doesn't enjoy a nice big bowl of buttery, salted popcorn while watching

VITAMIN

When most people feel a cold coming on, they start doubling and tripling the amount of Vitamin C they are taking in, in hopes of knocking it out. Unfortunately, you might be helping the cold, but you could be bringing on the stones.

In an article published in *JAMA Internal Medicine,* Swedish researchers found a connection between the formation of kidney stones and the use of vitamin C supplements.

During an 11-year time period, more than 23,000 Swedish men were studied and about 2 percent of them developed kidney stones. The study found that those who took vitamin C supplements were twice as likely to have kidney stones. Vitamin C is an acid that can be metabolized to oxalate, which will turn into a kidney stone.

a movie? Kidney stoners put your hands down. Taking in too much sodium increases your chance of developing a kidney stone. High levels of sodium can also be found in canned vegetables, deli meats, flavor packets and condiments, frozen meals, vegetable juices, and other processed foods. Sodium causes your kidneys to excrete more calcium into your urine and, again say it with me, too much calcium in the urine may combine with oxalate and phosphorus to form stones.

A Cup of Joe and a Stone

A morning cup of coffee might not seem like such a big deal, but if you rely on the beverage to get you through the day, and then follow it up with iced tea at dinner, an energy drink to push you through the night, and a drink when you go out with friends, you might be walking yourself right into my office or that of another urologist. These beverages are known as natural diuretics, which can cause increased urination and dehydration. As you know from my own personal experiences, becoming dehydrated can lead to stone formation.

Signs of Dehydration

Do not wait until you're thirsty to think that you are actually dehydrated. Thirst doesn't give a clear indication of dehydration. Instead, the color of your urine is a much better indicator. Clear or light-colored urine means you're well hydrated, whereas a dark yellow or amber color usually signals dehydration.

According to the Mayo Clinic, mild to moderate dehydration is likely to cause:

- Dry, sticky mouth
- Sleepiness or tiredness — children are likely to be less active than usual
- Thirst
- Decreased urine output
- No wet diapers for three hours for infants
- Few or no tears when crying
- Dry skin
- Headache
- Constipation
- Dizziness or lightheadedness

Severe dehydration, a medical emergency, can cause:

- Extreme thirst
- Extreme fussiness or sleepiness in infants and children; irritability and confusion in adults
- Very dry mouth, skin and mucous membranes
- Little or no urination — any urine that is produced will be darker than normal
- Sunken eyes
- Shriveled and dry skin that lacks elasticity and doesn't "bounce back" when pinched into a fold
- In infants, sunken fontanels — the soft spots on the top of a baby's head
- Low blood pressure
- Rapid heartbeat
- Rapid breathing
- No tears when crying
- Fever
- In the most serious cases, delirium or unconsciousness

At this point, it might seem that anything you put into your mouth can cause you to increase your risk of kidney stones, but that's not the case. I discuss diet more thoroughly in a later chapters, but there are food alternatives that will not increase your risk of forming kidney stones. The most important thing to remember is that everything you eat should be done in moderation. Too much of anything, including water and even veggies and salad, can cause potential problems. Remember, when it comes to reducing your risk of kidney stones, your diet is one of those factors that you can control.

Don't worry, because you won't feel deprived when you learn how to eat properly to prevent kidney stones. I, even, tell my patients that it's okay to go out with friends, have a few drinks and play some beer pong, but make sure to stay hydrated.

Here's a tip: For every one glass of wine or beer have a glass of water. If you go to the bathroom and see that your urine is starting to turn a darker yellow, it's a sign that you need to drink more water. It's all about choices. If you watch what you're doing, you could, potentially, avoid getting another stone.

How to Make Positive Changes

We all know that change is hard. For most of us, going cold-turkey can be especially challenging. Your best bet is to have a clear plan on how you will make the change, but be reasonable and realistic with yourself. Here are some tips that I find useful.

Make a list. Don't just say it, write it down. Define all of your goals, in order of importance, and display them somewhere prominent—on your bathroom mirror, refrigerator, or maybe create a vision board and post it on your bedroom door.

List your motivations. What is your overall objective? Likely, it is to avoid pain and perhaps surgery. Also list what you have to gain once you achieve your goals.

Set one goal at a time. Don't overwhelm yourself with too many changes. Stay focused on one goal at a time until it becomes habit. Then, move on to the next goal.

The buddy system. Ask a friend or family member to buddy-up to achieve your goals together. Perhaps your buddy wants to quit smoking, and you want to adopt a low-oxalate diet. Your goals may be different, but you can still check in with each other daily, either by phone, text or email, to see what successes and challenges you may be experiencing. Encourage each other to move past any failures and celebrate your milestones.

Squash negative talk. Are you telling yourself, "This is too hard"? Or asking, "How am I ever going to do this?" Stop. Those thoughts are derailing your plan. Every time a negative thought enters your mind, replace it with a positive one, like "I know it's possible," or "I deserve a life free of kidney stones."

Ask for support. Let your family members and friends know what goals you have set, and ask them to help you. They can make sure water is at-the-ready, or ensure you are eating the right foods to prevent kidney stones. Make a grocery and meal list and keep it handy for the cook of the house.

Reward yourself. Each time you successfully make a change, reward yourself. Perhaps you'll go to a movie, baseball game, or buy a new bike.

> **"**Your net worth to the world is usually determined by what remains after your bad habits are subtracted from your good ones.**"**
> – Benjamin Franklin

Get enough sleep. When we are tired, we tend to do what's easy, not what's right. Make sure you are well rested so you can think clearly about your choices, and make any extra effort needed to choose wisely.

Professional help. If you are truly struggling, a few sessions with a psychologist may prove beneficial. Psychologists can help to pinpoint triggers or emotional issues that are preventing you from reaching your goals, and help you get back on track. Nutritionists and dietitians can, also, be of help if you are finding it hard to lose weight.

Above all, don't get down on yourself if your plan goes awry. We all fail at times. But if you can forgive yourself, get back on track, and move forward, you can succeed.

The Choice is Yours

When it comes to developing stones, some patients are simply dealt a bad hand, but they play it well. For example, 46-year-old John is in the high risk category, because both his father and his grandfather have suffered from kidney stones on multiple occasions and, as you know, family genetics increases your risk as well. To add fuel to the fire, John was also diagnosed with Crohn's disease, an inflammatory disease of the intestines.

Fortunately, John knows that his lifestyle and dietary choices can contribute to an attack, which is something he wants to avoid at any cost. He takes good care of his health by making smart food choices, drinking plenty of fluids, especially water, and watching his stress levels. He is dramatically reducing his odds of getting another attack.

Then there are other patients who know they are at risk for a stone because it runs in the family, yet they do not follow the steps necessary to prevent it from happening.

Now let's talk about the patients who have already come to me with a horrific episode of kidney stones. For the first couple of months after the attack, they do incredibly well following the prevention guidelines. Then, something happens. The farther they go from the initial event, the more they start to slip a little. They don't drink as much water as they should or they start eating the wrong foods. Like I said, that's the reason 50 percent of the patients are back in my office within three years with another stone. They start to forget how painful and excruciating it was. I know it's hard to make major life modifications. It's like going on a diet – it's hard to change bad habits and, ultimately, people gain back the weight.

Here's a sad story about one of my young male patients. He had cystinuria, an inherited disorder in which the body is unable to process certain building blocks of proteins properly. He admitted that he was not good at sticking to his diet, and constantly made bad choices, so he became responsible for funding my kids' college tuition. What I mean by that, is he had 20 or so operations over the last few years. His stones kept dropping into his ureter and he constantly wound up in the emergency room.

In this situation, I have to be concerned about his narcotic intake. It's okay to take morphine for pain for a few days here and there, but imagine if you are like my patient and forming a stone every month and this goes on for a five-year period. You have to be careful and think about addiction and all of the side effects.

My patient ended up on disability because he would not adhere to any diet, gained weight and became a diabetic. Every six to eight weeks he had another operation to remove a kidney stone. I'm very surprised that rather than adhere to a diet, take medications and stay hydrated, he said, "I am going to live my life. I am not modifying my diet or downing tons of water to stay hydrated." Sadly, within five years he lost some kidney function. He didn't need kidney dialysis at that point in his life – he was in his 30s – but by the time he is in his 50s and 60s, I can almost guarantee he will be on dialysis.

I've also heard of patients who have a minimal risk of forming a stone, completely muck up their chances of avoiding one by making irresponsible choices that will almost guarantee them a visit to a urologist. For example a high school wrestler who needs to meet the weight requirement for his class may take laxatives to remove pounds prior to weigh-in. An occasional laxative is fine if you need it for medical reasons, but this abuse of the substance can leave you severely dehydrated and a prime candidate for kidney stones.

I have another male patient who had a low risk for kidney stones, but he decided to chance fate by not

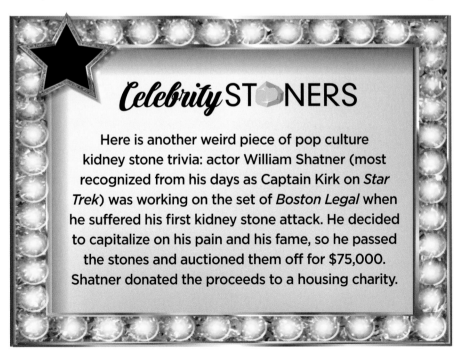

Celebrity ST◆NERS

Here is another weird piece of pop culture kidney stone trivia: actor William Shatner (most recognized from his days as Captain Kirk on *Star Trek*) was working on the set of *Boston Legal* when he suffered his first kidney stone attack. He decided to capitalize on his pain and his fame, so he passed the stones and auctioned them off for $75,000. Shatner donated the proceeds to a housing charity.

drinking enough of water during his workouts. He was already prone to urinary tract infections and, the health nut that he is, he ate a lot of dark, green leafy vegetables and salads. So here is a patient who, you would think, was taking good care of himself and reducing his chance of illness, but he wasn't drinking enough of water and, combined with UTIs, he catapulted himself to the top of the at-risk list and ultimately had to be treated for a kidney stone.

I speak from experience that nobody wants this pain, so why would you put yourself in that position if you know there's a risk you'll get a stone? I talked to a cardiologist who has told me that he has patients who, after a quintuple bypass, ask for a cigarette in the recovery room!

You can avoid the pain and the problems by simply making smarter lifestyle choices. Yes, while there are definite genetic predispositions for getting kidney stones, there are factors you can control. It's your body and how you treat it will determine exactly what will ultimately happen to you.

Ideally, you should aim for at least eight 8-ounce glasses, which equals about 2 liters, or half a gallon. This is called the 8x8 rule and should be easy to remember. The goal is to produce about two liters of urine per day.

CHAPTER 09

PREVENTING CALCIUM-BASED STONES

By now you have presented with symptoms of kidney stones at either your doctor's office or the emergency room and, after a series of tests, you either passed the stone or went through a procedure to have it removed. Of course, you never want to go through that again! But since you already had one stone, your risk is now considerably higher that you will have another (and even possibly another) stone, so what do you need to do to keep this from happening again?

At this point, you should know what type of stone you have and to do that, the stone first has to be captured and examined. This information is important, because your prevention plain will be tailored to exactly what type of stone you have. A doctor can take an x-ray and at least hypothesize about what kind of stone it might be based on how it looks. But the doctor cannot make a final diagnosis until the stone is passed or removed and sent to a pathology lab for a final diagnosis.

If you passed the stone on your own, you should try and catch it and then bring it in to the doctor's office, so it can be analyzed. In order to catch it, you need to collect your urine every time you pee. Then, you need to strain the urine to see if there any stones or undissolved crystals left behind. There are companies that sell special kidney stone filters for just a few dollars or you can create a makeshift kidney stone filter of your own by collecting your urine in a jar and then straining it through a very fine mesh wire basket or a coffee filter. Of course, collecting and straining your urine is not something anybody really wants to do, but finding out what the stone is made of is essential to creating a personalized kidney stone prevention plan.

Once your doctor knows what type of stone you have, additional tests may be ordered to provide a complete analysis of what's happening in your body. First, for my patients, I initially order a complete 48-hour urine chemistry analysis to find out exactly what your pH and other levels are. This isn't the time that you to should be on your best eating and drinking behavior. On the contrary, your doctor needs to get a true sense of what you do in your life and what you really eat and drink in a 48-hour period. If, over this period, you decide you are going to eat well, watch your sugar and salt intake and drink tons of water to impress your doctor, it will probably work and most likely your urine and metabolic test results are going to come

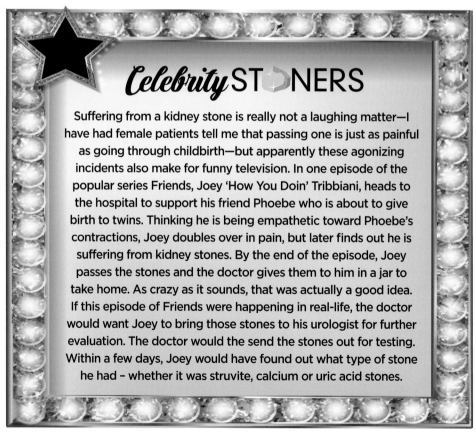

Celebrity ST◈NERS

Suffering from a kidney stone is really not a laughing matter—I have had female patients tell me that passing one is just as painful as going through childbirth—but apparently these agonizing incidents also make for funny television. In one episode of the popular series Friends, Joey 'How You Doin' Tribbiani, heads to the hospital to support his friend Phoebe who is about to give birth to twins. Thinking he is being empathetic toward Phoebe's contractions, Joey doubles over in pain, but later finds out he is suffering from kidney stones. By the end of the episode, Joey passes the stones and the doctor gives them to him in a jar to take home. As crazy as it sounds, that was actually a good idea. If this episode of Friends were happening in real-life, the doctor would want Joey to bring those stones to his urologist for further evaluation. The doctor would the send the stones out for testing. Within a few days, Joey would have found out what type of stone he had – whether it was struvite, calcium or uric acid stones.

back at normal levels. But, you are not doing yourself any good, because you know that these results are a fluke. Once you return to eating and drinking the way you usually do, you will be back at the doctor's office or emergency room at some point with another kidney stone flare up. So the bottom line is: this is one test that you do not want to cheat on.

Comprehensive Metabolic Panel

Blood will also be drawn and a Uric Acid Test and Comprehensive Metabolic Panel (CMP) will be ordered, which is a group of blood tests that provide information on your body's chemical balance and metabolism. See chapter three for more information on the CMP tests.

Parathyroid Hormone

Since you have been diagnosed with a calcium stone, your doctor may also order a test on your parathyroid hormone, or PTH. The parathyroid is four small glands that sit next to the thyroid in your neck and are responsible for maintaining the level of calcium in your body. If the glands over produce parathyroid hormone, a condition called hyperparathyroidism can result. Hyperparathyroidism can lead to the development of excess calcium in your urine and an increased risk of calcium kidney stones.

I do not see it too often, but sometimes I will have a patient that comes to me who has a history of multiple kidney stones and, once I check the parathyroid hormone levels, it is discovered that their levels are through the roof because they have a parathyroid tumor. Most parathyroid tumors are benign, but unfortunately they cause kidney stones to be produced.

Uric Acid

I will also order a uric acid level, particularly in patients with a history of the gout in order to see how well their disease is controlled. Sometimes, it is necessary to adjust allopurinol levels if the serum uric acid level is very high.

Your Diet

While drinking too much milk or eating too much ice cream cannot lead to calcium stones, eating and drinking other foods can. For example, if you are someone who enjoys a bottomless glass of cold, refreshing iced tea, you may be at risk for a higher oxalate level in your body. Black tea is a rich source of oxalate and contains 50 to 100 mg per 100 ml. You should especially take note of that fact if you reside in the warmer states. Known as the "Kidney Stone Belt," the south's higher temperatures can force residents to sweat more and, therefore, lose more fluids. As a result, they are at an increased risk for dehydration and kidney stones. And what do they commonly drink to quench their thirst? You got it. Their famous sweet tea. Drinking a lot of the sugary sweetness might refresh you, but the tea can cause the minerals to bind together to form a stone.

A physician from Little Rock, Arkansas wrote about his patient in a 2015 issue of the *New England Journal of Medicine*. The patient was a 56-year-old man who came to the emergency room with weakness, fatigue, body aches, and an elevated serum creatinine level. His urine showed a high level of calcium oxalate crystals in it. When the doctor questioned the patient's food and beverage habits, he owned up to drinking 16 eight-ounce glasses of iced tea every day! With 16 cups of tea in his daily diet, the patient's daily consumption of oxalate was more than 1,500 mg — a level that is higher than the average American intake by a factor of approximately three to 10. (Just so you know, hot tea can increase your oxalate level too, but since most people drink hot tea in smaller quantities, kidney stones do not happen as much as with cold iced tea.)

In addition to watching how much iced tea you drink, there are other dietary changes you should make to decrease your risk of getting another calcium kidney stone:

Can the soda: A 2013 study found that downing even one sugary-sweet soda a day can increase your odds of developing kidney stones by a whopping 23 percent. Researchers think the fructose (which can be found in table sugar and high fructose corn syrup) in sweetened drinks can cause an increase in kidney stone-causing chemicals.

Honestly, I'm more concerned about the knockoff flavored sodas and energy drinks like Red Bull.

Increase your water: What you really should do is forget the sweet drinks altogether and stick to drinking plenty of water. Water flushes out toxins that produce stones. If, however, you hate the way plain water tastes and bottled water doesn't do it for you either, there are other options to make it more flavorful. You can buy so many different flavors of water now and even add in your own natural fruit flavors for taste. You can also add a teaspoon, or more depending on taste, of real lemon juice to an extra-large glass of water with no sugar. Or, try water enhancers to add flavor to plain water. Whatever you do, keep trying until you find something that works for you to get your daily water requirements.

Ideally, you should aim for at least eight 8-ounce glasses, which equals about 2 liters, or half a gallon. This is called the 8×8 rule and should be easy to remember. The goal is to produce about two liters of urine per day.

Many patients understand the benefit of drinking more fluids, but unfortunately it impinges on their lifestyle. For example, one of my patients is a school bus driver who has had two kidney stones. She starts her workday at 6 a.m. and is in the bus for two hours. She cannot leave her students to go to the bathroom. I have another patient who makes microchips and, in order to do this, he has to wear a bodysuit and complete a sterilization decontamination process. During the day he only gets one 15-minute break. So, when I ask how much water they are both drinking, they tell me that they aren't. They just can't.

Golfers are in the same situation. A typical game of golf takes four hours and it only takes 90 minutes or less to form a stone. You can't play nine holes of golf in 80-90 degree weather without staying well hydrated, but that's what golfers do. They do not want to drink a lot of water and then have to pee while they are on the course. Yes, male golfers can, feasibly, duck behind a tree to relieve themselves, but female golfers can't, so they end up dehydrated.

As I stated, it only takes 90 minutes for the kidney stone crystallization process to begin. Luckily, most of these tiny crystals will wash away. But the bus driver, microchip processor, and golfer are already setting themselves up for a bad situation. As men get older, their prostate gets bigger too, so they go to the bathroom more frequently.

Substitute the salt: Cutting back on salt can be difficult to do with the typical American diet, since most Americans already consume too much sodium in their diet thanks to processed, canned, and fast foods. A 2013 study released by the U.S. Centers for Disease Control and Prevention in 2015 showed that during a two-year period (2011 to 2012), the average daily sodium intake among U.S. adults was 3,592 mg, which is well above the public

Calcium-Rich Foods

- Collard greens, frozen
- Broccoli Rabe
- Broccoli, fresh, cooked
- Kale, frozen
- Soy beans, green, boiled
- Bok Choy, cooked, boiled
- Figs, dried
- Oranges
- Sardines, canned with bones
- Salmon, canned with bones
- Shrimp, canned
- Milk, skim, low-fat, whole
- Almond milk, rice milk or soy milk, fortified
- Pudding, chocolate, prepared with 2 percent milk
- Ricotta, part-skim
- Yogurt, plain, low-fat
- Yogurt with fruit, low-fat
- Yogurt, Greek
- Mozzarella, part-skim
- Cheddar cheese
- American cheese
- Feta cheese
- Parmesan
- Cottage cheese, 2 percent
- Frozen yogurt, vanilla
- Ice cream, vanilla
- Orange juice and other fruit juices, fortified
- Waffle, frozen, fortified
- Oatmeal, fortified
- English muffin, fortified
- Cereal, fortified
- Mac & cheese, frozen
- Pizza, cheese, frozen
- Beans, baked, canned
- Tofu, prepared with calcium

health target set by the U.S. Department of Health and Human Services (HHS) of 2,300 mg. A healthy diet should include no more than 1,500-2,000mg of sodium per day. The study surveyed 180,000 American adults in 26 states, Washington D.C., and Puerto Rico. The findings were then published in the CDC's Morbidity and Mortality Weekly Report.

Reducing your salt intake is not an insurmountable task. Here are some tips to help you:

▶ **Go low:** Look for low-salt or unsalted versions of your favorite foods, but be sure to read the labels and see how much sodium you are actually taking in. Regulations say that foods touted as "reduced in salt" must contain at least 25 percent less salt than the original food, a competitor's product, or another reference. If the food claims it is "light in sodium" or "lightly salted," it must contain 50 percent less sodium than the original food, a competitor's product, or another reference. If the food claims it is "low in sodium," it can only have 140 mg or less sodium (natural or added) per serving.

Finally, foods that are labeled as "unsalted" or "no salt added" are not necessarily salt-free. Instead, this labeling means that the product has not had salt added to it during its processing.

▸ **Watch your serving sizes:** For example, let's say the label of your favorite canned soup says that there is more than 500 mg of sodium in just one chicken noodle serving, but the can actually holds two servings. You enjoy the entire can in one sitting and have now have taken in 1,000 mg of sodium in just one meal. Add in the other sodium-laden foods you eat throughout the day and you can see how the numbers can quickly add up.

▸ **Substitute:** Giving up salt does not mean you have to give up flavor. When you cook your favorite meals at home, substitute other low- and no-salt herbs and seasonings in place of traditional salt in your recipes. You might find new flavors you love.

▸ **Sidestep it:** If you are eating out, don't be shy. Ask for condiments that are typically salty, such as gravy or sauce, to be left off your food and put on the side so you can just use it as needed. Also, it is okay to ask that there not be any salt added to your meats and fish.

▸ **Salty drinks:** You might not realize it, but there is salt in drinks as well, including vegetable juices, energy drinks and powdered hot cocoa mixes.

Count on calcium

I said it before, but I'll say it again: How much calcium you get through the foods you eat has almost, nothing to do with how your kidney stones are formed. As a matter of fact, your body still needs the recommended amount of calcium that you get from your daily diet. Limiting your calcium intake may actually increase the chance that stones will form. In addition, this reduction of calcium can also leave you susceptible to osteoporosis, a disease of the bones that happens when you lose too much bone, make too little bone, or both.

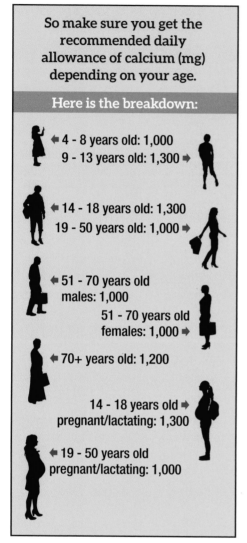

So make sure you get the recommended daily allowance of calcium (mg) depending on your age.

Here is the breakdown:

- 4 - 8 years old: 1,000
- 9 - 13 years old: 1,300
- 14 - 18 years old: 1,300
- 19 - 50 years old: 1,000
- 51 - 70 years old males: 1,000
- 51 - 70 years old females: 1,000
- 70+ years old: 1,200
- 14 - 18 years old pregnant/lactating: 1,300
- 19 - 50 years old pregnant/lactating: 1,000

Orange You Eating Better?

If you have already had a kidney stone, it's imperative that you make sure to include citrate, or citric acid, in your diet to try and stop more from forming. You can get citrate as a supplement or in some med- ications. Or, the next time someone offers you an orange, "fuggedabout" what happened to those who took one in the classic movie "The Godfather" and enjoy.

When life gives you lemons, eat them, add them to your meals, or turn them into lemonade if you want to prevent kidney stones from forming. Foods like lemons and that are rich in naturally-occurring citric acid, con- tain citrate, according to the U.S. Food and Drug Administration (FDA). Pure lemon juice has 1.44 grams per ounce of citrate while lemon juice concen- trates contain an average of 1.1 grams per ounce. Commercially-prepared, ready-to-drink beverages contain .03 – to – .22 gram per ounce.

Lime juice, another source of citrate, contains 1.38 grams per ounce while concentrate made from lime juice can contain as much as 1.06 grams per ounce. Other citric fruits, especially grapefruit and oranges, including their juice and concentrate, contain citrate as well, according to the U.S. Department of Agriculture (USDA), though in lesser amounts than lemons and limes. Various forms of pineapple and its byproducts—fresh pineapple, pineapple juice, pineapple concentrate, pineapple toppings, and products sold as a pineapple mix- ture—can all contain citrate as well.

Citrate can also be found in other foods where you might not expect it, such as processed cheeses, bottled cheese spreads, and canned cheeses. Citrate is also used as a dough conditioner in a variety of frozen foods including:

- Frozen bread dough
- Bagels
- Waffles
- Pancakes
- Dumplings
- Prepared cookie mixtures
- Cakes, brownies, pies,
- Cornbreads
- Biscuits
- Rolls
- Croissants
- Pizza dough
- Canned biscuits
- In-store bakery items

Citric Acid Boost

As the name implies, citric acid is found in citrus fruits and juices. The fruits with the most citric acid are lemons and limes, which are the best fruits to eat (or drink) to boost the citric acid content in your urine. Other good sources are oranges and grapefruit. Some berries—although they are not considered citrus fruits—also contain citrus acid, including strawberries, raspberries and cranberries. But lemons and limes are your best bet.

There are also prescription and over-the-counter citric acid tablets. For example, you could be prescribed potassium citrate in tablet form. But lemons have as much or more citric acid than either of these options. In fact, prescriptive tablets are costly and you may need to take a dozen tablets each day. You are better off drinking 4 ounces of lemon juice (that's just half a cup), which will give you as much citric acid as those 12 prescribed tablets. The reason is because the citrate contained in the citric acid in lemon juice will alkalinize a person more than the citric acid tablets. But how much citrate excretion increases depends on the amount of citrate and the pH of the beverage—the higher the pH, the more citrate versus citric acid. Crystal Light is an attractive option because of the high citric acid content and because the pH is higher than lemonade, meaning more citric acid is in the citrate form.

> Please note: Citric acid is often confused with Vitamin C, but they are not the same.

Love Those Lemons

Want some fun and simple ways to add citric acid into your diet? Try these.

✳ Dribble lemon over apples to keep them from browning

✳ Add lemon to guacamole to keep it fresh and green, not to mention adding a zest of flavor

✳ Go Greek and try lemon-packed avgolemono soup (an internet search will bring up recipes)

✳ Make lemon, lime or lemon-lime ice cubes. Add to a glass of water and you have a refreshing drink packed with kidney-stone fighting goodness.

✳ Drink lemonade with meals every day. You can make your own by adding 4 ounces of lemonade to a pitcher and sweeten with sugar, or better yet, sugar substitute. Another tasty option is Crystal Light™.

✳ Spruce up your salads by opting for fresh lemon juice instead of salad dressings (it's a great fat and calorie saver too!)

✳ Squirt lemon juice over baked fish, such as salmon.

TIP Eat and drink calcium and oxalate-rich foods together during a meal. Oxalate and calcium are more likely to bind to one another in the stomach and intestines before the kidneys begin processing, making it less likely that kidney stones will form.

▶ **Shrink your protein:** As you've already learned from the previous chapters, excessive protein in your diet can increase the amount of both calcium and oxalate in your urine, so it's important to reduce how much you eat on a daily basis. It doesn't mean that you need to eliminate it from your diet. On the contrary, you need protein, but in small amounts throughout the day. So forget the massive steak or the Dagwood-sized hamburger with bacon you want to enjoy at dinner. Instead, cook up a sampling of steak or a small-sized slider. Milk also contains protein, so limit your milk and milk products to two servings per day.

▶ **Keep it low fat:** Low fat diets keep your stones at bay.

▶ **Reduce the soy:** Consuming soy products, such as tofu, tempeh, edamame, soymilk and miso are on the rise because of their high nutritional value. However, soy also comes with a high concentration of oxalate, which plays into an increased risk of calcium kidney stones. Research has shown, however, that soy foods also contain phytate, which is a potential inhibitor of calcium oxalate kidney stone formation. As a result, soy foods that contain low concentrations of oxalate and high concentrations of phytate may be advantageous for kidney stone patients or anyone with an increased risk of kidney stones.

▶ **Skip the supplements:** Do not take extra calcium or vitamin D, vitamin C or fish oil supplements, unless the doctor who is treating your kidney stones specifically recommends it.

▶ **Beware the antacids:** If you have heartburn or acid reflux and you're chewing Tums or other antacids like they are candy, you might be doing yourself more harm than good, especially if the antacids are loaded with calcium. Calcium-enhanced antacids may lower the oxalate in your urine but they will also increase the calcium in your urine, which (repeat after me) can lead to kidney stones. There are also brands of antacids that are calcium-free, but talk to your doctor first about which ones are right for you.

A Low-Oxalate Diet

By now this should be a no-brainer. If you have calcium oxalate stones, you may need to limit foods that are high in oxalate. I've broken oxalate foods into three categories: high-oxalate foods to avoid; foods with moderate amounts of oxalate to limit; and little to no oxalate foods that are safe to eat. If you do opt for a high- or moderate-oxalate item, be sure to drink a glass of water before and after to help flush it out.

Please note that I found many inconsistencies when researching oxalate contents of various foods, so the attached chart may differ from your own research.

Medications

In addition to drinking plenty of fluids, watching your salt intake and eating a balanced diet of foods that are low in oxalate, thiazide diuretics can also help to prevent calcium stones from forming. Thiazide diuretics, also known as water pills, are medications that are typically used to treat high blood pressure (hypertension) and reduce fluid accumulation in the body. They work by reducing the ability of the kidneys to reabsorb salt and water from the urine and into the body, thereby increasing the production and output of urine (diuresis). They also lower the amount of calcium excreted in the urine. Side effects of thiazide diuretics are dose related and include:

- Dizziness and lightheadedness
- Blurred vision
- Loss of appetite
- Itching
- Stomach upset
- Headache
- Weakness

However, it's a catch-22 when it comes to this medication. On the one hand, thiazide reduces your fluid levels, but on the other hand, it causes you to lose potassium, which can reduce your citrate levels and can increase the risk for stones. Patients taking thiazide pills should also take potassium citrate to prevent this from happening, such as K-Lyte, Polycitra-K, or Urocit-K, but this is given only to patients who have normal urine calcium levels. With potassium citrate, most stones will not reoccur, but some patients cannot tolerate this medication because of its side effects, which include nausea, vomiting, diarrhea, and stomach pain. Taking it after meals will help prevent this from happening.

When it comes to preventing calcium kidney stones, the bottom line is this: Smart patients who don't want to end up with another kidney stone will follow these pretty easy, straight-forward guidelines—drink more water, eat better, and take their medication. Otherwise, I'll see you again.

HIGH-OXALATE FOODS & DRINKS TO AVOID

DRINKS

Black Tea	Frozen Lemonade	Prune juice	
Carrot Juice	made from concentrate	Rice Dream	
Chocolate Milk	Hot Chocolate	Soy Drinks	
Dark Beer	Instant Coffee	Tomato Juice	
	Ovaltine	V8	

VEGETABLES

Bamboo shoots	Dandelion greens	Okra	Potatoes
Beets	Eggplant	Olives	(baked, boiled, fried)
Beet greens	Escarole	Parsley	Red Kidney Beans
Beet root	Fava beans	Parsnip	Refried Beans
Carrots	Green beans	Peppers	Rhubarb
Celery	Kale	(chili and green)	Rutabaga
Chicory	Leeks	Pokeweed	Spinach
Collards	Navy beans		

FRUIT

Avocado	Dewberries	Lemon peel	Prunes
Blackberries	Elderberries	Lime peel	Raspberries
Blueberries	Figs	Oranges	Rhubarb
Carambola	Fruit cocktail	(& orange peel)	Strawberries
(star fruit)	Gooseberry	Pineapple	(canned variety)
Concord grapes	Grapefruit	(canned & dried varieties)	Tamarillo
Dates	Kiwis		Tangerines

BREAD & GRAINS

All-Purpose Flour	English Muffin	Rice bran	Wheat berries
Blueberry Muffin	(whole wheat variety)	Pancakes	Wheat bran
Brown Rice	French Toast	Cereal	Wheat germ
(cooked)	Grits	(bran or high fiber)	Whole Wheat Bread
Brown Rice Flour	Lasagna	Rice bran	Whole Wheat Flour
Cornmeal	Millet (cooked)	Rye bread	(whole grain)
Couscous	Miso	Soy flour	White Rice Flour
		Spaghetti	

Almonds
Buckwheat
Cashews
Peanuts
Pecans
Pistachios
Walnuts
Pumpkin Seeds
Sesame Seeds
(Tahini)
Sunflower Seeds
Nut butters

NUTS & SEEDS

Brownies
Cake
Candy bars with nuts
Chocolate chip cookies
Chocolate syrup or hot fudge
Pretzels
Potato Chips

DESSERTS & SNACKS

Soy cheese
Soy milk
Soy yogurt
Soy burger
Soy nuts
Tempeh
Tofu with magnesium or calcium

SOY

KEEP IT LOW FAT:

Low fat diets keep your stones at bay.

MODERATE-OXALATE FOODS & DRINKS TO LIMIT

You should limit these items to about two per day, which
have 2 to 10 mg of oxalate per serving.

DRINKS

Brewed coffee
Cranberry juice
Draft beer

Grape juice
Orange juice
Rosehip tea

VEGETABLES

Artichokes
Asparagus
Broccoli
Brussel sprouts
Carrots
(cooked and
canned varieties)

Corn
Fennel
Hot chili peppers
Lettuce
Lima beans
Mixed vegetables
Mustard greens

Onions
Peas
(canned variety)
Tomato
Turnips
Watercress

FRUIT

Apples
Applesauce
Apricots
Cherries (canned)
Coconut

Cranberries
Mandarin orange
Peaches
Pears
Pineapples

Plums
Prunes
Strawberries

**BREAD &
GRAINS**

Bagels
Biscuits
Bran muffins
Brown rice
English muffins
(multi-grain or
wheat varieties)

Oatmeal
Rye bread
Tortillas
(corn or flour)
White bread
Wheat bread

DAIRY

Yogurt

**DESSERTS
& SNACKS**

Cinnamon pop tart
Milk chocolate candy
Pie
Pudding pops
Sponge cake
Tortilla chips

MEAT

Liver
Sardines

LOW-OXALATE FOODS & DRINKS YOU CAN HAVE

Here's the good news—foods you can eat!

Low-oxalate foods have less than 2 mg of oxalate per serving.

DRINKS

Apple cider	Grapefruit juice	Lime juice
Apple juice	Green tea	Milk
Apricot nectar	Herbal tea	(fat free, 1%, 2% and whole)
Buttermilk	Lemonade	Pineapple juice
Cherry juice	Lemon juice	Powdered milk
	Limeade	Wine

DAIRY

Butter	Eggs
Cheese	Frozen yogurt
(American, Cheddar, Cottage, Low-fat and Mozzarella)	Ice cream
Cream cheese	Mayonnaise
Egg beaters	Salad dressing

BREAD & GRAINS

Barley malt flour	Corn bread	Oatmeal bread
Cereals	Corn flour	Oat bran bread/muffin
(corn or rice varieties)	Egg noodles	White rice
Cheerios	Hummus	Wild rice
Chicken noodle soup	Macaroni	

FRUIT

Bananas	Grapefruit	Melons	Pears
Blackberries	Grapes	Nectarines	(canned variety)
Blueberries	Huckleberries	Papaya	Plums
Cantaloupe	Kumquat	Peaches	Raisins
Cherries	Mangoes	(canned variety)	Watermelon

VEGETABLES

Alfalfa sprouts	Corn	Radish
Bok choy	Endive	Scallions
Cabbage	Green pepper	Sauerkraut
Cauliflower	Mushrooms	Yellow squash
Chives	Peas	Zucchini
Cucumber	Pickles	

continued on page 110

LOW-OXALATE FOODS & DRINKS YOU CAN HAVE

Here's the good news—foods you can eat!
Low-oxalate foods have less than 2 mg of oxalate per serving.

MEAT

Antelope	Chicken liver	Meatballs
Bacon	Corned beef	Moose
Beef	Ground beef	Pork
Bologna	Ham	Shellfish
Buffalo	Hot dogs	Turkey
Chicken	Lamb	Venison
Chicken dog	Liver	Wild game

FISH

Fish sticks (frozen)	Founder	Salmon
Alaskan King Crab	Halibut	Shrimp
Bluefish	Mackerel	Swordfish
Clams	Oysters	Tuna
Cod	Pollack	Whiting

DESSERTS & SNACKS

Chocolate pudding	Graham crackers	Rice cake
Crackers (Ritz, Saltines, Triscuits, Wheat Thins)	Hard candy	Rice crispy treat
	Jell-O	Rice pudding
Cream-filled snack cake	Oatmeal cookies	Sherbet
Custard	Popcorn	Tapioca pudding
Fruit roll-ups	Popsicle	Vanilla pudding

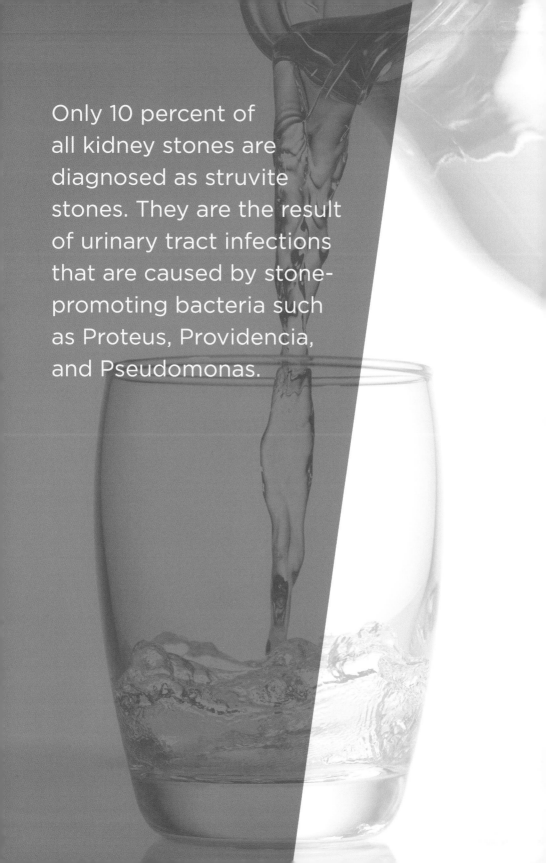

Only 10 percent of all kidney stones are diagnosed as struvite stones. They are the result of urinary tract infections that are caused by stone-promoting bacteria such as Proteus, Providencia, and Pseudomonas.

CHAPTER 10

PREVENTING STRUVITE STONES

If you have been diagnosed with a struvite kidney stone, you have the unfortunate circumstance of having a stone that can grow quickly and fill your entire kidney, carry bacteria through your system and even, in some cases, cause death. As a result, it is extremely important to learn how to prevent these stones from forming.

Only 10 percent of all kidney stones are diagnosed as struvite stones. As I mentioned in chapter four, they are the result of urinary tract infections that are caused by stone-promoting bacteria such as Proteus, Providencia, and Pseudomonas. These bacteria produce certain enzymes that raise the level of ammonia and pH in your urine. The higher these levels are, the more at risk you are for struvite stone crystals to form. To prevent this, you must first have the stones removed and then work to prevent the urinary tract infection from coming back.

You can actually have a urinary tract infection without having any symptoms, but most of the time, you will have at least a few indicators. For example, you might feel pressure or burning when you urinate or pressure in your abdomen. When you pee you might see that your urine is cloudy or has a strong urine smell. If the UTI is left untreated and the bacteria travels from the urinary tract to the kidneys it can cause a condition called pyelonephritis, which is a very serious kidney infection. The symptoms of pyelonephritis may include fever, nausea, vomiting, chills, and back pain.

Women are prone to urinary tract infections more than men because they have a shorter urethra than men. This gives bacteria a quicker route to the bladder. A UTI can also happen if bacteria moves from the anus to the vagina. Having sex can introduce bacteria into the urinary tract, too.

You are also at risk for a urinary tract infection if you:

- Have diabetes: People who have diabetes may have changes in their immune system which may make it easier for them to get UTIs.

- Have an enlarged prostate: An enlarged prostate can block the flow of urine, keep the toxins inside the urethra, and ultimately cause a UTI.

- Are an infant with an abnormality of the urinary tract.

- Have a long-term catheter or tube placed in your bladder.

CAUTION! Beware if you are pregnant. UTIs are more serious during pregnancy because the bacteria are more likely to travel to the kidneys. If you are pregnant and think you might have a UTI, consult with your gynecologist. A UTI can be treated successfully during pregnancy without causing kidney damage or damage to the fetus.

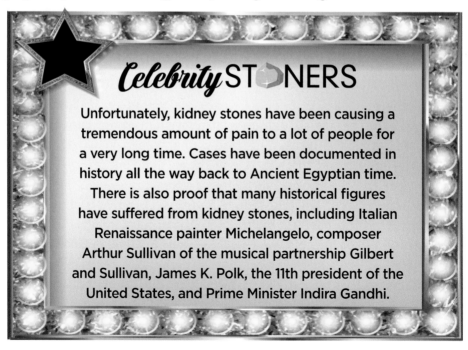

Celebrity ST◉NERS

Unfortunately, kidney stones have been causing a tremendous amount of pain to a lot of people for a very long time. Cases have been documented in history all the way back to Ancient Egyptian time. There is also proof that many historical figures have suffered from kidney stones, including Italian Renaissance painter Michelangelo, composer Arthur Sullivan of the musical partnership Gilbert and Sullivan, James K. Polk, the 11th president of the United States, and Prime Minister Indira Gandhi.

However, UTIs caused by problems like an enlarged prostate gland or a kidney stone can lead to kidney damage if the problem is not corrected and the infection continues.

Your Diet

If you are prone to urinary tract infections, there are a few steps you can take to reduce your risks of getting another one.

▶**DRINK PLENTY OF FLUIDS:** I cannot stress it enough that water helps to flush out the toxins in your urine and reduces the risk that bacteria will form. If you do not like to drink a lot of water, here are some ways to add more into your daily routine:

1 Ease into it: Start by adding one glass of water into your daily routine every day for a week. You can also replace one of your other beverages with just one glass of water. Then, the next week, drink two glasses of water every day for a week and repeat this routine until you are drinking at least six eight-ounce glasses of water every day.

2 Find a routine: Perhaps you prefer to have a glass of water in the morning, but not with meals or you prefer your cup of Joe in the morning and your water in the afternoon. Find a routine that works for you and stick to it.

3 Carry it with you: When you are thirsty and do not have water with you, you may be tempted to buy your favorite soda or coffee. Instead, be prepared wherever you go by filling up a reusable bottle or thermos so you will have it with you at all times.

4 Spice it up: Water doesn't have to be bland, especially with today's flavored waters and enhancers. You can also add fruit and vegetables, such as lemon, cucumber, or some other natural flavors to the glass. Try to make it different every time you drink it.

5 Eat it: Yes, eat it. There are fruits and vegetables that have a higher water content than others and can help you to stay hydrated.

FOODS TO HELP YOU STAY HYDRATED

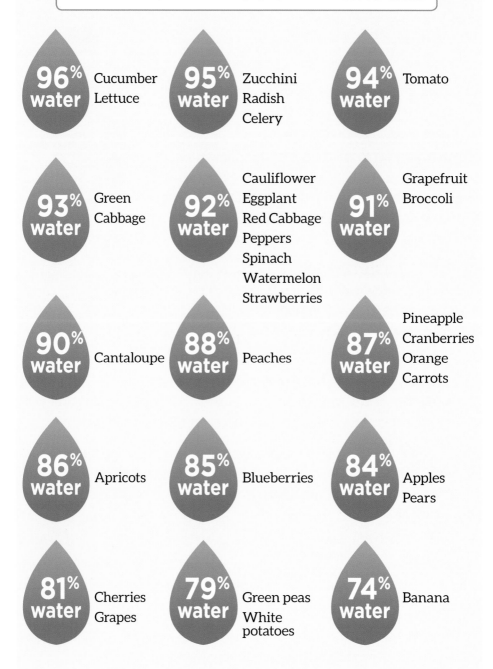

96% water — Cucumber, Lettuce

95% water — Zucchini, Radish, Celery

94% water — Tomato

93% water — Green Cabbage

92% water — Cauliflower, Eggplant, Red Cabbage, Peppers, Spinach, Watermelon, Strawberries

91% water — Grapefruit, Broccoli

90% water — Cantaloupe

88% water — Peaches

87% water — Pineapple, Cranberries, Orange, Carrots

86% water — Apricots

85% water — Blueberries

84% water — Apples, Pears

81% water — Cherries, Grapes

79% water — Green peas, White potatoes

74% water — Banana

When you gotta go, GO!

Do not hold your urine for lengthy periods of time. When the urge hits that you have to pee, go do it. Holding back your urine because you are too busy to stop and tinkle keeps the toxins in your system for a longer amount of time than it should. As a result, this is the perfect atmosphere for the creation of kidney stones. And, no matter how tired you are, make sure to empty your bladder before climbing into bed at night.

▶**WIPE RIGHT:** The correct way to wipe after urinating is from front to back, not back to front. This prevents the bacteria from getting into the urinary tract.

▶**CLEAN YOUR GENITALS EVERY DAY:** You might be surprised, but this is something I have to remind patients to do. Please do it.

If you research the internet for information on struvite stones, you may find that some doctors recommend washing the urinary tract with a solution of organic acids, in order to make the urine more acidic. This has been recommended if the patient has not responded to other medications. I do not recommend this because it does not work.

▶**URINATE AFTER SEX:** After you have had intercourse, make sure you head straight to the bathroom and pee, especially if you are a woman and are having unprotected sex. Urinating helps remove the bacteria that can get into your system from having sex.

If you have already been diagnosed with struvite stones and have a UTI, the proper course of treatment is to first get rid of the stone and then treat any infection. To make sure this doesn't happen again, you need to prevent future UTIs.

SIDE NOTE: I would also advise that when you are going to the urologist's office, clean yourself and change your underwear. Some patients, especially the older ones, come to me without having changed their underwear for days. I can tell!

Medications

If you have already had struvite stones, you may be placed on ongoing rounds of antibiotics to make sure there isn't any bacteria building in the urine. Some are taken every day as prophylaxis. Acetohydroxamic acid (also known as Lithostat) can be used in combination with antibiotics to also reverse bacterial growth. It blocks the enzymes that bacteria release, and has been effective in preventing stones. This drug is only for patients with healthy kidneys and is not to be used by pregnant women. It is not commonly prescribed unless other treatments have failed.

The side effects of Acetohydroxamic acid include:

- Anemia (low iron levels)
- Nausea
- Vomiting
- Depression
- Anxiety
- Rash
- Persistent headache
- Small blood clots in the legs

After treatment, careful follow-up and urine testing is extremely important. A high-pH urine indicates low acidity and an increased risk of infection.

While it is very rare for kidney stones to cause kidney failure, these stones can completely form inside the kidney and destroy it. If left untreated, it can lead to chronic infections and may result in death, so prevention is vitally important.

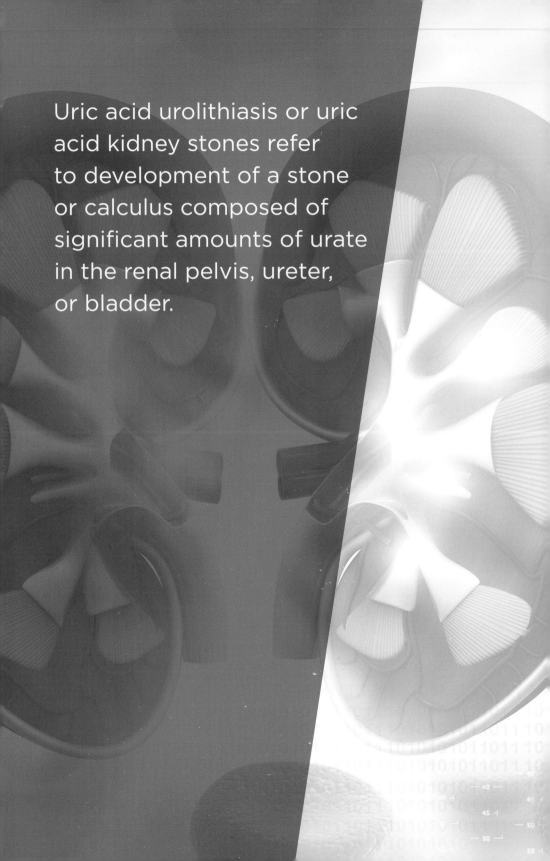

Uric acid urolithiasis or uric acid kidney stones refer to development of a stone or calculus composed of significant amounts of urate in the renal pelvis, ureter, or bladder.

CHAPTER 11

PREVENTING URIC ACID STONES

Simply put, if you have been diagnosed with a uric acid stone, it means that your urine is too acidic.

Uric acid is the breakdown of any form of purine. Foods with high purine content include beef, chicken, fish and beans. So the prevention of uric acid stones is simple – you need to reduce the amount of purine you take in.

And, I've mentioned it before, but it's worth mentioning again. If you are following one of those popular high-protein diets or downing protein shakes to meet your protein requirements or add muscle to your body, you are at an increased risk of getting a uric acid kidney stone.

This also goes for some protein supplements that contain purine because the high protein leads to an increase in acid. This results in a low urine pH and therefore a risk of uric acid stones.

Every day, Americans assault their bodies with a huge amount of protein that the body can't handle and, as a result, it can lead to excess uric acid buildup, which can lead to stones.

Your Diet

The ideal size of a protein serving is the size of your fist. If you want to have protein in your diet, it's best to have several smaller helpings versus one huge serving. So, if you're headed out to eat, don't go to a steakhouse and inhale a huge ribeye or go to the deli and chow down on a corned beef and pastrami sandwich (which comes with enough meat to feed an entire family). This is not a good idea.

You want to have small portions of protein throughout the day.

Do not fall into the trap of eating too many carbs as a replacement for protein. You will ultimately gain weight. It's not always easy to find the balance, especially if you love protein-based foods, but in the long run a low-protein diet is better for you than being doubled over in kidney stone pain. Vegetable or plant proteins are low-value proteins. Examples of low-value proteins are: bread, cereals, dried beans, nuts, rice, pasta or noodles, and vegetables.

The National Kidney Foundation offers these low-protein suggestions:

- Fill up sandwiches with lettuce, alfalfa sprouts, cucumber, chopped celery, apple, parsley, or water chestnuts.

- Use meats that are sliced very thin, which can be spread out to look like a larger portion.

- Choose bread that is thickly sliced and consider more flavorful breads, such as sour dough or rye bread.

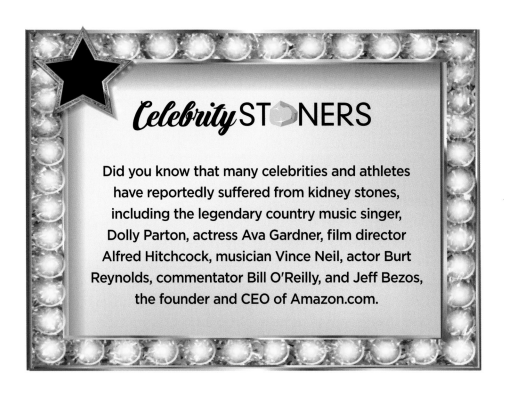

Celebrity STONERS

Did you know that many celebrities and athletes have reportedly suffered from kidney stones, including the legendary country music singer, Dolly Parton, actress Ava Gardner, film director Alfred Hitchcock, musician Vince Neil, actor Burt Reynolds, commentator Bill O'Reilly, and Jeff Bezos, the founder and CEO of Amazon.com.

Soups

- Choose lower-protein foods, such as rice and pasta to add to a soup without adding much protein.

- Use milk substitutes that are low in protein when making cream soups.

Main Dishes

- Use vegetables and grains as the main dish and meats or other high-value protein as the side dish.

- Try kebabs, using smaller pieces of meat and more vegetables or fruits.

- Prepare dishes with small pieces of meat or chicken mixed in with rice or pasta. Fried rice dishes or ground meat with pasta work well.

- Toss together a chef salad with lettuce and crisp vegetables, adding smaller strips of meat and egg.

- For casseroles, use smaller amounts of meat than the recipe calls for and increase the starch (rice or pasta). Also use low-sodium soups in all casserole recipes.

- Allow yourself extra portions or larger servings of bread, rolls, pasta and rice to help meet your calorie needs without increasing your protein intake by very much.

- For a stronger cheese taste with a smaller amount of cheese, buy sharp cheddar, Parmesan, or Romano cheese. A little bit of these cheeses will go a long way.

Calorie Boosters for Low-Protein Diets

It is always important to stay at your healthiest weight for your body size, but when you are eating less protein, you may also take in fewer calories. This may cause you to lose weight. To keep from losing too much weight, you can "make up" some of the calories lost when cutting down on protein by eating foods with higher calories.

Heart-healthy fats include mayonnaise-type salad dressings, canola oil, olive oil, corn oil, safflower oil, soybean oil, and sunflower oil. These can be used in large amounts to fry or season foods.

Candies such as hard candies, gumdrops, jellybeans, chewy fruit flavored candies, and marshmallows can be used as desserts or snacks. Sweeteners such as honey, jams or jellies, and white sugar can be added to foods or drinks to increase calories. (Please consult your dietitian if you are diabetic.)

The pH Numbers Game

Preventing uric acid stones from developing is also a pH numbers game. You have to keep your urine pH level greater than 6.5. Medications can help you to do that, including sodium bicarbonate, which is otherwise known as baking soda.

Sodium Bicarbonate

Sodium bicarbonate comes as a tablet and powder to take by mouth. It's taken one to four times a day, depending on the reason you take it. Take sodium bicarbonate exactly as directed. You can dissolve sodium bicarbonate powder in at least 4 ounces (120 milliliters) of water. Measure powdered doses carefully and do not take more than prescribed by a doctor. It's important to not use sodium bicarbonate for longer than two weeks unless your doctor tells you to. If sodium bicarbonate does not improve the level of pH in your urine, call your doctor.

Whatever you do, to not open a box of Arm & Hammer and try to self-medicate. There are side effects to taking sodium bicarbonate, so tell your doctor if any of these symptoms are severe or do not go away:

- Increased thirst
- Stomach cramps
- Gas

If you have any of the following symptoms, stop taking sodium bicarbonate right away and call your doctor immediately:

- Severe headache
- Nausea
- Vomit that resembles coffee grounds
- Loss of appetite
- Irritability
- Weakness
- Frequent urge to urinate
- Slow breathing
- Swelling of feet or lower legs
- Bloody, black, or tarry stools
- Blood in your urine

The general idea is that you should raise your urine pH to help dissolve your stones in the short term. However, you can end up raising your urine pH too much. Risk begins when pH is 6.5. Once pH is 7.0 there is very little benefit to raising pH higher, and calcium phosphate stone risk will increase as pH goes from 7 to 7.5. It's important to monitor your pH level at home with special urine pH test strips. Do this consistently for several weeks. If you are a good patient and follow the guidelines, you can avoid a

potential surgical procedure or you can reduce a large stone enough to turn an invasive procedure, like a percutaneous procedure, into a utereroscopy.

A more palatable way of increasing your pH and citrate levels is to drink Crystal Light lemonade because it has a fair amount of citrate in it. But don't overdo it.

One beverage to avoid is carbonated water as it also has carbonic acid. It's all about balance and other things you're taking in.

You want to avoid a program where your pH is raised all the time. That would be difficult on your body, which is always trying to get an acid base balance and sometimes it needs to secrete acid. In the short term, it's fine, but in the long term you need to focus on lifestyle changes.

At this point it's hard to tell you how much to drink and for how long to keep your pH levels up. Every patient is different so that will be determined by your doctor.

Dalmatians and Kidney Stones

According to the Dalmatian Club of America, Dalmatians form urinary stones. They write, "Dalmatians, humans and apes are unique for the way in which they metabolize 'purine-yielding foods." Not every human will form urinary stones and neither will every Dalmatian. The amount of dietary protein may contribute to the problem but, more importantly, the type of protein can be more damaging. For many Dalmatians, diets containing high amounts of purine – yielding foods should be avoided. Certain foods such as liver and other organ meats are very high as purine – yielders; other foods like eggs and most vegetables and fruit are acceptably low as purine – yielders.

When some humans ingest foods high in purines, they develop gout or kidney stones. When some Dalmatians ingest those foods, they develop urinary stones and in particular those known as "purine" or "urate" stones. Dog foods containing high amounts of meat, beef and meat- or beef-"by-products" should be carefully evaluated for Dalmatians as well as other formulations creating an abnormally high acidic urine.

Of all stone-forming Dalmatians, the vast majority form urate stones but a few may form other types. Treatment can be the exact opposite for each type of stone so your veterinarian will run tests in order to prescribe the most effective treatment. Also, feeding most types of table scraps to dogs is perhaps one of the worst disservices to their good health, especially to Dalmatians.

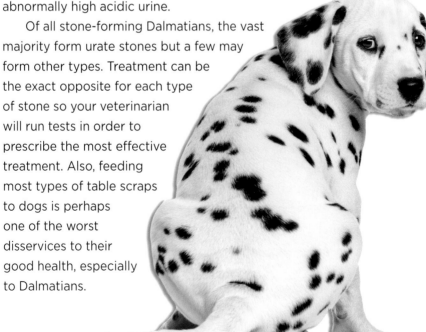

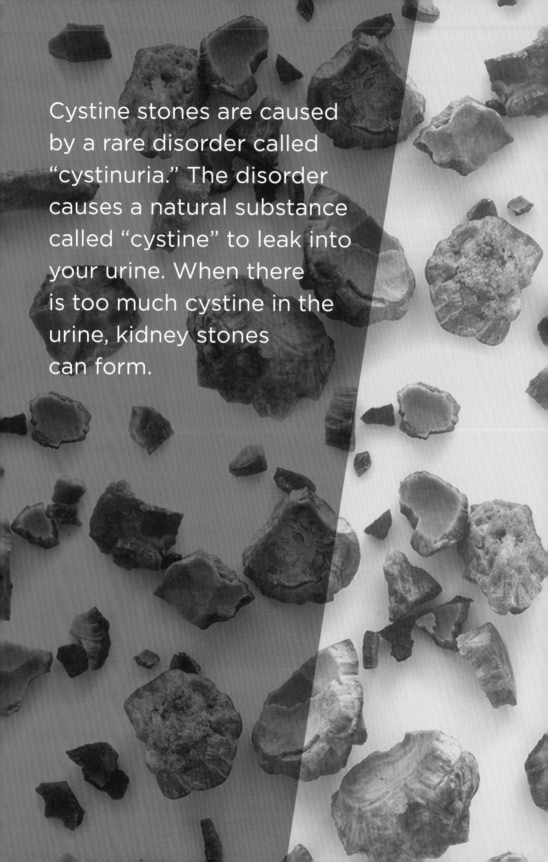

Cystine stones are caused by a rare disorder called "cystinuria." The disorder causes a natural substance called "cystine" to leak into your urine. When there is too much cystine in the urine, kidney stones can form.

CHAPTER 12

PREVENTING CYSTINE STONES

As we mentioned in chapter five, cystine stones are very rare forms of kidney stones and are due to a defect in your body's transport of amino acids. To be diagnosed with cystine stones, you need to carry the gene for cystinuria. Unfortunately, if you do, there is only one thing you can do to try and prevent these stones from forming and that's to drink a large amount of fluids. However, even that is no guarantee that it will stop these stones. Cystine stones are very difficult to treat, and you may want to see a sub-specialist, if you form these types of stones, as they are rare.

Your Diet

Cystine stone patients must avoid diuretics such as tea, coffee, and alcohol that can make the urine more acidic.

While many patients who suffer from cystine stones swear that water is the only thing they drink, others say it doesn't matter as long as you are drinking a lot of acidic drinks, such as orange juice, which can also raise pH levels. Crystal Light may also raise pH, although this hasn't yet been proven. Regardless, no beverage will be as effective as potassium citrate pills.

Methionine

In addition to drinking a tremendous amount of fluid, there has been some indication that reducing the amount of methionine in your diet may help cystine stone patients. Methionine is the amino acid that produces cystine and it can be found in animal protein, such as meat, limited milk, yogurt, cheese, and other dairy. Therefore, you should eliminate eggs and fish, and opt for a diet filled with green veggies, beans, and nuts. There is no guarantee that this diet will help, but it is worth a try.

Raise Your pH

Cystine kidney stones are more likely to form in low pH urine. You can significantly reduce your risk by keeping your urine pH levels up to a level of 7.5 to 8.0. There are products such as Urocit-K, Polycitra, sodium citrate, potassium citrate, and sodium bicarbonate that help increase your urine's pH. You can check urine pH levels with special strips that you can get from your urologist or purchase at a drugstore and use at home.

Medication

Tiopronin

There are medications to help prevent the formation of cystine stones, including Tiopronin (Thiola) and Penicillamine. You should not take Tiopronin if you are pregnant or plan to become pregnant or have a history of blood disorders, including aplastic anemia, agranulocytosis, or thrombocytopenia (this medication can cause these disorders too).

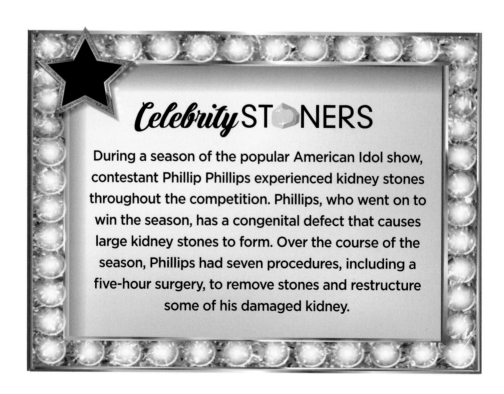

Celebrity STONERS

During a season of the popular American Idol show, contestant Phillip Phillips experienced kidney stones throughout the competition. Phillips, who went on to win the season, has a congenital defect that causes large kidney stones to form. Over the course of the season, Phillips had seven procedures, including a five-hour surgery, to remove stones and restructure some of his damaged kidney.

You must be monitored while you are on this medication because of the potential side effects, which may include:

- An itchy rash
- Drug hypersensitivity that includes fever, joint pain, and swollen lymph nodes
- Decreased sense of smell
- Nausea
- Vomiting
- Diarrhea or soft stools
- Loss of appetite
- Abdominal pain
- Bloating
- Gas
- Sore throat
- Mouth sores
- Hives
- Warts
- Swelling of the throat
- Difficulty breathing
- Shortness of breath
- Fatigue or weakness
- Muscle or joint pain
- Swelling in your legs
- Fluid build-up in the lungs
- Lung or kidney problems
- Blood or high amounts of protein in urine

- Patients also report wrinkling or thin, fragile skin during long-term treatment

Seek immediate attention if you have a fever, sore throat, chills, bleeding, easy bruising, coughing up blood, muscle weakness, blistering or raw areas on the skin or mucous membranes, joint pain, swelling of the lymph nodes, or swelling in your legs.

Penicillamine (Cuprimine, Depen)

Penicillamine is commonly used to treat people with rheumatoid arthritis. But it can also help prevent cysteine stones. That's because Penicillamine binds to cysteine, which decreases the urinary excretion of cysteine. Side effects include:

- Itching or a rash
- Nausea, vomiting and diarrhea
- Poor appetite
- Ear ringing
- Difficulty tasting food or beverages
- Mouth sores
- Wounds that won't heal correctly
- Skin wrinkling

Captopril (Capoten)

Although rarely prescribed, Captopril is another medication that is used to bind to cystine and keeps it from forming stones, but like every medication it also comes with side effects, which include dry cough and headache. Captopril may also interact with other medicines such as nonsteroidal anti-inflammatory drugs (NSAIDs), antacids, potassium supplements, certain diuretics, and lithium. Be sure your doctor knows about all prescription and over-the-counter medicines and dietary supplements you are taking. Do not use this medicine if you are pregnant, breastfeeding, or planning to get pregnant. If you need to use this medicine, talk to your doctor about how you can prevent pregnancy.

Call 911 or other emergency services right away if you have trouble breathing, hives, or swelling of your face, lips, tongue, or throat. Call your doctor if you have:

- Irregular heartbeats (this could be caused by too much potassium in your blood)
- Dizziness or lightheadedness or fainting

Follow Up

When you are taking these medications, make sure to follow up with your doctor who will check your potassium levels and kidneys to make sure they are functioning properly.

For more information on Cystinuria and cystine stones, visit the Rare Kidney Stone Consortium at www.rarekidneystones.org. It is an organization with international collaboration focused upon research and education aimed at improving care.

Fraudulent health products are not always easy to spot. If you're tempted to buy an unproven product or one with questionable claims, check with your doctor or other healthcare professional first.

CHAPTER 13

LIVING WITH STONES

Whether you have passed one kidney stone or multiple kidney stones, your entire life has changed. From this point on, you will always wonder if that little twinge you feel is the onset of your next stone.

Deciphering Truth from Quackery

Coping with the aches and pains of any medical condition, but especially kidney stones is a struggle. On some days, you may find that you are able to manage the discomfort, inflammation and, depending on the severity of the stone, the lack of mobility. On other days, it might seem overwhelming. You may feel so desperate for an immediate solution or a cure for the pain that you'll try anything, but how do you distinguish between the hype and the helpful? After all, some truly useful medical therapies do come from outside of mainstream medicine.

Advertisements for miracle medical cures typically claim that you can eliminate the pain of stones by eating this or drinking that. Some ads tout:

"THIS is a leading natural product that targets kidney stones by featuring a proprietary formula that has been carefully researched and developed with the highest quality ingredients."

They will say things like:
"THIS is the PREFERRED choice among those who suffer from kidney stones. Thousands of people have successfully used this product!"

The offer to cure your kidney stones sounds so good that all you need to do is mail a check to receive your first shipment of a "cure-all" medication or a device that will melt your pains away. Your body aches and, with desperation setting in, you mail your check immediately.

Unfortunately, you may have just put your health at risk. These self-proclaimed cure-alls are anything but, and many of these products that allege to be breakthroughs are unproven, and possibly dangerous, remedies. If you have already fallen for one of these deceptive cures, do not feel foolish. Many smart, educated consumers are lured into buying these products because of suggestive wording.

The U.S. Food and Drug Administration estimates that more than 40 million Americans use a fraudulent health product each year. Billions have been spent on quack products or treatments.

So-called miracle cures are far more likely to:

- Waste your money.
- Cost you time from getting early, professional treatment.
- Cause side effects.
- Endanger your life.

There are proven treatments that can help alleviate your kidney stone symptoms, but your health is in your

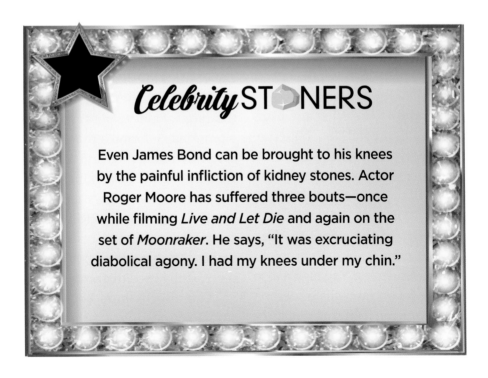

Celebrity STONERS

Even James Bond can be brought to his knees by the painful infliction of kidney stones. Actor Roger Moore has suffered three bouts—once while filming *Live and Let Die* and again on the set of *Moonraker*. He says, "It was excruciating diabolical agony. I had my knees under my chin."

own hands. Do not try anything to ease the pain. Learn fact from fiction when it comes to treating your body so you have the confidence to make the right decisions that protect both your wallet and your health.

Tip-Offs and Rip-Offs

The Food and Drug Administration (www.fda.gov) offers some tip-offs to help you identify rip-offs of medical products:

One product does it all. Be suspicious of products that claim to cure a wide range of diseases. A New York firm claimed its products marketed as dietary supplements could treat or cure senile dementia, brain atrophy, atherosclerosis, kidney dysfunction, gangrene, depression, osteoarthritis, dysuria, and lung, cervical, and prostate cancer. In October 2012, at the FDA's request, U.S. marshals seized these products.

Personal testimonials. Success stories, such as, "It cured my diabetes," or "My tumors are gone," are easy to make up and are not a substitute for scientific evidence.

Quick fixes. Few diseases or conditions can be treated quickly, even with legitimate products. Beware of language such as, "Lose 30 pounds in 30 days," or "eliminates skin cancer in days."

"All natural." Some plants found in nature (such as poisonous mushrooms) can kill when consumed. Moreover, the FDA has found numerous products promoted as "all natural" contain hidden and dangerously high doses of prescription drug ingredients or even untested active artificial ingredients.

"Miracle cure." Alarms should go off when you see this claim or others like it such as, "new discovery," "scientific breakthrough," or "secret ingredient." If a real cure for a serious disease were discovered, it would be widely reported through the media and prescribed by health professionals—not buried in print ads, TV infomercials, or on Internet sites.

Conspiracy theories. Claims like, "The pharmaceutical industry and the government are working together to hide information about a miracle cure," are always untrue and unfounded. These statements are used to distract consumers from the obvious, common-sense questions about the so-called miracle cure.

Even with these tips, fraudulent health products are not always easy to spot. If you're tempted to buy an unproven product or one with questionable claims, check with your doctor or other healthcare professional first.

TRAVELING with STONES

It is hard to say this, but if you suffer from regular kidney stone attacks, the last thing you want is to do is put yourself in any situation where you either end up in the emergency room or cannot get the help you need. Traveling is a wonderful thing, but just imagine what will happen if you're on a remote island in the Caribbean and have an attack? Or you're on safari in Africa and you start feeling that all-too-familiar pain down your side? How will you get help or get to the hospital for treatment? Think ahead before you book any exotic trips and have a plan of action just in case.

At the same time what do you do if you're in the car, driving across the country and you are in crippling pain? The best course of action is to call 911 and have them take you to the nearest hospital. Your kidney stone symptoms can't tell you whether you have a 1mm stone or a 7mm stone. You must get evaluated. Odds are that if it is a 7mm stone, you are not going to pass it.

Consumers can also subscribe to the FDA RSS feed that will send information on fraudulent products to your smart phone or computer and help you from being duped or hurt by these products.

Keeping track of what's helpful and what's hype is tricky. One thing to remember is that the FDA approval is not the only criterion to go by. Of course, your doctor should be your main go-to when deciding what medications and products to use. All the FDA approval means is that the substance has been tested in a laboratory, but many folk remedies aren't tested.

Folk Remedies

Folk medicine consists of typically homemade remedies, sometimes herbal in nature and often based on superstition. All share the characteristic of being derived from folk, rather than Western scientific, tradition.

Apple cider vinegar is one common example of a folk remedy that has been extolled as a solution for just about everything over the years, including a solution for kidney stones. Those snake oil salesman tell you to combine it with baking soda, lemon juice, olive oil or water. Unfortunately, these and other folk remedies have claimed to cure kidney stones or eliminate the pain, but they do not.

Online Medical Information

You probably obtain your medical information from your doctor, friends and family, medical reference books, and maybe newspaper and magazine articles. Of course, today most people have turned to the internet as a source of medical information. However, just because the internet is a wealth of information does not mean it makes the most accurate or reliable source of information. Be careful what you're reading. In general, watch for biased information on some dot-com websites. You may find more reliable, up-to-date information on dot-gov websites. There is also a list of websites I recommend on various topics in the Resources section at the end of the book.

Finding Support

Online Support

And, when you are smack in the middle of an attack, you'll likely wonder how you will handle work, take care of the kids, eat, and other simple tasks when you are in so much pain and you can't even get off the couch. Add nausea to the mix, and it's simply overwhelming. Not to mention how impossible commuting and traveling are when all you want to know is where the nearest bathroom is.

You're not alone. Remember there are millions of Americans who have been in your shoes and know exactly how you feel. A simple internet search and you will find other kidney stoners with stories similar to yours. The Urology Care Foundation website is a good source of information

For example, one woman writes about her husband's experiences: "He's had them at least three times, twice since we've been married. The first time, the doctors determined that the stones were too large to pass naturally, so they (the stones, not the doctors) were pulverized via ultrasound. The most recent time was this summer, in the midst of a whole boat load of other stuff going on. I was on my way home from seeing my daughter in a New York hospital when he called me on my cell phone to tell me he was in our local hospital. The pain was so excruciating that he went to the ER to get painkillers; the routine ones we had around the house were ineffective. This is a guy that almost never takes an aspirin or an Advil. Of course, you can't just walk into an ER and say, 'Gimme some Percocet!' When I got there, he was white as a sheet and all but crying out with the pain, which he said was constant and unremitting.

Career CHOICE

When it comes to work, if you are a chronic stone former, there are some occupations to stay away from because they are not conducive to your condition. Remember the school bus driver who was stuck on the bus for hours at a time and couldn't drink enough water to keep his stones at bay? Or the microchip processor who had to go through a decontamination process? She couldn't take the suit off every half hour to urinate, so she didn't drink enough of water. Odds are, she was bound to have more stones, so consider your profession if you suffer from stones.

I can tell you that you're not likely going to be a commercial airline pilot or an astronaut or someone who travels a lot. The FAA now requires that pilots who suffer from kidney stones be examined by their physician and certified by an Aviation Medical Examiner to issue a medical certificate for kidney stones. Pilots need to provide to the aviation medical examiner the worksheet completed by their treating physician. If they do not meet the criteria, they cannot fly.

But the ER folks, of course, have to first take care of those who were in actual danger of dying before those who just feel like it.

"He eventually got his pain meds, and a scan for diagnostic purposes, and later a visit to his urologist, which yielded more pain pills and some med that was supposed to either help the stones dissolve or relax the passageways so that they could pass. These stones were not of the size that would benefit from ultrasound, so he just had to wait it out. When the pain was bad, all he could do was take the strong pain meds and sack out on the couch. It was weeks before the thing(s) eventually left him. I thought his suffering was far, far worse than anything I had ever experienced, including childbirth."

You can find forums online for you to communicate with others, as well as resources and suggestions on how to live with kidney stones.

Here's a lighter view on the topic from another online support group.

"The first time was very scary.

I was walking from my bedroom to the kitchen for a drink. Suddenly this unbelievably excruciating pain dropped me to the ground.

My thoughts were as follows:

'Oh my god, I am having a heart attack! No wait, this is my heart, wrong area. I think one of my kidneys is failing, damn, damn, damn!

I called for help. I finally got my fiancé to awake and she called 911.

I remember being in the ER for hours. Banging on the wall somehow made me feel better. I was admitted, stuck with an IV, and stuck in the hospital for several days. I eventually went home and passed the stone with the help of a lot of water, a few beers and a love making session.'

Online you will also find that patients share tips on pain relief and how they deal with the unbearable symptoms. Some patients swear by only using medications while others say a heating pad and a walk can lessen the pain. In these groups you can complain, vent, or look for suggestions on doctors, treatments, and recipes.

Support System

It is very important that you develop your own support system for when you have an attack. If you have children or a loved one who depends on you, you will need a backup plan when you are laid up. Know who you are going to call to pick up your children, cook dinner for them and get your medications (you might be unable to drive). Make sure that you have all of this ironed out long before you feel the slightest twinge of a kidney stone pain.

Do not try to do things alone when you are not feeling well. Instead, rely on loved ones who want to help. For example, they can rub your back or press their hand or fist firmly into the painful kidney to help alleviate the pain. They can get you a pillow to put under your pelvis. They can also drive you to the hospital if you can't take the pain anymore. This will also give your loved one a sense of being useful when they see you are hurting Though you are experiencing extraordinary pain, your family and friends are experiencing the pain of not being able to do anything to help you.

Support Groups

Patients have a tendency to suffer from depression due to the severity of this condition caused by the significant amount of pain and disruption to everyday life. There are doctors' appointments, x-rays, and possible hospital stays and treatments—not to mention the amount of time spent in the bathroom because of the water they drink to keep their stones at bay. Rest assured there are support groups available.

Depending on your circumstances and personality, it may be beneficial to turn to others for help. You may feel less alone with your illness when talking with others who face or have faced similar challenges. There are online and in person support groups for you to attend.

In-person support groups are a community of patients, family members and friends who meet on a regular basis to share stories, advice and, emotional support. Check with your urologist or your local hospital to find support groups that meet in your area.

If a face-to-face support group is not for you, you may want to try one of the many online support groups. Here you can chat with people who have the same condition, but in the privacy and comfort of your own home. You can find a list of online support groups that may be right for you in the Resources section at the end of this book.

In addition to support groups, there are a variety of books and online resources that you can turn to for additional information. We made a list of some of them in the resources chapter, but you may find others by conducting your own internet search.

Hopefully, by following the guidelines in this book and your doctor's advice and reaching out to support groups for more information, you will never have another attack again.

RESOURCES

AIDS
The mission of AIDS.ORG is to help prevent HIV infections and to improve the lives of those affected by HIV and AIDS by providing education and facilitating the free and open exchange of knowledge at an easy-to-find centralized website.
www.aids.org

Cystinuria
The International Cystinuria Foundation aims to support a growing and strong group of patients, families, professionals, and friends by providing educational and health related resources to affected individuals worldwide. It also aims to promote knowledge of cystinuria within the research and medical communities in order to reduce kidney destruction, renal impairment, and subsequent health, vocational, and economic impact.
www.cystinuria.org

Incontinence
The National Association for Continence (NADC) is a national, private, non-profit organization dedicated to improving the quality of life of people with incontinence, voiding dysfunction, and related pelvic floor disorders. NAFC's purpose is to be the leading source for public education and advocacy about the causes, prevention, diagnosis, treatments, and management alternatives for incontinence.
www.nafc.org

The mission of the Simon Foundation for Continence is to: "Bring the topic of incontinence out into the open, remove the stigma surrounding incontinence, and provide help and hope to people with incontinence, their families and the health professionals who provide their care."
www.simonfoundation.org

Interstitial Cystitis
The Interstitial Cystitis Association (ICA) advocates for research dedicated to discovery of a cure and better treatments, raises awareness, and serves as a central hub for the healthcare providers, researchers and millions of patients who suffer with constant urinary urgency and frequency and extreme bladder pain called IC, or interstitial cystitis.
www.ichelp.org

The Interstitial Cystitis Network

The Interstitial Cystitis Network is a woman-owned, "social advocacy" health education company dedicated to interstitial cystitis, overactive bladder and other pelvic pain disorders. It provides critical 24/7 support to patients in need, develops new educational materials, conducts vital research, provides webinars and lectures, and creates Interstitial Cystitis awareness campaigns, all at NO COST to the patients who visit the website.

www.ic-network.com

The Cystitis and Overactive Bladder

The Cystitis and Overactive Bladder (COB) Foundation gives support to people with all forms of cystitis, overactive bladder and continence issues together with their families and friends. UK-based.

www.cobfoundation.org

Kidney Cancer

The Kidney Cancer Association (KCA) is a charitable organization made up of patients, family members, physicians, researchers, and other health professionals globally. It is the world's first international charity dedicated specifically to the eradication of death and suffering from renal cancers.

www.kidneycancer.org

Kidney Disease

The National Kidney Foundation is the leading organization in the U.S. dedicated to the awareness, prevention and treatment of kidney disease for hundreds of thousands of healthcare professionals, millions of patients and their families, and tens of millions of Americans at risk.

www.kidney.org

The American Association of Kidney Patients

The American Association of Kidney Patients (AAKP) has been the patient voice – advocating for improved access to high-quality health care through regulatory and legislative reform at the federal level. AAKP is leading the effort to bring kidney patients together to promote community, conversations and to seek out services that help maximize patients' everyday lives.

www.aakp.org

Primary Hyperoxaluria, Oxalosis

The Oxalosis and Hyperoxaluria Foundation (OHF) is the leading organization in the world dedicated to the awareness, understanding and treatment of Primary Hyperoxaluria, Oxalosis and related Hyperoxaluria Kidney Stone Conditions for thousands of healthcare professionals, patients and their families. OHF aims to share our knowledge so that everyone – patients, medical professionals, government officials, the general public and industry has accurate information about the advances in our disease.

www.ohf.org

Prostate

The Prostatitis Foundation aims to educate the public about the prevalence of prostatitis and encourage and support research to find the cause and a cure for prostatitis.
www.prostatitis.org

The Prostate Cancer Foundation

The Prostate Cancer Foundation (PCF) is firmly committed to curing prostate cancer and is the leading philanthropic organization funding and accelerating research globally. For the men and their families fighting prostate cancer globally, PCF is a primary source for new standard-of-care and research information.
www.pcf.org

The Prostate Cancer Research Institute

The Prostate Cancer Research Institute is a charitable not-for-profit organization whose mission is to improve the quality of men's lives by supporting research and disseminating information that educates and empowers patients, families, and the medical community.
www.pcri.org

The Center for Prostate Disease Research

The Center for Prostate Disease Research conducts basic science and clinical research programs that strive to combat diseases of the prostate.
www.cpdr.org

The Prostate Health Education Network

The Prostate Health Education Network (PHEN), Inc. is a non-profit organization that was founded in 2003 by Thomas A. Farrington, a prostate cancer survivor and author of the books, "Battling the Killer Within," and "Battling The Killer Within And Winning," PHEN is governed by a board of directors, and works with advisory boards, sponsors, partners and volunteers to implement its programs and initiatives.
www.prostatehealthed.org

Prostate Conditions Education Council

Prostate Conditions Education Council (PCEC) is a national organization committed to men's health and is the nation's leading resource for information on prostate health. The PCEC is dedicated to saving lives through awareness and the education of men, the women in their lives, as well as the medical community about prostate cancer prevalence, the importance of early detection, and available treatment options, as well as other men's health issues.
www.prostateconditions.org

Rare Kidney Stones

The Rare Kidney Stone Consortium facilitates cooperative exchange of information and resources among investigators, clinicians, and patients, and researchers in order to improve care and outcomes for patients with rare stone diseases. The consortium promotes ready availability of diagnostic testing, pooling of clinical experiences, and availability of tissue banks in order to advance the science. Our goals are to:

- Establish and expand registries and collaborate with patient organizations for the rapid dissemination of knowledge

- Stimulate generation of testable hypotheses regarding mechanisms of renal injury in these diseases through registry findings, tissue resources, and pilot projects

- Develop cohorts of well-characterized patients for future clinical studies

- Attract and train investigators to rare diseases research in nephrology

www.rarekidneystones.org

Sexually Transmitted Disease
American Sexually Transmitted Diseases Association is an organization devoted to the control and study of sexually transmitted diseases. Its objectives are: to support the control, prevention and ultimate eradication of STD; to support research in all aspects of STD, including medical, epidemiologic, laboratory, social and behavioral studies; to recognize outstanding contributions in STD control and prevention; and to disseminate authoritative information concerning STD.
www.astda.org

SUPPORT GROUPS

There are many in-person and online support groups. These are just a few. Ask your doctor for recommendations to additional groups.

www.dailystrength.org/group/kidney-stones

www.mdjunction.com/kidney-stones

www.drugs.com/answers/support-group/nephrolithiasis

www.medhelp.org/forums/Kidney-Stones/show/1207

www.exchanges.webmd.com/kidney-disorders-exchange

www.aakp.org/community/support-groups.html

Note: This website provides a list of in-person support group meetings throughout the United States.

Acidosis: Too much acid in the body.

Acute: Of abrupt onset, in reference to a disease.

Adrenal glands: Sit on top of the kidneys and are responsible for controlling hormones, including testosterone and cortisol levels. Also help to regulate your electrolytes.

AIDS: Acquired Immune Deficiency Syndrome. The final and most serious stage of HIV disease, which causes severe damage to the immune system.

Allopurinol: A drug used to prevent gout attacks and kidney stones caused by uric acid.

Anabolic steroids: Very powerful synthetic substances developed in the late 1930s to treat a condition where the testes do not produce sufficient testosterone.

Anus: The opening where waste leaves the body.

Benign Prostatic Hypertrophy (BPH): An enlarged prostate.

Bladder: Pear-shaped sac in the pelvis that stores urine. When it has filled up enough, it sends a signal to your brain that it's time to go to the bathroom.

Calcium: A mineral found mainly in the hard part of bones, where it is stored.

Calculi: The plural of calculus.

Computerized tomography: Pictures of structures within the body created by a computer that takes the data from multiple x-ray images and turns them in pictures.

Cystinuria: A condition passed down through families in which stones made from an amino acid called cystine form in the kidney, ureter, and bladder.

Cystoscope: A fiber optic camera that is inserted into the urethra and up to the bladder to make sure there is no damage to the penis.

Endourology: Is a minimally invasive technique available to treat kidney stones.

Gout: Condition characterized by abnormally elevated levels of uric acid in the blood, recurring attacks of joint inflammation (arthritis), deposits of hard lumps of uric acid in and around the joints, and decreased kidney function and kidney stones.

Hematuria: Blood in the urine

Hyperparathyroidism: A disorder in which the parathyroid glands in your neck produce too much parathyroid hormone.

Hypercalciuria: Excess calcium in the urine.

Incontinence: Loss of bladder control.

Interstitial Cystitis (IS): A condition with an unknown cause that can affect both men and women who are typically older than 30. Symptoms include chronic pain between the vagina and the anus, and a constant need to urinate (someone with IS can urinate dozens of times during the day), and pain during sex.

Intravenous Pyleogram (IVP): Is an x-ray that uses a dye to obtain pictures of the kidney, bladder, and ureters and can show if there is a kidney stone.

Kidney Stones: A small, hard deposit that forms in the kidneys and is often painful when passed.

Lithotripsy: A procedure to break a stone into small particles that can be passed in the urine.

Meatus: Opening of your penis.

Nephrolithiasis: The process of forming a kidney stone in the kidney or lower down in the urinary tract.

Prostate: About the shape and size of a walnut and is located under the bladder and in front of the rectum. It's a soft gland that's part of your reproductive system, which runs through your urethra and helps to make semen.

Prostatitis: Swollen prostate, a common complaint in middle-aged men, is caused by potential tumors, prostate cancer, food allergies, yeast infection, uric acid disorders, and prostate stones.

Purines: The end products of digestion of nucleic acids in the diet. Some purines are made in the body. Purines are in many drugs and other substances, including caffeine. Too much blood uric acid may occur in people who are not able to use up and release purines, leading to gout.

Rectum: The final section of the large intestine, terminating at the anus.

Renal: Having to do with the kidney. For example, renal cancer is cancer of the kidneys.

Renal Tubular Acidosis: A disease that occurs when the kidneys don't properly remove acids from the blood into the urine.

Retrograde Urethrogram: Test to check the penis. A special solution is injected through the urethra and x-rays are taken to see if the solution leaks, which can identify trauma, etc. to the urethra.

Sepsis: The presence of bacteria (bacteremia), other infectious organisms, or toxins created by infectious organisms in the bloodstream that spread throughout the body.

Shock Wave Lithotripsy (SWL): Shock waves are used to break up kidney stones.

Stent: A tube designed to be inserted into a vessel or passageway to keep it open.

Torsion of Testes: A twist in the spermatic cord. This cord brings blood to the testicle, and it can rotate and twist, cutting off the testicle's blood supply.

Ultrasound: Also called a sonogram, diagnostic sonography, or ultrasonography, it uses high frequency sound waves to create an image of some part of the inside of the body.

Urethra: The tube that runs through your penis and is responsible for carrying pee and semen to the outside of your body.

Ureter: One of the two tubes that carry urine from the kidneys to the bladder. Each ureter arises from a kidney, descends, and ends in the bladder.

Urinary: Having to do with the function or anatomy of the kidneys, ureters, bladder, or urethra. For example, the urinary tract is the collection of organs of the body that produce, store, and discharge urine.

Urine: Liquid waste produced by the kidneys.

Urologist: Physician with knowledge regarding problems of the male and female urinary tract and the male reproductive organs.

Ureteroscope: Used on smaller kidney stones. It's equipped with a camera that is passed through the urethra and bladder and up to the ureter. The stone is then grabbed and broken into pieces so it can be passed out and a temporary stent is put in.

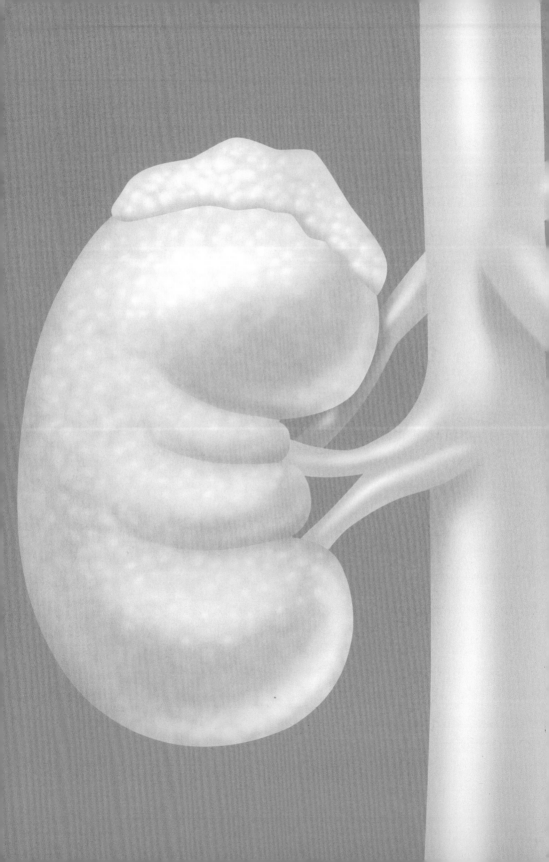